Middlefield
and the Settling of
the New York Frontier

GEORGE CLARKE, 1768-1835

Samuel F. B. Morse, American, 1791-1872; *George Clarke*, 1833; oil on canvas; 43 1/8 in. x 34 3/4 in.; Saint Louis Art Museum, Friends Fund and funds given by Mrs. Mark C. Steinberg by exchange 17:1975.

Middlefield and the Settling of the New York Frontier

A Case Study of Development in Central New York, 1790-1865

Dominick J. Reisen

Square Circle Press
Voorheesville, New York

**Middlefield and the Settling of the New York Frontier:
A Case Study of Development in Central New York, 1790-1865**

Published by
Square Circle Press LLC
137 Ketcham Road
Voorheesville, NY 12186
www.squarecirclepress.com

First hardcover edition 2009.
Printed and bound in the United States of America on acid-free, durable paper.
15 14 13 12 11 10   2 3 4 5

ISBN 13 (hardcover): 978-0-9789066-3-4
ISBN 10 (hardcover): 0-9789066-3-2

ISBN 13 (paperback): 978-0-9789066-4-1
ISBN 10 (paperback): 0-9789066-4-0

Library of Congress Control Number: 2009929844

Publisher's Acknowledgments
The mural painting on the cover is located in the former Joshua Pinney tavern in Middlefield and attributed to itinerant painter William Price. Cover photograph, ©2009 Dominick J. Reisen. Both the paperback edition cover and hardcover dustjacket designs are by Richard Vang, Square Circle Press, using the Corel suite of graphics software (www.corel.com).

The text of this book was created and formatted by Square Circle Press using OpenOffice.org, a free suite of office software (www.openoffice.org). The type is set in Garamond and Book Antiqua.

Sources for illustrations and maps are listed with each. The author's personal and professional acknowledgments appear at the end of the preface.

To Rodney E. Johnson

my mentor, my friend

Contents

PREFACE   *ix*

One	THE MANORIAL VISION	3
Two	THE DEVELOPMENT OF THE HAMLET	21
Three	PROSPERITY AND SOCIAL EPIPHANY	45
Four	THE CHANGING OF THE GUARD	87
Five	A STEADY PROSPERITY	124
Six	AN ABSTRACTION CALLED WAR	163
	CONCLUSION	175

Appendices

1	THE KIDNAPPING OF DANIEL MCCOLLUM (1878)	187
2	MIDDLEFIELD TOWN SUPERVISORS AND CLERKS (1797-1877)	188
3	POSTMASTERS FOR MIDDLEFIELD (1815-1967)	189
4	PETITION FOR MIDDLEFIELD MASONIC LODGE (1823)	190
5	BAPTIST CHURCH PEW AUCTION RESULTS (1826)	191
6	LIST OF STUDENTS, ACADEMIC SCHOOL (1827-28)	193
7	NUMBER OF STUDENTS PER CLASS, ACADEMIC SCHOOL (1827-28)	194
8	SCHOOL BILL, ACADEMIC SCHOOL (1827-28)	195
9	CIVIL WAR ENLISTEES FROM MIDDLEFIELD (1860-65)	196

NOTES	199
INDEX	223

Illustrations follow page 80

Maps follow page 179

PREFACE

The development of Clarksville, the modern day hamlet of Middlefield, is the story of the growth of a small hamlet in central New York. Hamlets are significantly different from towns and their stories are markedly different. Hamlets develop naturally as people settle in a place and set up the myriad businesses and services that interconnect to form an independent unit. Towns are political devices designed for the easy administration of government. Hamlets came first. It was only after the settlement of these communities that political boundaries—towns—were designated. In some cases, these town boundaries encompassed multiple hamlets, as was the case in the town of Middlefield, in which Clarksville was only one of several hamlets. Hamlet boundaries were fluid, growing and contracting as their component businesses grew and contracted in number and physical space. Town boundaries were firmly fixed and did not fluctuate. The only exception was when a town was divided into several others, as when the town of Middlefield was divided from Cherry Valley.

Hamlets grew throughout central New York as settlers moved into this region after the Revolutionary War. Although it is true there were several such communities in central New York prior to the Revolution, most settlement occurred after that date. Many people who migrated into the area traced their roots from the eastern states of Massachusetts and Connecticut. In some cases, these migrants had moved from the eastern states to the Hudson River valley before moving further west into what became Otsego County. Similarly, many migrants eventually left Otsego County and Clarksville and moved further west to the vast areas opened by the Erie Canal and thence to Ohio.

The examination of the Antebellum development of Clarksville bears remarkable similarity to so many other hamlets strewn across the region. In this way, Clarksville serves as a case study in understanding why and how these communities coalesced. To understand this westward migration, in which Clarksville was a relatively brief stopping point for some and a permanent home for others, one must answer certain questions. First among these is why people came to Clarksville. It is not enough to know that they came. To some it was opportunity that beckoned by way of fresh, rich farmlands. To others, it was to follow family members who had come before. Many saw a chance to prosper as local agriculture prospered. Still others left to make a fresh start, free perhaps of shadows in their past.

Once upon the frontier, where settled New York was far to the east and wilderness was to the west, little enclaves of people and isolated farmsteads formed interdependent relationships. To refer to these people as self-sufficient is a rather romanticized view, and gives the impression that they made all they needed to survive. That is not entirely true. The earliest settlers had no ability to forge tools and cooking utensils, they could not grind grain, they certainly could not saw trees into lumber to build houses, and feeding themselves in their first year on the frontier could be problematic. Very shortly after arriving in this region to settle, people could certainly have made their own furniture and clothing, and they could have grown crops on which to subsist, however, there was still a need for outside assistance. Most people refused to even settle on land unless there was a blacksmith, grist mill, and saw mill within some reasonable distance. Through much of the first quarter of the nineteenth century, these little communities, which were fast becoming recognizable as hamlets, co-existed in a symbiotic way, with people traveling between them to take advantage of a store here, a blacksmith there, and a mill down the road.

This is not to imply that travel was easy. The opposite was true. A short trip over rough roads, if there was a road at all, could require the better part of a day. Depending on the season, such trips could be grueling. The spring, with its depths of mud, could be very time consuming and agonizingly slow. To travel any distance in the winter must have been nearly unbearable with the bitter cold, even though traveling on frozen ground and, in many cases, along frozen rivers and lakes, made travel faster. However, as difficult and awful as travel may have been at these times of the year, the fact is that it was a necessary part of life on the frontier. To argue that people did not travel simply because it was difficult misses the point of necessity.

It was during the early nineteenth century that any real semblance of self-sufficiency in these central New York communities came into being. Self-sufficiency required the ability to be able to meet all of one's needs. Hamlets developed to do just that for a group of people. Within these hamlets there was every necessary service from blacksmithing to tinsmithing to milling. People became carpenters, doctors, and lawyers to fill necessary occupations, but they also became tailors and shoe makers. People built churches and schools in close proximity to taverns and distilleries. Stores opened in these communities to bring goods from distant parts of the state and country to the hamlet. These same stores allowed local farmers and craftspeople to have an outlet to barter or sell their excess produce and other wares. Serving as a link to the outside was the postal service.

Separating the many hamlets across the region were vast stretches of farmland dotted with individual farmsteads. The economy of these hamlets was built largely on the prosperity of these surrounding farms. Even though the economy had a certain level of internal momentum, they would have withered away had it not been for the farmers. That is to say, the economies in these hamlets developed an internal dynamic in which the component businesses of the hamlet grew and flourished on the strength of each other. That phenomenon notwith-standing, the surrounding farms with their many needs for products and services drove the hamlet economies forward. The merchants and professionals of these hamlets grew prosperous, and in some cases, wealthy, as the fortunes of the local farm economy ebbed and flowed.

Clarksville exemplifies this progression. Although, as with any hamlet in any part of central New York, there will be a certain degree of uniqueness, the story of Clarksville is not all that dissimilar from other hamlets. There were personal dynamics at work among the residents, and there were individual and community concerns which would not be replicated in other hamlets. This, however, does not change the fact that the businesses and services that were established, indeed in some cases the physical positioning of certain buildings and businesses in Clarksville, was mirrored in innumerable hamlets. Distilleries and tanneries were kept to the outskirts of the hamlet, whereas schools, stores, and taverns tended to the center. Mills were necessarily near a large source of water and cemeteries were kept at a distance.

Perhaps one of the most unique features of the history of Clarksville revolves around its name. Originally named after the great local landowner, George Clarke, the spelling was Clarkesville. Sometime, imperceptibly, during the second quarter of the nineteenth century, the "e" which ended George Clarke's name was dropped from the hamlet's name, leaving it as Clarksville. In the third quarter of the nineteenth century, beyond the scope of this work, the name of the hamlet became synonymous with the name of the town. Middlefield came to mean either the entire town or just this hamlet, depending on the context. This slow transformation in the spelling of Clarksville has been mirrored in the text of the present work. The early chapters include the "e," but later chapters drop this letter. The attempt has been made to closely follow social usage in Otsego County.

As with much of the central New York region, the second quarter of the nineteenth century was a time of economic and social consolidation in Clarksville. By the time of the Civil War every business and service necessary to area residents was to be found within the confines of the hamlet. The hamlet had become as self-sufficient as was possible; much more self-sufficient than it had been at the dawn of the nineteenth century. By the outbreak of war, it was scarcely necessary for the average person to leave Clarksville during their lifetime. All that they needed was to be found within the bounds of the hamlet. Indeed, many nonessential, luxury goods could be found there as well. Socially, people intermarried within the communities more and deep family ties were formed. This, too, grew out of the lack of need to travel. In an earlier time when travel was necessary, and hence perhaps more common, marriage and family ties could be sustained over longer distances. As the need for travel declined, so too did the tendency to form relationships across longer distances.

The picture of Clarksville in 1865 was that of an independent organic unit.

It was self-sustaining and stable. Growth in infrastructure had reached its apogee. Indeed, one of the last buildings ever constructed in the hamlet was erected in 1859. People tended to their personal and business relationships at a relative distance from the rest of the world. So complete was this self-sufficiency that a cataclysmic event such as the Civil War, which threatened to rend the nation in two, could be viewed as an abstract event from within Clarksville. To refer to this as a simple time is to miss the point. People wrestled with the big social questions of the day such as slavery and intemperance, business dealings were not always based on a friendly handshake, and religious, political, and familial ties bound people together. Many of these issues were viewed by residents of Clarksville through the microcosm of their world and, hence, their personal experiences. Intemperance was a greater horror to them than slavery, because they had, by 1860, first hand experience with intemperance whereas slavery was just an abstract idea.

The world was not simpler to the people of Clarksville than it was to people in larger, more urban areas, it was just smaller. The study of this smaller, organic unit serves to highlight human behavior as people band together to build a community. It serves to exemplify how relationships develop through familial and business bonds, and how some people manage to make great successes of themselves on the worldly stage through hard work and perseverance, and perhaps a bit of luck.

I would be remiss if I were not to extend my gratitude to the many people who have helped me with this work. First and foremost among all these people are Rodney and Jeanne Johnson, whose assistance in so many aspects of this work could never be tallied. Their patience through long conversations and their willingness to share their vast stores of knowledge make me greatly indebted to them. Wayne Wright and Jo-Anne Van Vranken at the New York State Historical Association Library were invaluable. Additionally, the staffs at the Otsego County Clerk's Office and the Otsego County Surrogate's Court proved themselves always gracious and helpful. Special thanks need to be tendered to Thomas Savini of the Chancellor Robert R Livingston Masonic Library and the staff at the Cornell University Library. Of special note is the assistance of Les and Dorothy Rathbun who graciously allowed me access to the minute books of the First Baptist Society in Middlefield. Virginia Schoradt, New Lisbon Town Historian, for making the New Lisbon Congregational Church records available to me. My friends who tirelessly read the manuscript and made thoughtful suggestions deserve my gratitude: Sandra Bullard, Rodney Johnson, Les Rathbun and Joseph Sisk. Lastly, I must express my appreciation to my parents, who have always been supportive of all my work with words of encouragement.

Middlefield
and the Settling of
the New York Frontier

Chapter One

THE MANORIAL VISION

I n the early hours of 11 November 1778 the residents of the settlement of Cherry Valley were awakened from their slumbers suddenly and violently. The settlement was under attack by a force of Iroquois Indians and Tories led by Joseph Brant (or Thayendanegea) a Mohawk, and Walter Butler. When the dust had settled and the smoke dissipated, many of Cherry Valley's inhabitants were slain and much of the village was burned. The Indians and Tories responsible vanished into the wilderness. Although Fort Alden remained intact, the settlement was abandoned until after the war.[1]

It would not be until much later that these Indians gathered at their *niskay-una*, or council rock, to camp for the night. This spot on the Cherry Valley Creek was close to the edge of a trail running in a southwesterly direction from the settlement. This trail would later be designated State Route 166 and this council rock may still be found very near the present Dubben Farm along the Dubben Cross Road. The hieroglyphics which once covered it are now entirely obliterated by virtue of its shale composition. Out of this violent and isolated wilderness grew up the town of Middlefield.

The eighteenth century was a period of rampant land speculation. As early as 1698, the government in England had begun trying to regulate the granting of land patents in the colony of New York. The Lords of Trade had given directives to the colonial government stating that, among other things, no more than two thousand acres could be granted to one person and the grantee must settle some part of this land within three years. However, in 1708 the colonial assembly of New York passed an act which effectively nullified the two thousand acre restriction. This paved the way for wealthy individuals and land companies to gather into their hands large tracts of land. By the second quarter of the eighteenth century it had become apparent to some that this method of land granting was causing serious problems in the settlement of New York. Lewis Morris, who served as Chief Justice of New York with James DeLancey, noted this in 1733, "the consequence of all this is, first, the engrossing great tracts into few hands; second, rendering it very difficult if not impracticable for any but a certain class of men to come at them; third, rendering them so dear that . . . it will not be worth the while even of those few that can come at them to meddle with them, there being better lands and much cheaper to be purchased in Jersie and Pennsylvania."[2]

Under these conditions it was relatively easy for wealthy individuals to purchase large tracts of land in central New York in order to parcel up and lease or sell to settlers. George Clarke, Lieutenant Governor of the province of New York from 1736 to 1743, and James DeLancey, the aforementioned Chief Justice, serve as two early examples of the common practice of men exploiting their official position and personal connections for private gain on the New York frontier. Clarke began acquiring land in 1705 with the Oriskany Patent. He proved quite adept at locating good land and had amassed approximately 120,000 acres by the 1740s.[3] By 1741 most of the present hamlet of Clarkesville was held by Volkert Outhout, possibly on behalf of Clarke, in his land patent granted by King George II. Due to its long and narrow dimensions it was known as the Long Patent. Clarke also held large portions of the Godfrey Miller Patent which bordered the Long Patent to the north.

There were already several houses along this stretch of land, making it one of the first areas settled in the town of Middlefield. It was in 1734 that much of this patent was conveyed to George Clarke through his agent John Lindsay. John Lindsay had been appointed Sheriff of Albany County in 1732, an appointment which bespeaks his influential connections. Through his services, Clarke and James DeLancey also acquired the Cherry Valley Patent. Lindsay received a 200-acre lot in Cherry Valley as compensation for his assistance to Clarke and DeLancey, and sometime between 1738 and 1740 he moved to these holdings with his family. Through Lindsay, Clarke was introduced to the Reverend Samuel Dunlop, a graduate of Trinity College, Dublin and a Presbyterian minister, who agreed to recruit settlers for Clarke's lands. For his services, it was agreed that if Dunlop succeeded in settling 2,000 acres within twenty years, he would receive a 400-acre lot. He was instrumental in bringing some of the first settlers to Cherry Valley in 1741. This group numbered about thirty and included David Ramsay, William Galt, James Campbell, Patrick Davidson, William Dickson and their families.[4] Settlement was crucial to making land speculation profitable because all who speculated in land knew the one fundamental maxim: land was only valuable if it was settled. The desire of these speculators was to get people on the land to work it as tenant farmers.

Before William Cooper's somewhat novel idea of selling small parcels of land on terms of easy credit to impoverished settlers, most speculators were bent on renting land to settlers in the hopes of building manors as existed in England. Owning large tracts of land in colonial New York was a mark of gentility among the growing aristocracy of the province. The quasi-feudal manor system that was growing up along the Hudson, first instituted by the Dutch, then naturally adopted by the English, was merely an attempt to ape their genteel cousins in Europe. However, it proved more difficult to lure settlers into central New York, away from the easy transportation network along the Hudson and into the wild frontier where dangers posed by Indians and beasts were of equal concern. It was, therefore, not a contradiction to actually give land to a person who could induce settlers to large portions of vacant lands. Improvements they would make and rents the landlord would receive would more than compensate for the cost of giving land to that key individual.

The idea of building manor farms in central New York was problematic. Due to the sheer quantity of available land, speculators either had to make lease terms enormously attractive to settlers, or be willing to sell the land outright. Most men knew that they could acquire a freehold, particularly if they were among the first settlers to the area. Those who came to the frontier earliest, when it had the fewest improvements, expected, and often received, the most favorable terms. Goldsbrow Banyar, who was not only Secretary of the Province of New York in the 1750s, but who also managed Clarke's Cherry Valley holdings, which included the Cherry Valley, Godfrey Miller, and Long patents, noted to Dunlop in August 1761:

> In a Country where there is such Plenty of unsettled Lands, I am sensible People who can afford it would rather purchase than be burthen'd with a perpetual Rent even tho. low.[5]

In many ways, it was prospective tenants who had the upper hand; a classic supply and demand equation. There was simply more land available than there were willing settlers. This had the effect of keeping rents moderate and land prices low, for those landlords prepared to sell land, compared to other colonies. Peter Martin, who settled in what became the hamlet of Middlefield Centre, but was first known as Newtown-Martin in the 1760s, was typical when he told Banyar that settlers would want Clarke to provide a grist mill, saw mill, meetinghouse, and school.[6] These items would not only be considered necessities, but would only be constructed at considerable expense. Simply transporting the equipment required for a grist mill and saw mill would be a tremendous task in light of the primitive condition of the roads traversing the area. It was not without precedent for the dominant land owner or landlord to build these facilities as aids to encourage settlement and as businesses to augment his income. It is interesting to note that by 1769, about six miles from Newtown-Martin, in Cherry Valley, Richard Smith, traveling to view the Otsego Patent, noted three grist mills and a saw mill.[7] A clear indication that Martin's words had not fallen on deaf ears. Although Clarke did not personally construct and run these enterprises, he did encourage their establishment.

Rents remained a constant concern. Martin, in a letter to Banyar in 1762 expressed the desire, on the part of settlers in Newtown-Martin:

> . . .that our Rentes may not be uncertain For if it should our Improvements will be of much less value than at present.[8]

Clarke heeded this advice and devised a rent system well suited to his tenants' needs. For the first ten years a tenant was liable for no rent. This allowed tenants to use their money to improve the land as best they could afford. It was believed that improvements would have a two fold effect. First, it would make the land more valuable and ease the way for later emigrants. Early settlers would construct roads and communication networks. Nascent enterprises, such as mills and stores, would be called into existence. Further, these first arrivals would bring a sense of peace and security to the frontier. All combined, this would allow the landlord to assess his land as more valuable to later arrivals. Second, tenants would be less willing to exhaust the land and leave it after a short time. Although elementary on its face, it was a very real problem in this period that some settlers would move onto frontier land, burn the trees and sell the potash, only to move further into the frontier a few short years later after erosion and heavy cultivation had exhausted the soil. Once a tenant had occupied his lot for seven years, Clarke assessed his rent at three pence per year per acre. Only after a full fourteen years did rents reach their full amount of six pence per year per acre. This rent system changed slightly as the area became more settled and conveniences such as roads and mills were built. By the late 1760s or early 1770s, Clarke had begun to shorten the rent-free period from ten to seven years. Using this method, Clarke attracted twenty-five tenants to 3,350 acres on the Cherry Valley and Long patents by 1773.[9]

Favorable lease terms were not the only inducement to a person to become a tenant rather than a freeholder. There were other, more pressing, economic considerations which tempered one's idealism. It has been estimated that by 1750 it would require £200-£500 to start farming a freehold.[10] Clearly, without even the burden of purchasing land outright, a move to the frontier would require more than muscle and an adventurous spirit. Leasing land allowed the settler to invest their available capital in setting up a farm, clearing land, purchasing seed, building a house and barn, etc. Without a doubt, it would be easier to take a long lease, as offered by the landowners, rather than purchase one's land initially. It is a simple fact that the average farmer coming to the frontier had very little specie left after purchasing the bare necessities to start farming and paying to transport his family to the wilderness.

Further, not all men were inclined to set up farms; others sought to lease land and use their capital to set up businesses. Among the earliest necessary businesses was a mill, as noted by Martin. Setting up a mill could cost £350-£400 and as early as the 1730s it had been estimated by William Johnson of the Mohawk Valley that such a mill could produce £30 in income a year.[11] Other early business ventures included pot and pearl ash works. An ash works provided a way for settlers to quickly make money from their lands. The ash created from burning the trees from their land could be sold. In 1769 a ton of pearl ash could net a settler £40. It would require about ten acres to produce that ton. This ash, once properly boiled and baked to pearl, could be transported to Albany and thence to New York City where it sold for $125 to $150 per ton,[12] providing a nice profit all around. People moving to the frontier would require enormous sums of cash if they hoped to purchase their land and set up a farm or business. It seemed more logical to most people to lease land for long periods (a life lease) and invest their money in the equipment required to begin their farm or business.

Clarke visited his holdings in Otsego County occasionally, but in 1745 he traveled to England, never to return. Dunlop sent notification to Clarke in 1761 that he had settled the agreed upon lands and he was promptly given four 100-acre lots in Cherry Valley.[13] In Clarke's absence, his attorney from New York City managed his property and his rent collector in Albany forwarded the rent receipts to him and, after his death, to his heirs. This arrangement, an absentee landlord employing others to manage his property, was not uncommon since many wealthy landlords had no desire to live on the rough frontier. This system was not without its pitfalls, though. Dunlop, as intermediary between Clarke and his tenants, often became embroiled in disputes with the tenants. Finally, in a dispute with a tenant over the use of pasture land, Dunlop, as the minister, refused to baptize the tenant's child. Banyar, who helped resolve the issue (in favor of the tenant) was appointed by Clarke to replace Dunlop as overseer.[14] It was crucial that landlords employ agents able to get along well with the tenants in order to keep peace and maintain order on the frontier as well as to encourage further settlement.

The other problem with the establishment of a manor system was that these frontier regions stood in constant danger of Indian attack. The Cherry Valley Massacre is the most horrible, but not only, example of such dangers. There is also the frightening story of the two year old Daniel McCollum, son of Alexander McCollum of Newtown-Martin, being kidnapped by an Indian in the spring of 1778. He was gone for nine years before he was recognized in Lake George and restored to his family. Having been raised by Indians, he knew their customs and spoke three Indian languages, but barely any English. In later life he wrote a narrative of his captivity. These and other harrowing experiences were fresh in people's minds. This resulted in a reluctance of people to settle this far into the wilderness. Furthermore, as the Revolutionary War approached, fears of Indian attacks were compounded by fears of British hostilities. So precarious was life on the frontier that it has been estimated that Tryon County's population of approximately 10,000 in 1772 dropped to about 3,500 during the Indian and Tory raids of the 1778-1781 period.[15] As Dunlop made clear to the Tryon Committee on Safety.

. . .the inhabitants of Cherry Valley, being assembled yesterday at a public town-meeting, and among other things taking the present critical situation of affairs into consideration, looked upon ourselves, and the neighborhood around us, Springfield and Newtown-Martin, as a frontier, lying very open and unguarded, and very much exposed to the enemy, in case an Indian war should break out, or any party of the enemy should take it into their heads to come down upon us; and that it would be absolutely necessary to have a party of men sta-

tioned here among us, in order to keep a sharp look-out, and to scout all around our frontiers; lest at any time we be taken by surprise.[16]

The Committee was unable to comply with this request due to both the lack of funds and the presence of only tepid support for the American cause of independence in the area. Consequently, many residents, including Samuel Dunlap, Samuel Campbell, James Scott, Robert Wells, James Richey, James Moore, and Samuel Clyde, petitioned the Provincial Congress of New York for assistance.

The humble petition of the inhabitants of Cherry Valley, Newtown-Martin, and Springfield, in the County of Tryon, humbly showeth: That we, the aforesaid inhabitants, from the most authentic intelligence we have received from our missionaries and Indian friends, learn that we are in imminent danger of being cut off by savages, our enemies whom we understand are bribed by Sir John Johnson and Col. Butler to execute the same. Know also honorable gentleman, that the spirit of our inhabitants has been such for the American cause, that out of the small and scattered bounds of Cherry Valley and Newtown-Martin, no less than thirty-three have turned out for immediate service and good of their country, and thereby left us in a defenseless condition.[17]

The use of the names of Sir John Johnson and Colonel Butler, known loyalists, was sure to incite the congress to take whatever action it could. Also, the quantification of the number of men who went to serve in the American cause, although an exaggeration, was calculated to garner sympathy. It is of no small irony that this intelligence of an impending Indian attack came from Indians, which only goes to demonstrate the split allegiances in the area.

Faced with a clear and present danger to current inhabitants, as well as the specter of vanishing profits for landlords and land speculators, pressure was exerted on the Continental Congress to act. In 1779 General Washington was asked to assist in securing the area from Indian and British attack. A clear prospect was at hand to not only deprive the British of a food source and native ally for the loyalist troops, but also to appease those of power and influence in the region and secure their support for the Colonial cause. It must be borne in mind that central New York, particularly Tryon County, then comprising the Mohawk Valley and the Otsego area,[18] was not a rebel stronghold and there were many pockets of influential loyalists. It was estimated by the Tryon County Committee in 1777 that over half of the residents of the county were loyalists. Indeed, it has been estimated that in the entire Province of New York one half to two-thirds of the population were pro-British. The loyalists were so strong that assistance was requested of the Continental Congress.[19] The family of Sir William Johnson, Superintendent of Indian Affairs for the Province of New York and an enormous landowner along the Mohawk River, stands out as one of the most prominent examples. There was also John Butler, a large landowner along the Susquehanna River and an interpreter at the Fort Stanwix treaty negotiations of 1768. These and other large landowners were inclined to support the

British because of the stability that established government brought with it. It was not just the wealthy who supported the Crown. Many tenant farmers flocked to support the British including about 1,000 of Johnson's. It has been estimated that over a third of all loyalist properties seized in New York were in Tryon County.[20] This fact indicates a huge loyalist population in the area. This cannot be concluded by merely noting the extensive territory the county comprised. It would require a large proportion of the overall population to be loyalist to account for seizures of this magnitude.

In addition to the number of loyalists in the area, there was also the Indian sentiments which were a concern to the American cause. The Indians of the area were convinced that their survival would best be assured through adherence to the British. Brant instructed his Indian brethren "to defend their Lands & Liberty against the Rebels, who in a great measure began this Rebellion to be sole Masters of this Continent."[21] George Washington was well aware of the importance of the area in the War for Independence. The British stronghold in nearby Canada, with their impregnable fort at Niagara, the natives allied with the British, and a wavering population which could change its allegiance based on self and financial preservation were all concerns weighing on the rebel leader's mind. All these factors, when combined with New York's central location in the colonies, meant that New York must be secured to the rebel cause. If New York was lost to the British, it would effectively split the colonies in half geographically and seriously jeopardize the American cause.

Under the command of General John Sullivan, Washington devoted one third of his army to secure the region from Pennsylvania to Canada. Sullivan, with the bulk of the force, was to drive up from Easton through the Poconos to Tioga. General James Clinton with 1,600 men, 250 boats, and two three-pounders would start at Otsego Lake, push down the Susquehanna, and meet Sullivan in Tioga. By damming Otsego Lake at the mouth of the Susquehanna River, Clinton was able to raise the water level considerably. Upon destroying the dam, he was able to float his forces and equipment down the river. Meanwhile, Colonel Daniel Brodhead would traverse the Allegheny to Genesee. At Newtown the American forces met and engaged the British and Indian forces. After a flanking maneuver, the enemy fled in disarray leaving the Seneca country open. As a result, the villages of the Senecas and Cayugas, forty-one in total, were destroyed, their crops burned (estimated at 200,000 bushels of corn), and their orchards were ruined. This effectively ended the usefulness of this region as a food source for the British. Importantly for the rebel cause, though, it ended the hopes of the British in splitting the American forces by driving a wedge from Canada to New York City. Unfortunately, it did not succeed in ending the internecine warfare between American loyalists and rebels. By the time the war was over Tryon County was decimated. It has been estimated that "seven hundred buildings had been burned, twelve thousand farms abandoned, hundreds of thousands of bushels of grain destroyed, nearly four hundred rebel women made widows, and some two thousand children of revolutionaries orphaned."[22]

When peace was secured, ending the War of Independence, many of the surviving inhabitants of the Cherry Valley settlement returned to pick up their lives. Soldiers were paid with tracts of land throughout the wilderness and land speculation carried on again more eagerly than before. By the 1790s it was not uncommon to see advertisements for large land sales. Henry Bowers, of New York City, advertised such a sale in the *Otsego Herald* in 1795 when he sought to sell 100 lots in his Bowerstown area of Newtown-Martin.[23] Purchasers of such parcels had to be prepared for a rough life, lacking many of the comforts of more settled areas. Otsego County was heavily wooded, particularly with maple, beech, birch and elm trees of very old growth. To just clear the land was an enormous task, taking between seven to ten days for a man to clear an acre. It has been accepted by many historians that a man could hope to clear and sow up to ten acres in his first year.[24] A daunting task by any measure.

Among these enterprising and wealthy land speculators was George Clarke, great grandson of the Lieutenant Governor, who came to America in 1789. He had been raised at Hyde Hall, in Cheshire, England where his family had made its home upon his great grandfather's return to England in 1745. Hyde Hall had passed to Lieutenant Governor Clarke upon the death of his wife, Anne Hyde Clarke, on 19 May 1740. In January 1789 Clarke arrived at Swanswick, the family's sugar plantation in Jamaica which his father had been managing. Clarke's father, also named George, dispatched letters to James Duane and Goldsbrow Banyar making clear that his son intended to come to America upon reaching his majority and asking how he should best proceed in light of the fact that these men had acted as the family's agents and attorneys in America. George Clarke (the son) also sent a similar letter at that time as well.[25]

As co-heir to his great-grandfather's lands in America, along with his younger brother Edward, George's intention was to stay permanently in New York and become a naturalized citizen. Becoming a citizen would enable him to take possession of his inheritance since non-citizens at this time could not hold land in New York. In October 1790, Clarke was called abroad unexpectedly and on his behalf, his attorneys Goldsbrow Banyar and James Duane, both of whom were also large land owners in New York, submitted a petition to the New York State legislature asking that Clarke be permitted to hold lands in New York State in spite of his not being a citizen. This petition stated:

> *That your Petitioner was born in England, and is Great-grandson of George Clarke, formerly Lieutenant Governor of New York; that he resided in the City of New York for about a Year preceding the Month of October last, with Intention, at the End of two Years to have been naturalized under the Statute of the United States; that he was unexpectedly called abroad on important Business, but expects to return in the Course of the ensuing Summer; and as his Naturalization must now be unavoidably suspended, to the great embarrassment of his Affairs, your Petitioner humbly prays that his Name may be inserted in the Bill before the honourable the Legislature, to grant a similar Privilege of holding Lands*

within this State, notwithstanding the want of Naturalization, and your Petitioner shall ever pray.

George Clarke

To avoid confiscation of his lands by New York State, an act that would have been based on Clarke being a British subject during the Revolution, Clarke claimed special status as a minor and non-belligerent during the war. By the simple act of not taking up arms during the war he claimed that his rights to his inheritance had not been forfeited. The act was passed on 22 March 1791 by a state legislature eager to not disturb property rights and titles to land in a way that could potentially cause trouble to other landlords in the state.[26] This gave Clarke the right to hold, buy and sell lands in New York as a citizen. However, more important than that, it allowed him to take possession of lands that were his by inheritance. Upon his arrival back in England, he purchased Edward's share of the American lands and sent the deeds to Duane for filing in New York in December 1791.[27]

This trip to America included a wide-ranging tour of his lands, starting with his sugar plantations in Jamaica and thence to New York. Clarke's account books clearly indicate where he went and how he traveled. In June of 1789, he took a sloop up the Hudson River to Red Hook, paying three pounds, twelve shillings for himself and his servant. It is unclear how many servants Clarke had with him. He indicates paying for wages and washing of one servant, but also records making numerous gifts to the servants of Banyar. It would not have been uncommon for a traveling aristocrat to have "borrowed" a servant from a local friend for use while on an extended trip. After touring his lands in the Hudson region, he continued overland to Otsego to inspect the Long, Godfrey Miller, Springfield, and other land patents he held along Lake Otsego. While in Otsego he stayed at the inn of Griffin and Richey in Cherry Valley for four pounds, twelve shillings, and three pence. He must have taken an immediate interest in the development of this area. While in Cherry Valley, he lent Benjamin Griffin eighty pounds to build a malt house for which Clarke held a mortgage. The mortgage is recorded as being paid by 6 February 1790, certainly indicating that Griffin met with success in his venture.[28]

Clarke had the Long Patent subdivided into parcels of 100 acres each. Parcel numbers 17 and 18 of Great Lot 12 of this patent was the area which became the hamlet of Clarkesville. This parcel was of more than just passing interest to Clarke, even at this early stage of development.

The Southerly Part of this Lot is considerably Hilly & Stony but the Northerly Part contains some good Land It is Watered by a small Brook Timber Maple Beech Birch Basswood Hemlock & Ash - a good stand for Business & Country Store and Tavern 4 roads join.[29]

It was along the southwest corner of this junction, where the Long Patent

Road and the Cooperstown Road met, that Clarke arranged for the construction of an imposing edifice. This was a wood frame house with a fully developed five bay façade. Its considerable size and the tastefulness of its Federal ornamentation mark it as quite a sophisticated example of architecture in early Otsego County. Significantly, it was situated back from the road on all sides, not directly along the road. This was in keeping with the contemporary philosophy that houses for people of great importance should have space around them, marking them and their occupants as being apart from the common. This three-story house would become one of the more important buildings in the hamlet, serving as host to numerous community groups and being called home by some of its leading citizens. Clarke had a marker placed in the exact center of the crossroads to mark out smaller parcels in Lot 18. This marker was still present in the mid-twentieth century when Carlton Hinman noted its location.[30] From this marker, Clarke would be able to divide parcels for sale in the hopes of luring settlers to the area. His plan was clearly for a cluster of houses and businesses at this crossroads, rather than renting the whole parcel as one farm as he had done elsewhere along the Long Patent.

Clarke used as his surveyor a man named Benjamin Gilbert. Gilbert was a phenomenal man and figures large in the early history of both Middlefield and Otsego County. He was born in Brookfield, Massachusetts in 1755 and served with distinction during the Revolutionary War, obtaining the rank of Lieutenant. After the Revolution, he was taught surveying by an old friend and commander, General Rufus Putnam, in March of 1784. When Gilbert was discharged he had traveled back to his native Brookfield, but he seems to never have had any intention of staying there, even though most of his family and friends lived there. He despaired of having "so many enemies in that place who wish to destroy my character, Interest, and Life…" This tirade against the people of his town was a result of a scandal in which Gilbert was embroiled. He stood accused of having gotten Patience Converse, the daughter of Colonel James Converse and the sister of a good friend, pregnant. Upon first hearing of her state, he had seemed to accept his responsibility. However, as her delivery came closer, he disavowed that he was the father of this child. This notwithstanding, when he left the army in November of 1783 and returned to Brookfield he was arrested "on Patience Converse's account." Even though he maintained his innocence, he nonetheless saw fit to settle with Colonel Converse and Patience for thirty pounds, fifteen payable immediately and fifteen due in twelve months. He did not pay that remaining fifteen pounds until 16 February 1786, shortly after he had married Mary Cornwall.[31]

In 1784 he purchased 219 acres in Otsego County from John Bullock of Albany for £250. This is a significant transaction in light of the additional expenses that would have been attendant to setting up a farm. It is reasonable to assume that Gilbert came to Middlefield with considerable capital. However, even in his circumstances, he still was thankful of the gift of farm tools from his father, totaling £3 4s. 4d. which he brought with him from Brookfield.[32] Shortly after his arrival he found he needed additional farm tools and asked his father to make a gift of those as well.

> *I find myself very short of farming Tools. Shall be at Brookfield the first Jany. next. Shall want a midling sized stubble plow shear, a Crow Bar, a stubbling Hoe, a Post Ax, a Sett of Betle Rings, a Chain twice as big and a third longer than the one I brought from there last spring. If you find your circumstances such as to enable you to give me those articles as an encouragement, I wish you to have ready by the first of Jany. next . . .*[33]

This gift totaled three pounds, eighteen shillings, and ten pence. It must be borne in mind that, in addition to hoping for financial assistance from his father, Gilbert was requesting these items from Brookfield, Massachusetts because they were not readily available in Otsego. Settlement in the area was still in such an infant stage as to make local manufacture of these types of tools nearly non-existent.

In May of 1785, while just beginning to set up his farm in Middlefield, Gilbert met with the inhabitants of Cherry Valley and agreed to set up and teach a school for ten months at a rate of £23 6s.8d. It was already clear to his neighbors that Gilbert was well-educated and capable of teaching (he had taught a school in Warrens Bush in 1784). As was common practice, during the ten months school was in session, Gilbert would board with various residents in Cherry Valley. In order to make additional money, Gilbert used his knowledge as a surveyor, building a reputation in that craft long before he was introduced to Clarke. On 20 August 1785 he noted in his diary that after keeping school in the morning, he surveyed twenty acres for £4.[34]

In the winter of 1785 Gilbert was anticipating the advent of a good growing season and a plentiful harvest. He felt financially secure enough to take Mary Starr Cornwall of Danbury, Connecticut as his wife in 1786 and bring her back to Middlefield.[35] As his fortunes took root, Gilbert was able to use his social and political connections to become one of the leading citizens of Middlefield and Otsego County. He was appointed Sheriff of Otsego County in the spring of 1792. This appointment came from the New York State Council of Appointment and bespeaks his waxing political influence. A member of the council, Stephen Van Rensselaer, was a good friend of William Cooper of Cooperstown. Cooper and Gilbert were great friends, with Gilbert being a staunch political supporter of Cooper. He would later lose this commission at the hands of his political foes on 11 March 1793. However, he regained his appointment in 1794 for a term of one year, and again in 1799. Gilbert had received his commission initially due to his political neutrality in the local and state battles between the more populist Clintonians and rather elitist leaning Federalists. After his appointment, he was accused of showing partisan favor toward the Federalists, whose county leader was Judge William Cooper. Gilbert, as sheriff, had confiscated the ballot boxes for Otsego, and was later accused of stuffing these boxes.[36] The charges were never satisfactorily proved and he was exonerated, as testified by his re-appointment.

Gilbert's political fortunes in Otsego County were on the ascendant during this decade. As the Federalists were swept into power, the support of Gilbert and his friends helped propel Cooper to his seat in the U. S. House of Representatives. In 1794 Gilbert's prestige in the county was sufficient to win him election to the New York State Assembly as its sole representative, taking office from Jacob Morris. He was re-elected in 1799 to serve with his Federalist friends Joshua Dewey and Francis Henry, as well as their political rival Jedediah Peck, of Burlington. During this time, these Federalists were embroiled in a heated political struggle with the leveling forces in the county as represented by Peck and his friends. Gilbert, having come from a prominent Massachusetts family, was a man of genteel pretensions as were his friends Joshua Dewey, a Yale graduate who conducted a school in the academy building on the corner of Third and West (now Church and Pioneer) Streets of Cooperstown, Elihu Phinney, who was a publisher and owner of the *Otsego Herald* of Cooperstown, and Francis Henry, who ran a tavern in Cooperstown. Although Gilbert lived in what would soon be known as Newtown-Martin, his close friends were men from Cooperstown. These men, and those like them, tended to be at odds with the political aspirations of the hinterland farmers[37] whose sense of egalitarianism was a result of the ideals espoused during the recent revolution. It is illustrative of this point to briefly explore who these men were.

In 1795 Elihu Phinney founded the first newspaper in Otsego County, the *Otsego Herald*. This weekly was widely read, partially explained by the fact that Phinney would accept farm produce for subscription payment. Concurrent with this business, Phinney established a printing business and bookstore. By 1800 he was advertising 350 titles available in his store. To further his book business, he devised wagons to carry his books into the countryside for sale over a wide area.[38]

Joshua Dewey, who conducted the Otsego Academy, a secondary school, was equally learned and enterprising. The Otsego Academy was set up in 1795 and counted forty-two people among its initial subscribers, who pledged a total of $1,441 to establish the school. Dewey would later receive a position as Assistant Teacher at Hartwick Seminary for the 1815-1816 year. The original board of trustees for the Cooperstown academy included William Cooper and General Jacob Morris, the two preeminent local landowners, speculators and businessmen. However, also on the board were Benjamin Gilbert, Elihu Phinney, Moss Kent Jr. and James Averell. Of these men, only Gilbert could be called a farmer and even that was a stretch in terminology. He was destined to become too wealthy to have anything in common with all but the most affluent in Otsego County. Indeed, by this point, he preferred to refer to himself as a surveyor, a position considered to be of vital importance on the frontier. To the establishment of this school, he contributed twelve pounds. This is less than the twenty pounds James Averell contributed and the sixteen pounds Elihu Phinney contributed, but more than the ten pounds Moss Kent Jr. gave.[39] Certainly Gilbert's contribution was no trifling sum and was sufficient to rank him among the forefront of the leading citizens of Cooperstown, the center of the county.

Moss Kent Jr. stands out as a personage destined for greatness, unfortunately not in Otsego County. He was the brother of Chancellor Kent and a good friend of Gouverneur Morris, the early American statesman and diplomat. Kent was an enterprising businessman, establishing a pot and pearl ash works in Springfield, and was an attorney and secretary to Cooper. However, in 1804, after being defeated in his run for re-election to the state Senate, he relocated to the Lowville area. In 1814 he represented that area in Congress.[40] In Otsego County however, he, like Gilbert, Phinney, and Dewey, exemplified culture and learning on the frontier.

It is not surprising that many of these men were responsible for founding one of the first social, non-religious organizations in Otsego County. The Freemasons of Cooperstown obtained their charter and convened their first meeting at Elihu Phinney's house on Lake Street in March 1796. Elihu Phinney was installed as the first master and Benjamin Gilbert as the first treasurer, an office he held through 1798. Other early residents of Middlefield who joined as founding members of this group were Lewis Edson, who was installed as the junior deacon and became one of the first three school commissioners for Middlefield, and Ezra Eaton, who was tyler in the first year, an office he held twenty-nine times.[41] He was the last surviving charter member when he died in 1837 at the age of eighty-seven. In June of 1797 this group erected their first building at a cost of 300 pounds on the corner of Front and West Streets (present day Lake and Pioneer Streets). The bond that was obtained stipulated that "100 pounds was to be paid on raising the frame, 100 pounds on the completion and glazing the same, and 100 pounds on the completion thereof, provided that said work be approved by Tho's Tanner, Timothy Barnes, and Elihu Phinney".[42]

When the building was raised on 24 June 1797, the Freemasons held an impressive ceremony commemorating the event. Benjamin Gilbert delivered an oration "perfectly adapted to the occasion"[43] to those gathered to mark the celebration. A cut limestone corner stone was unveiled. Set in the stone was a copper plate with the inscription:

> *Anno Lucis VMDCCXCVII Die Junii XXIV*
> *Haec Aula Erecta Fuit, A Membris*
> *Otsego Latimorum Societatis E. P. M.*
> *Et Dedicati Usui Filiorum Lucis.*
>
> *Non Nobis Solum Nati Sumus*
> *Sed Partim Patriae Partim Amicis.*[44]

The men who founded this group and these early business ventures were many of the same men who were the leaders of this new community. The list of their social, political, and in some cases, marital, connections was extensive and would remain so with their descendants well into the nineteenth century. The leaders of Middlefield, as well as those of the county, were a fairly close-knit group of like-minded men. It was no coincidence that these men were the most literate, best educated, and wealthiest men of the area. Not surprisingly, they were also very well connected politically, with Cooper being regarded locally and state wide as the leader of the county.

It is probable that it was through Judge Cooper that Benjamin Gilbert first met George Clarke. It was only natural that these two great landowners, with holdings in such close proximity, would move in the same social circles in this tiny community. It is not unlikely that Cooper would have sought out Clarke's company as he was trying to recast himself more as a country gentleman much as Clarke appeared as an English gentleman. Alternately, it is not beyond the realm of speculation that Clarke sought out Cooper when he came to America to learn about the frontier and methods of successfully developing his lands. Cooper already had a far-reaching reputation for being able to successfully and quickly settle frontier lands. Gilbert was an important political supporter of Cooper's, as has been noted, as well as one of his surveyors, although the honor of surveying Cooperstown fell to Daniel Smith of Burlington in 1788. However, most importantly, Gilbert and Cooper were good friends, as is evidenced by Elihu Phinney in his letter of 1 February 1796 to Cooper in which he refers to Gilbert as "our good friend, the Sheriff".[45] In all likelihood, Cooper advised Clarke to retain Gilbert's services as surveyor. A move that made even more sense in light of Gilbert's first hand knowledge of the area of the Godfrey Miller Patent, on which Gilbert's house in Newtown-Martin was situated and much of which Clarke owned, as well as the Long Patent. Gilbert was responsible for surveying many of the early plots along the Long Patent, and three of his daughters and one son would later live in houses built on that patent in the hamlet of Clarkesville.[46]

In addition to the house he had built along the Long Patent Road, Clarke may also have instructed that a house be built closer to Cherry Valley. This house was built of brick and was similar to the house on the Long Patent both in terms of its tasteful and elegant Federal ornamentation as well as in its construction technique. There can be little doubt that both houses were built by the same person. Lacking firm documentary evidence, it remains a mystery why Clarke would have built these two houses. Knowledge of what other landowners were doing does provide some clues. There were already numerous tenants on these lands paying rent to Clarke and carving out farms. These farms were producing marketable commodities. Clarke would have toured the Hudson on his way to Albany and seen the great manors of the Livingstons, Beekmans, Van Rensselaers, Cortlandts and Philipses. In building these grand houses, it is probable that he had in mind the establishment of manor farms which he could then sell. William Davy, a traveler from Devonshire, England, upon viewing Samuel Wallis' homestead along the west branch of the Susquehanna at Muncy in the 1790s, could not help but compare it to the great manors he knew in England.[47] Clarke could easily have come to the same conclusion in light of his family relation to the Hydes of England, who were the Earls of Clarendon.

Clarke's grand tour of his American lands, particularly those in New York, and the impression it made on his tenants needs to be seen through the prism of the upheaval in New York resulting from the outcome of the revolution as it affected land ownership. During and after the Revolution, huge estates held by loyalists were seized and sold. In these sales, the large holdings were split into smaller, more marketable parcels. Clarke's lands were saved from this seizure by virtue of the fact that he was in England during this time. Although initially seemingly contradictory, living in England actually helped preserve Clarke's lands intact. Property of known and active loyalists was subject to confiscation. However, since it could not be determined if Clarke was an English loyalist or a colonial sympathizer, his lands were spared. Credit must also be given to Clarke's attorney, Goldsbrow Banyar, son-in-law of John Jay, who managed to maintain a persona of neutrality around the Clarke family. These confiscations and breakups did have the effect of weakening the feudal social system that had been growing up in New York.[48] As manors were broken and sold, often the buyers were the tenants. This same sort of democratizing obviously could not occur on Clarke's lands since they remained intact. Thus, he would have been able to entertain the notion of creating two manors around these houses with his already numerous tenants; tenants who may not have been privy to the activities further south.

To better understand Clarke's intentions it is helpful to explore the way land ownership was developing in New York. It is significant to note that the leasehold system of land ownership that had grown up along the Hudson River and allowed the colonial aristocratic families of New York to build their manors was transplanted inland with little difficulty. As this system gravitated to central New York, it encountered some resistance from the independent newcomers of Yankee origin, primarily from Connecticut and Vermont. However, economic necessity forced these tenants to accept lease terms as offered until they were able to purchase the land on which they had made their home or until they could move to regions further west where the leasehold system had not taken root among the land owners. The other side of this equation, as has been discussed, was the abundance of land in central New York. This had the effect of moderating the terms which landlords extracted, to the point of landlords commonly offering rent free years to entice tenants to set up farms. In the 1780s and 1790s Stephen Van Rensselaer offered his tenants seven rent free years allowing them time to clear land, construct houses and barns, fence their farms, and raise cash through crop sales. By 1793 most of the leases on his west manor in Albany County started paying and by 1800 most of the leases for his east manor had been signed. James Duane was able to entice settlers to sign similar leases on his lands. In the period 1785 to 1792 he had 229 leases signed stipulating rent free periods of five years. Thereafter, rent was fifteen dollars annually with water and mining rights reserved to Duane. The reservation of water and mining rights, which was not uncommon, not only acted to secure for the landlord future possible sources of income by exploiting these features, but it was also a way of clearly delineating the landlord/tenant relationship; the landlord controlled the land and its resources. However, it is important to note that throughout the 1790s competition from western lands in the Ohio River valley prevented these landlords from raising terms.[49]

By this time, the leasehold system was not without skeptics. James Duane's son-in-law, Colonel William North, also a large landowner, had his doubts about the profitability of leasing land.

> *This letting farms on shares and indeed for rent in money is a miserable business . . .Sell - money enough down to pay a years rent and credit for the rest - They will then work for the farm as for themselves and make it better - and after all, if they can not fulfill the contract, you are the gainer. Farms here which sell for 800+ will not rent for 20 — what a lot of interest.*[50]

These views were echoed by William Cooper in his *Guide in the Wilderness*, in which he advised that lands should be sold on terms of easy credit. Only in this way would the settler expend his money on excellent improvements and tend his land well, knowing that it is indeed his. Cooper would also allow the settler time to clear the land, erect his improvements, and have several growing seasons before requiring payment. However, even Cooper realized that there was an impoverished class of settlers who would still not be able to purchase their land under these terms. For these people, he advised the perpetual lease: this gave security of tenure to the settler and regular income to the landowner.[51]

The leases that George Clarke used on his lands were similar in many ways to Van Rensselaer's and Duane's, and differed slightly from those of the lieutenant governor. The farms tended to be subdivided in 100-acre lots and there was usually a rent free period, at least during this early period. These leases were typically three-life leases, meaning that the lease remained in effect during the lifetime of the three people therein named, with a guaranteed period of thirty-one years. His leases also bore other covenants; for example, tenants could only build one dwelling house and were required to plant one apple tree for every five acres and these trees were to be at right angles, thirty feet from each other. Finally, one sixth of the land was to be left as wood "for necessary Fencing & Fuel for One Dwelling House."[52]

Tenants were perfectly willing to accept such lease terms which were not deemed egregious at all. Actually, since water and mining rights were not clearly reserved, these terms were considered more lenient than most other landlords offered. Table 1 contains total rents received by Clarke and serves to show the growth in population on all of Clarke's New York lands over the twenty year period 1786 to 1806. Occupancy grew dramatically over this period, but so did improvements such as roads, mills, and inns, which allowed Clarke to charge higher rents to later arrivals. Indeed, such was the growth that rent receipts nearly doubled in the seven years 1790 to 1797.

TABLE 1: TOTAL RENTS RECEIVED

YEAR(S)	AMOUNT*
1786-89	£202 9s. 6½d.
1790	£326 13s. 4d.
1797	£634 18s. 4d.
1806	£838 15s. 14d.

* £ = pounds; s.= shillings; d. = pence.

Source: George Hyde Clarke Papers, box 143, folder 3, Cornell University Library, Division of Rare and Manuscript Collections, Ithaca.

A few points of significance need to be noted because they are the closest one can get to understanding Clarke's thoughts and plans for the area of Great Lot 12 in the Long Patent. He had already made it clear, by his loan to Benjamin Griffin, that he was willing to foster business in Otsego. This is made even more obvious by his not reserving water and mining rights, a restriction which was noticeable by its absence from his leases and a point certainly not lost on potential settlers. Clarke had no intention of setting up business enterprises as other landlords had done to increase their personal income, though. This is in keeping with the eighteenth century British aristocratic disdain for engaging in trade; the accepted mode of attaining wealth was through land and rents. Further, Clarke would show great willingness to rent parcels of significantly less than the normal 100 acres to people who would engage in business; Moses Rich is a good example with his mill and later his inn in Westville, and so is Joshua Pinney with his inn situated in Clarkesville on Parcel 18 of Great Lot 12. Finally, of greatest importance are Clarke's own notes which label this lot as being an ideal place for business, and his clear intention of subdividing this lot into smaller parcels. Certainly by building his house here and siting it back from the road, he anticipated this area as being a thriving center of activity.

Whatever his intentions may have been, the fact is that Clarke was never able to establish in Middlefield anything resembling the feudal manors of England, or even something resembling the manors as existed along the Hudson River. This despite the great increases in rental income he derived from the area. What he did set in motion by building these houses, particularly the house on the Long Patent, was a hub of activity around which a hamlet could grow. Much as William Cooper and Jacob Morris had established towns around their estates, Clarke's agents had successfully enticed a thriving population to the Long Patent. Already Benjamin Gilbert had shown what industrious efforts could produce; other men would soon replicate his success and bring talent, business acumen, and culture to the wilderness that was Clarkesville, as the area around Clarke's house on the Long Patent was quickly being identified. For his part, Clarke was able to claim significant income from properties he rented to farmers and business owners on the Long Patent. This, coupled with his other holdings in Otsego and surrounding counties, did achieve Clarke's primary goal: to live as a landed gentleman in the English manner, deriving the bulk of his income from the land he owned.

Chapter Two

THE DEVELOPMENT OF THE HAMLET

As social hierarchies were coalescing along the Otsego frontier, political institutions were taking root as well. The vast region which had been Tryon County gave way to numerous counties in 1791, of which Otsego was one. This county, surrounding Otsego Lake, consisted only of Otsego and Cherry Valley townships at this point. With large, post-war influxes of people swarming to the frontier, these two towns, of necessity, were divided into smaller populations and land areas. These divisions were meant to create political units with populations and areas that could be managed more efficiently. That is, town governments could form which would be able to address the needs of these burgeoning populations. These governments could also address the issue of the poor condition of roads and begin the regulation of trade by granting licenses for such things as taverns. Further, they would take on the task of two new issues of need on the frontier: the rural poor and education. These were all issues which were more easily handled with smaller towns.

It was on 3 March 1797 that a tract of land containing the hamlets Newtown-Martin (Middlefield Centre), Clarkesville, Waterville and Westville, comprising 37,456 acres, was separated from Cherry Valley.[1] In time additional communities would form in this town taking such names as: Whigville (Whig Corners), Lynchville (Lentsville), Bowerstown, and Phoenixville (Phoenix Mills). It was also in 1797 that the towns of Springfield and Worcester were separated from Cherry Valley as well. The hamlet of Middlefield Centre, joined later by the communities of Lentsville and Whig Corners, ran along the road from Cherry Valley to the rapidly expanding town of Cooperstown by way of the northern border of the new town, through the Godfrey Miller Patent. Lentsville derives its name from an early family in that area. Whig Corners was named reputedly because of a group of Whigs who routinely met there under an elm tree during the mid-nineteenth century. Bowerstown, on the Bowers Patent, was along the road leading out of Cooperstown. It was on the east side of the Susquehanna River and was named after Henry Bowers who held considerable amounts of land in the patent. Phoenix Mills was further down the Susquehanna near the southerly tip of the town. Clarkesville, Waterville and Westville were along the Long Patent Road which ran roughly in a north-south direction on the eastern edge of the town. Clarkesville took its name from George Clarke due to the building of his house in the center of that hamlet and Westville was named due to its location at the western end of the Long Patent. Waterville was between Clarkesville and Westville at the juncture of the Long Patent Road and the present day Norton Cross Road. The origin of this name is a mystery.

The town was often called Newtown-Martin because that was the largest of these eight hamlets. It was named after Peter Martin who had brought his family to settle in that area between Otsego Lake and Cherry Valley before the War of Independence. The Godfrey Miller Patent, as that area was first known, contained 9,000 acres which were divided into 100-acre lots. By 1769, when Richard Smith toured the area, he noted that there were twelve people living in this hamlet. In the 1770s Martin started having financial difficulties and began selling off lots from his holdings for between twenty-five and forty-four pounds.[2] His financial problems were only compounded by his loyalist sympathies. With the outbreak of the war and increasing attacks from the Indians, instigated in large part by the British, Martin deposited his family in the relative safety of Fort Plain and left his considerable land holdings to go to Canada where he later died.[3] It was common for loyalists to leave their families in New York where it was presumed they would be safe, while they joined the British in Canada to fight the rebels. It must be noted that the town was alternately called either Newtown-Martin or Middlefield at this time. Newtown-Martin would more correctly have designated the hamlet that became Middlefield Centre though, and Middlefield designated the whole town.[4]

One month after its separation from Cherry Valley, on 4 April 1797, at the first town meeting, Samuel Griffin of Middlefield Centre was elected supervisor of Middlefield, as the town was to be known. He held this post until 1802. Lewis Edson and Robert Campbell, along with Samuel Griffin, were elected the first school commissioners in the town. The office of school commissioner was one recently created by the New York State legislature in 1795. This legislation allowed for towns to elect school commissioners, levy taxes to support schools and to build schools. A school is mentioned as being in existence as early as 1790 in the Bowerstown area. Although little is known of its operation, it is known that it was conducted by Hannah Hubbell, an early settler to the area. This would probably have been considered a dame school. In an era when most school teachers were men, a school taught by a woman requires special mention. To say female teachers in this period were an anomaly would be incorrect. However, their duties usually were a combination of day care and the teaching of basic reading. Both of these tasks had been shifting from the home to such schools for over a century, first in England, then in New England, and by the late eighteenth century, to the New York frontier.[5]

In light of the timing of the school legislation, it may be assumed that this first school was not supported with public funds. Instead, it would have been financed privately by the residents, as was the school that Benjamin Gilbert taught in Cherry Valley in 1785. This speaks volumes about the sense of responsibility of these early settlers. Even while trying to carve a life out of a wild landscape, there was still enough concern for their children to set up a school at private cost to teach at least the rudiments of education. Such concern was not without precedent. Peter Martin had articulated a need for a school in the area in the 1760s. In about 1800, in the area of Middlefield Centre, a school was erected with Master Alpin as teacher. Early town records indicate that funds were allocated for schools at this time. Samuel Griffin, as supervisor, recorded receipt "of school money from the State for the town of Middlefield, forty-one pounds thirteen shillings. Also, twenty-one pounds twelve shillings raised by said town, making in the whole the sum of sixty-three pounds five shillings" on 22 August 1797.[6] Master Alpin's school probably received such funds.

These early schools were very small buildings, if indeed a building was erected for this specific purpose. When Samuel Dunlop taught school in Cherry Valley, it is said he did so while tending his crops. Benjamin Gilbert, however, put down in his diary, as stated above, that the residents of Cherry Valley did see fit to erect a school building in 1785. Master Alpin's school in Middlefield Centre was typical of these early, humble schools. Henry Clarke Wright, in his memoirs, made it clear that in the first decade of the nineteenth century on the Otsego frontier only the rudiments of education were taught: spelling, reading, writing and arithmetic.[7] For those parents who could afford to allow their children to pursue more advanced learning, there were academies in Cherry Valley and Cooperstown where logic, rhetoric, history, English composition, Latin and Greek were taught.

One of the first orders of business for this new town government was the improvement of the road system. A better road system was key to commerce, industry, and increased settlement, which, for those like Clarke, translated to increased profits from land speculation and tenant farmers. Thus, starting in the late eighteenth and continuing through the early nineteenth century there was increasing pressure to improve the highways. Most roads at this point were mere horse trails. In 1795 it could take a traveler an entire day to go from Cooperstown to Cherry Valley and a full five days to travel from Cherry Valley to Albany. Even as late as 1806 it was easier and more common to travel on foot or horseback as most roads were still impassable with a wagon.[8] This state of affairs would act as a serious impediment to commerce, causing great delays and expense to transport goods.

A better road system would serve to make overland transportation of crops cheaper. After a succession of harsh winters, bad harvests and intermittent warfare, only made worse due to the struggles with Napoleon, by the 1790s Europe was in great need of imported wheat. The low-lying area of Middlefield, along the Cherry Valley Creek, proved a good location for growing this crop. Generally, the riverbed areas of Otsego County could produce almost thirty bushels of wheat per acre.[9] The result was to siphon settlement from the Cherry Valley to Cooperstown corridor, encompassing Middlefield Centre, to the Long Patent area. This gave a boost to settlement of the Clarkesville and Westville areas as newly arrived settlers found fertile flat land in this valley to grow wheat for export at rapidly rising prices.

The farmers who grew this cash crop generally sold it to either their landlords in lieu of paying rents or to middlemen. In both cases these businessmen, and not the local farmers, were the men who would sell the crops to exporters in Albany. These enterprising businessmen would shoulder the cost of transportation. Therefore, it was these same people who were exerting pressure to improve roads on the premise that better roads would lead to cheaper transportation, and, hence, increased profits. Their goal was to make it as easy as possible to transport this wheat to Albany, where it could be sold and loaded onto ships for overseas transport.

Albany had become the central embarkation point of the wheat trade of upstate New York. By 1807 wheat was selling in Albany for $1.37 per bushel.[10] When multiplied by the reported 30 bushels per acre, it can be seen that farms were producing wheat with a retail value of $41.40 per acre. Although, it was the men who purchased this wheat from the farmers and bore the cost of transportation as well as the vagaries of the market who reaped the lion's share of the benefit from these prices, it is reasonable to assume that there was some competitive mechanism whereby farmers would reap greater financial rewards when prices were high.

It was the profitability of growing this crop and the fact that it grew best along the alluvial lands around Clarkesville which created the primary financial incentive that acted to draw people from Middlefield Centre and other previously more densely populated areas. The Parshall family serves as a prime example of this migration. James Parshall had traveled from Long Island to Middlefield Centre in 1796 with his wife and children during a period when this hamlet clearly showed greater promise of opportunity. He was followed the next year by his younger brother John and his wife Phebe Coddington. They purchased land from the McCollums on which to build their farm. However, by the first decade of the nineteenth century, John and his family had relocated to the hamlet of Clarkesville. They were soon joined in the hamlet by their nephew James Jr. It is a testament to the enduring opportunities which the hamlet of Clarkesville held for the bulk of the nineteenth century that this family took root and intermarried with so many of the local families including the Haydens, Baileys, Crandalls, Knapps and VanHusens. It was not long after his arrival in the hamlet that James joined the recently formed Baptist church, requesting fellowship from the Baptists in 1815 along with Gilbert Pinney, Sally Pinney, Mary Pitts, and Phebe Weed. On Sunday 15 October 1815, these people were all Baptized by Elder Sawin in the Cherry Valley Creek.[11]

The export of wheat was not the only commodity these settlers produced. In clearing the land as they moved to Clarkesville, large amounts of hardwood trees were felled and burned to produce pot ash. By boiling and baking these wood ashes, potassium salts were refined for use in soap, saltpeter, dyes, bleach, glass and some drugs. There was a very lucrative market in pot ash and England's factories were hungry for it. A pot ash works could hope to make between fifty and sixty pounds per ton in profit. Moss Kent set up such a works near Springfield and his business was thriving by 1792. Kent's friend William Cooper even built a road from Cooperstown to his works to make transport easier.[12] This was a calculated move, since Cooper would often receive fresh pot ash from settlers in exchange for credit at his store. The construction of this road made transport easier, hence increasing the profits from this ash for Cooper.

This barter system of Cooper's was illustrative of the economic dynamic of rural New York. Individual settlers and tenants did not often personally take part in the trans-Atlantic commerce of which wheat and pot ash are examples. These commodities were often purchased by or traded to large landowners, store keepers, or their agents. It was these wealthy individuals who took the risk of transporting these items. George Clarke, through his agent, engaged in the same sort of business with his tenants on the Long Patent. Like Cooper, Clarke's tenants could pay their rent in an equivalent value of wheat. Any production over and above that necessary to pay rent could be sold for cash to a willing buyer, or traded for credit at a store. It was in this way that landlords maintained the primacy of their position over their tenants. It was a symbiotic relationship but it existed within a structured, hierarchical framework. The similarities of this system to the feudal arrangement in England was more than just coincidental. Cooper even referred to his home in Cooperstown as the Manor House. Clearly, men like Cooper and Clarke were trying to create a manor system on this new frontier the way the Livingstons, Cortlandts, and Philipses had done along the Hudson before the Revolution.

The amount of profit in any commodity was closely tied to the ease of transport. This was so elementary that Cooper was easily able to enlist the help of merchants from Albany in lobbying the state legislature in 1790 to grant £400 to improve the road from Canajoharie to Cooperstown. Cooper was awarded this construction contract, along with two partners, and subcontracted the work to settlers. Not surprisingly, settlers could receive payment in cash or credit at Cooper's store.[13] This road would allow wagons to travel to the Mohawk River, and, thence by water to Albany. So firmly was the primacy of road construction and maintenance recognized that at the first Middlefield town meeting three commissioners of highways were elected: Andrew Wilson, Stephen Smith, and Moses Rich. These men were charged with laying out road districts, or wards. To judge the importance of this position, it is well to consider who these commissioners were; to this end, Moses Rich serves as a fine example. He had served in the Revolutionary War and had obtained the rank of colonel. He settled in Middlefield in about 1787. At this time he was living in the hamlet of Westville and is credited with erecting and operating the first grist mill in the town in 1795.[14] This mill was located on the Cherry Valley Creek as it ran through that hamlet. He later augmented his holdings by adding a saw mill. In the spring of 1798 he was licensed to keep an inn.

The commissioners of Excise for the Town of Middlefield have Licensed Moses Rich to keep an inn or Tavern, which I've acct'd to the Poor-Masters five dollars.

Samuel Griffin, supervisor.
Middlefield, May 26, 1798.[15]

With his economic prosperity and, indeed, survival so tied to a good road system it is no wonder that he sought to become a commissioner, and thus exert influence to ensure his financial well-being. Both the mill and the inn required a good road system to sustain a healthy business for obvious reasons. This enterprising man had managed to put himself into a position of authority over the road system and thus use tax dollars to indirectly help his business. However, he was not expending his capital on land either. Both the parcel the mill was on and the parcel the inn was on were being leased from George Clarke; one plot for four pounds, one shilling, and nine pence per year and the other for five pounds, fourteen shillings annually, both rents payable in December.[16] As has been noted, it was not at all uncommon to see a business man using his available capital for the furtherance of his business and not to use it to invest in fixed assets such as land. Both of these enterprises would have been strongly encouraged by Clarke and his agents as ways of luring additional settlers to his lands to increase rental income. It was just this sort of activity that helped to more that double Clarke's rental income in the 1790 to 1797 period (see Table 1, page 19).

Each road district was to be maintained by an overseer who reported to the commissioners. On February 14, 1798 these districts had been mapped as follows (according to Duane Hamilton Hurd's *History of Otsego County*):

No. 1   *Begin at Cooperstown bridge - ends 4 rods N. of James Ingals.*
No. 2   *Begin 4 rods N. of James Ingals, ends at bridge near Andrew Carman's.*
No. 3   *Begin at bridge near Andrew Carman's - ends at Cherry Valley line.*
No. 4   *Begin at State road near Phineas Wilson's - ends at Springfield line.*
No. 5   *Begin at State road near Samuel Anderson's - ends at Springfield line.*
No. 6   *Begin at State road a few rods N. of James Horth's - ends at Springfield line.*
No. 7   *Begin at State road between Jas. Ingals and Abel Parkers - ends at Ron't. Riddle's.*
No. 8   *Begin at State road running by John Cook's, Samuel Killpatrick's, and to the Cherry Valley line.*
No. 9   *Begin at State road near Samuel Anderson's - ends at the Long Pattent near Ephraim Brookins.*
No. 10 *Begin at road No. 9 - ends at the N. line of the Wm. Ruse's farm.*

No. 11   Begin at the State road near Hosea Brown's - ends at Nathan White's house on Long Pattent.

No. 12   Begin at Cherry Valley line - runs down the Long Pattent to Moses Rich's barn.

No. 13   Begin at a bridge near Jas. Murphy's - ends at N. line of John Thomas' farm.

No. 14   Begin at N. line of John Thomas' farm - ends at S. line of Middlefield.

No. 15   Begin at house of Arnold Burrell's - end at S. line of Mid. W. side of Cherry Valley Creek.

No. 16   Begin at Moses Rich's mill - end at Cherry Valley line E. side of Cherry Valley Creek.

No. 17   Begin at State road near nears Mrs. Butt's farm - end at crotch of road near Bowers Saw mill.

No. 18   Begin at State road near Bowers field - end at crotch of road near Thomas tract.

No. 19   Begin at school house - end at bridge below Bowers Saw mill.

No. 20   Begin at bridge near Thomas tracts - end at Jeremiah Irons.

The following nineteen overseers of highways were appointed by these commissioners: Isaac Green, Oliver Buel, Ebenezer Bennett, Oliver Stetson, Nathaniel Harley, Nathanial Gallop, Oliver Gibbs, John Sweet, George Boid, Daniel Temple, Samuel Killpatrick, Thaddeus Brookins, James Ingalls, Timothy Walker, Abijah Barnum, Cornelius Hendrix, Jonathan Bennett, Nathan Pearce, and Jonathan Smith.[17] This position was viewed as slightly lower in prestige than that of commissioner. Quite often the men who held the position of Overseer were respectable farmers of good standing and moderate prosperity. Oliver Stetson, for example, who rented his farm in the Long Patent from George Clarke for four pounds per year, seems to have paid his rent promptly, indicating that his farming efforts were such that he was able to keep current with his obligations. He did, however, skip years 1804 and 1805, paying current in 1806, and giving the farm over to James Murphy in 1807. This compares to such men as James Ingalls of Middlefield Centre who was sufficiently prosperous to be able to keep a hired hand by 1803 and became a director of the Second Great Western Turnpike.[18]

Overseeing highways and keeping roads in good repair was a very serious business. Those officials found negligent in their duties were subject to harsh treatment by courts. Each overseer would sign a contract with the town stating that he would ensure that people living along the road would work to keep the road clear and in a good state of repair. The individual's work requirement, *i.e.*, number of days of labor and tools he had to bring, were based on his assessment and tax. These were derived from the amount of land he owned. Universally, land leases stipulated that the renter was responsible for roadwork. It is interesting to note that individuals could commute their assessments by paying the corresponding tax, thereby freeing them from their labor.[19] It is worthy of note that when viewing these routes on a map it is clear that, wherever possible, steep grades were avoided. This was necessitated by the mode of transport: horse and wagon. It would be both difficult and dangerous to take a horse and wagon over a steep grade, which, in turn, would be an impediment to business.

These district descriptions note the location of two mills and Hannah Hubbell's school in the town. One mill was in Bowerstown owned by Henry Bowers; the other was in Westville owned by Moses Rich. There were several other businesses in Middlefield at this time, some of which had already been in operation for a significant time. Alexander McCollum of Middlefield Centre had established the first saw mill prior to the Revolutionary War. By the late 1790s he and Andrew Cameron were both operating inns as well. Further, Benjamin Johnson had opened the first store in about 1790.[20] The saw mill, store and both inns were located in Newtown-Martin (Middlefield Centre). The ability of this area to support such a level of commerce points to this as having been a very heavily traveled route. The opening of an inn was a logical way for the enterprising of nature to tap into the flow of outside money coming with travelers. However, the types of businesses established were also indicative of the needs of the residents. Most residents made what they could: cloth, soap, candles, etc. Saw mills, grist mills and stores catered to those needs which could not be fulfilled at home. They represented an enormous investment of capital and equipment to establish and sustain, and therefore, would have been built by men who settled in the area with some degree of financial means. These settlers were men of vision and fortitude ready to take a calculated business risk. Not all settlers were of limited means and/or education looking to start over, heading into the wilderness with nothing save what they could carry.

One fact of which these commissioners had to be cognizant was the beginnings of a shifting of Middlefield's population. In the 1790s most of the inhabitants and businesses were situated along the Cherry Valley to Cooperstown corridor, specifically in Newtown-Martin. This was logical by virtue of Cherry Valley and Cooperstown being the major population centers and business hubs on this frontier. However, it was the vast tracts of flat riverbed land along the Cherry Valley Creek encompassing Clarkesville and Westville that was attracting the attention of the enterprising. This was terrain well suited for the growing of crops, particularly wheat which was a prime cash crop. Throughout the 1790s this was the area that experienced a preponderant growth in population and business activity. Clarke had chosen this spot for his house on the Long Patent because he realized that this was a spot that could serve as the center of his manor farm and already there were numerous farms growing up in the area. Oliver Stetson's farm has already been mentioned. However, there were also Benjamin North's 117-acre farm on Lot Number 10 of the Long Patent, which he rented for four pounds per year, and John Moake's 126-acre farm on Lot Number 7 of the Long Patent, which he rented for four pounds, one shilling annually. In total, by this time 38 of the 68 lots on the Long Patent had tenants.[21] Further, there was the business activity of Moses Rich in Westville, as well as other enterprising men. These first commissioners recognized these facts as is evidenced by the sheer amount of attention they paid to the area of the Long Patent. They designated 30% of the road districts to that tract, *i.e.*, district numbers 9, 11, 12, 14, 15, and 16.

To gauge how effective these commissioners of highways were at improving the road system in the new town, it is useful to look at the changes in population and business activity. In 1800, the population of Middlefield was 1,042 persons. By 1810 the population had increased by 100.3% to 2,087 persons, and by 1820 it was augmented a further 22.9% or 477 persons. This brought the total population to 2,564. Considered over the space of this twenty-year period, the population grew by 1,522 persons, or 146%. By comparison with Otsego County as a whole, Middlefield was growing at a relatively brisk pace. The average growth in population in the county by town over this same twenty-year period was 1,665 persons, or 109.7%.[22] The town was growing at a faster than average rate compared to the county's other towns. This was a direct result of an improved road system which was able to improve accessibility to the town's resources and, therefore, business opportunities in the town. The bulk of this population increase was due to immigration from other parts of the country, primarily Connecticut and Massachusetts. There must have been some recognition that opportunity abounded in the Middlefield area. This opportunity was in the form of easy land lease terms, good agricultural land, and an improving road network. All these factors helped foster other businesses such as the mills, taverns, and stores cropping up in Middlefield.

These population figures do not include persons held as slaves. There are only sketchy records enumerating the number of slaves in the town for the year 1800, but it is known that slavery was present. Henry Bowers, for example, is known to have had slaves. The records of the Presbyterian Church of Cooperstown state that in December of 1803 "a black boy of Mr. Bowers" died of a slow fever. There is also the case of "a black boy of James Averell Jr. dying in January 1804". Presumably, both boys died of similar causes.[23] Although there seems to be no indication that slave holding and trading was extensive in the area, it did occur. In 1799, there was an advertisement for the sale of an unmarried slave girl for $200.[24] However, already the slave issue was getting attention from such socially conscious people as Jedediah Peck, of Burlington, Otsego County, who, as a member of the Assembly, proposed a bill for the abolition of slavery in 1799. Further, numerous slave owners were in the habit of freeing slaves after they had served an agreed upon length of time as is evidenced by a certificate issued to a slave named Bob by his owner, Abraham Roseboom, in 1818.[25]

In addition to simple population trends, it is illustrative of the point to consider trends in wealth. It would be expected that increases in overall population would lead to increases in the number of taxpayers in the town. Indeed, the period 1805 to 1820 saw such an increase (see Table 2, next page). Specifically, the number of taxpayers increased by 17% while the average value of their wealth increased by 7%. Comparing the town to the average growth in the county, it is again clear that Middlefield was ahead of the average. The average wealth per taxpayer in the county for the same period was $832 by 1820, an increase of 12% over the fifteen year period whereas in Middlefield it had grown to $865. The apparent shift downward in aggregate wealth and wealth/taxpayer from 1815 to 1820 has a dual cause and needs to be considered more an anomaly than a trend. The period 1815 to 1820 saw, not only a steep increase in population, but also a rural financial crisis resulting from a depression that curtailed the money supply and, hence, depressed land values. Most wealth in the county was held in the form of land, which makes the 1820 wealth figures deceptively low. Further, a depression in land values had a disproportionate effect on only the most wealthy residents, not the population as a whole.

TABLE 2: TOWN OF MIDDLEFIELD RESIDENT TAXPAYERS AND AGGREGATE WEALTH

YEAR	1805	1810	1815	1820
RESIDENT TAXPAYER	282	306	288	330
AGGREGATE WEALTH	$227,660	$227,790	$383,933	$285,378
AGG. WEALTH PER TAXPAYER	$807	$744	$1,333	$865

Source: Alan Taylor, *William Cooper's Town: Power and Persuasion on the Frontier of the Early American Republic* (New York, 1996), 433.

This population growth and its attendant accumulation of wealth provided attractive business opportunities for enterprising individuals. One such man, Joshua L. Pinney, an acquaintance of George Clarke, saw his future financial success in this wilderness. By 1803 Pinney had relocated from his Albany home, where he first met Clarke, to the hamlet of Clarkesville. Pinney took up residence in Clarke's stately house on Lot 18 of the Long Patent and operated it as a tavern. Clarke assessed Pinney a rent of seven pounds, nine shillings for the house along with two acres and one rood of land.[26] Significantly, comparing this rental assessment to Oliver Stetson's rent of four pounds per year for an entire farm indicates that Clarke considered a business venture on Lot 18 to have great potential (a note made when he first viewed the lot) and probably that there was other settlement on this spot by that time. Further, the amount of Pinney's rent demonstrates the value Clarke placed on his house on that parcel.

Clarke was an astute man of business who no doubt considered renting his house to Pinney as a practical step in terms of augmenting his income and developing his lands in Otsego. Since 1797 he had been traveling over his New York lands having them mapped and leased by competent surveyors and agents. He did not take well to errors in these endeavors as is witnessed by a sharp letter he sent to William Cockburn, who was also the land agent for Robert Livingston of Clermont, the holder of one of the largest landed estates in New York. In 1797 Clarke sternly asked if the mistakes made by James Cockburn had been corrected. He clearly stated that he wanted these corrected maps when he arrived in Oriskany on his way to Cherry Valley. Only with well drawn maps would he be able to properly have his lands settled and developed, thus assuring his future income. He demanded the same attention to detail when he had the hamlet of Clarkesville mapped. As a result, when Barnabus M. Gilbert, grandson of Benjamin Gilbert, remapped the hamlet in 1851 he was able to clearly mark the original subdivisions in black and overlay the current subdivisions on those lines.[27]

Through Clarke's efforts the hamlet was already proving an important stopping point for travelers, creating a need for lodging and board. Taverns and inns were common in the early nineteenth century, as is evidenced by the number already mentioned as operating in Middlefield by this time. They were necessitated by both the condition of the roads and the mode of transport which made a trip from Clarksville to Albany take five days or so. Taverns served as places for men to gather and discuss business and politics as well as other topics which might not have been suited for such community gathering places as the church or meeting house. Unfortunately, inns could also become settings for scenes of drunken depravity. Pinney, being an industrious man, saw an enticing business opportunity in these simple facts; as one contemporary commented, being a tavern keeper was the "surest road to public honours and riches."[28] Pinney would continue to prove to be an enterprising man in the future, having a stake in numerous businesses in the hamlet. As a socially conscious and philanthropic man, he used his wealth to improve the hamlet as well.

The first decade of the nineteenth century saw some dramatic developments in the hamlet of Clarkesville, both in terms of settlement and construction, and settlers who would shape the future of the hamlet. It was during this decade that two houses of great significance were built. The significance of these houses was tied to the future role they would play as the hamlet developed into an important stopping point for travelers; both houses would later become hotels. The first house was built by Hosea Cummings on land he rented from George Clarke on the north side of the Cooperstown Road two building lots down from the crossroads. This house was a two story wood structure with a five bay façade. Its perfect symmetry was in keeping with the aesthetic of the Federal taste. The back of the house was constructed against an embankment with a rear ell extending from the second floor, which, due to this embankment, would have been at ground level. This architectural device gave birth to the term "bankhouse." The Hosea Cummins house is the only structure in the hamlet known have had entablatures over the windows. This would have been considered quite an extravagance for the period.

Very little is known about Hosea Cummings. His rental relationship with Clarke can only be surmised from the land deeds which record a sale from Clarke to Cummings on 8 April 1822 for 20 perches and 37/100 of land for the amount of $27. Further, on that same day Cummings sold the property to Hannah Howard for $400. Clearly, Cummings had been renting the land from Clarke and built his house, then sold the entire parcel to Howard with the improvements. Whether or not Clarke held a private mortgage with Cummings prior to this date is unknown, but certainly the pressing impetus for Cummings to purchase the parcel from Clarke in 1822 was his desire to sell it to Howard. It is very likely that it was Howard who first opened the house as a hotel as a means of supporting herself. It was a very unusual occurrence for a woman to be so proactive in endeavoring to support herself during this period. However, her husband, Nathan, seems to have been a scoundrel. Some years later she would accuse him of adultery to successfully procure her divorce. Since the property was purchased in Hannah's name, it is tantalizing to surmise that the Howards may have already been estranged. It is probable that Joshua Pinney assisted Howard in buying this property since, many years later, the property was referred to as having been called Pinney & Howard.[29]

As odd as it may seem for Pinney to have assisted in establishing another tavern that would compete with his own tavern, it must be kept in mind that Pinney would throughout his time in Clarkesville show himself to ever be a charitable person to those less fortunate. Howard's marriage to a rake would have recommended her to Pinney's charitable sentiments. Beyond these magnanimous sentiments, though, it is equally certain that Pinney would not have acted in a manner that would have adversely impacted his own financial interests. Without a doubt, any monies he would have advanced to Howard to assist in this purchase would certainly have been lent out at interest.

The other house of note that also became a hotel, was built across the street from the Cummings house by James Jones. Jones, like so many others, left very scant information about himself. His house was of modest dimensions with a three bay façade and standing only one and one half stories high. Its front-facing gable is uncharacteristic of the Federal period, but the delicacy of the house's moldings and its construction technique clearly mark it as an early house of this period. It would not be until the 1840s that this house was dramatically enlarged to become a hotel.

As this construction was occurring, certain people key to the future of the hamlet were laying roots. Four of these people would loom large at this time: Joshua Pinney, Benjamin Gilbert, Elder Benjamin Sawin, and Dr. Sumner Ely. George Clarke, and his descendants, continued to hold large tracts of land in the town. However, much of his attention was being focused on legal proceedings and the building of Hyde Hall, his stately Regency-style mansion on a bluff overlooking Otsego Lake. These endeavors necessarily limited his involvement in the development of Clarkesville. He did, however, see fit to augment his holdings as the opportunities arose. In 1810, for example, he purchased three farms totaling 342 acres from Richard Cooper, the son of Judge William Cooper and older brother of the author James Fenimore Cooper. These farms were designated as: Farm A 115 acres, Farm B 102 acres, and Farm C 125 acres. Clarke paid $1,200 for all three farms, which were conveyed on one deed. They were already rented to tenants and located in the town of Middlefield.[30]

Clarke, who owned over 100,000 acres throughout New York, like many other such landlords in New York, was encountering considerable opposition from his tenants. The influx of large numbers of Yankees from Connecticut specifically, but from other New England states as well, brought a fierce sense of independence to the farmers of central New York. These people came to resent the entire landlord/tenant relationship. Agrarian unrest on these manors was nothing new. However, in the past this unrest had focused largely on obtaining better lease terms. In 1795, tenants tried a new tactic. In that year about 210 Livingston tenants in the Hudson River valley actually petitioned the state legislature to revoke the 1686 Dongan Patent on which the Livingstons based their land titles. Even though they were unsuccessful they were undeterred. They tried the same tactic again in 1811, when about 153 tenants of the Livingston Manor petitioned the state legislature to invalidate the Livingston family's colonial patent again. The legislature rejected this petition as they did the one in 1795. In that same year, on behalf of his tenants in Otsego, as well as Montgomery, Delaware, Dutchess, and Saratoga counties, numerous appeals were made to the state legislature questioning Clarke's land claims. The basis of these claims was that during the revolution Clarke was an English born subject of the Crown and, thus, an alien enemy of the American cause.[31] This claim was made despite Banyar's efforts during the revolution to cloak Clarke with the shield of neutrality and in spite of the legislature's passing of an act in 1792 allowing Clarke to hold land in New York even though he was not a citizen.

George Clarke was an obvious target for the ire of disgruntled tenants and their political leaders. They saw in him the consummate English aristocratic landlord, which was a persona he helped to foster by keeping aloof from the bulk of his tenant farmers. He preferred associating with those he viewed as his equals: Goldsbrow Banyar, James Duane, Stephen Van Rensselaer, *et al.* This distancing of himself from his tenants even manifested itself in the siting of his house in Clarkesville in the 1790s and, later, Hyde Hall. To answer these appeals, the New York Senate created a committee to look into the various allegations of Clarke's tenants and recommended that the governor begin proceedings against him. Clarke, for his part, strictly maintained his right of inheritance and refused to even testify before the senate committee. Legal proceedings ensued and the war of words heated up. DeWitt Clinton, a staunch Jeffersonian, launched such vicious attacks against Clarke and the manor system he was building that Clarke felt compelled to challenge Clinton to a duel. In 1811 the state legislature recommended that Clarke's titles be vacated. It was not until 1818, in the case of *Jackson v. Clarke*, heard before the United States Supreme Court, that the issues were finally settled in Clarke's favor.[32]

Clarke's decision not to take an active role in the early organization of the town is more a result of his preoccupation with tenant unrest and these legal issues and not that he had given up on his manorial vision. The evidence, indeed, points in just the opposite direction. The idea of building a manor similar to the pre-Revolutionary manors along the Hudson was still in the forefront of his mind. Obviously, he envisioned a manor as a source of rental income, devoid of the feudal obligations from tenants that New York manors once included. Well into the nineteenth century, the Clarke family continued to hold large tracts of land in Middlefield and the neighboring town of Springfield, as well as other areas in New York State. These holdings, as stated above, were augmented as the opportunities arose. Further, Clarke continued to lease this land to farmers and businessmen, deriving the bulk of his income from rentals very much as an English nobleman might. There was, however, a qualitative difference between the attitude of Clarke to his tenants and other landlords, like William Cooper, to their tenants. Clarke chose to live on a secluded spot on Otsego Lake, rather than in his house on the Long Patent. This is in stark contrast to the Cooper family's preference for living in the heart of their namesake village and is emblematic of Clarke's desire to keep a distance between himself and his tenants. His attempt to create a baronial atmosphere around himself and his family in this way was largely successful.

The siting and development of Hyde Hall needs to be discussed in order to shed light on the attitudes of Clarke. In 1816 Clarke had considered building a house in Albany, even going so far as to have an architect design the house. This architect was Philip Hooker, who had attained some fame in Albany; having designed the New York State Capital in 1806 and Catherine Duane's residence, Featherstonhaugh House, in 1812, as well as numerous other buildings. Indeed, by the early nineteenth century, Hooker was credited with having designed seven of the most prominent buildings of Albany. When Clarke met this architect is unclear although it is known that they were both members of the Society for the Promotion of Useful Arts in 1814. Clarke never had the Albany house built but with modifications the garden front of that house became the south, or lake, front for his cottage on Otsego Lake. Construction on this cottage started in 1817 and it was ready for Clarke's family to move into by 1819. It is this cottage that developed into the grand house that Clarke christened as Hyde Hall.

The spot chosen was a secluded bluff overlooking the lake a full mile from the road. The front of the cottage commanded "a full view of the lake, and the handsome village of Cooperstown". Inspiration for the piazza that wrapped around the cottage came from the house Pierre Pharoux had designed for M. Chorand in Coxsackie in 1795, and represented a novel architectural feature in America. The east front, facing Clarke's lands along the lake, was designed to be austere so as "to have a good appearance at a distance, from which it will be generally viewed." The floor plan of the main section of the house followed the plan for a villa designed by John Plaw in his book *Rural Architecture* published in 1785. Plaw was an architect with whom Clarke was familiar, having at least one of his books in his library.[33]

Clarke's house stood out as one of the grandest houses in America at this time with the east façade, when completed in 1834, measuring a full ninety-seven feet across. Within this section of the house was contained "two of the finest rooms constructed in a private house in America before 1840," to quote Edward Root, an early twentieth century historian and art collector. He was referring to the drawing room and dining room which were behind this austere east façade. Both rooms had elaborate suspended plaster ceilings. The drawing room ceiling very similar to the ceiling designed by Inigo Jones for the double cube room at Wilton, which had been designed in 1649.[34] It was meant to impress and to display both wealth and status. Clarke was not interested in mingling with his tenants and the local residents. He wanted to overawe them and at the same time keep a distance between them and his family. He had hinted at this in building his house on the Long Patent, siting it as he did back from the road. Everything about Hyde Hall, though, showed the full fruit of that vision. This was in perfect keeping with the normal order of things Clarke would have known from his English genteel upbringing; the lord's family and manor house were at a distance from his tenants.

Viewing frontier development from this prism it can be seen that when considering any influence Clarke exerted on the early government of Middlefield, it would have been very much in a clandestine manner in the form of "wise counsel" spoken to his tenants at appropriate times. In this way, Clarke knew that a landlord could have considerable influence over his tenants by exploiting the esteem and respect the tenant might have for the landlord, or, conversely, by cajoling the tenant based on his position of dependence in relation to the landlord. Although it is hard to know what influence Clarke wielded over his tenants or how he wielded it, it would be naive to assume that just because there is no clear documentation explicitly stating he used his power to influence political outcomes that he did not do so. That this was a common practice may be gleaned from William North's statement to Benjamin Walker referencing activities on the Van Rensselaer Manor during the gubernatorial election of 1801, that "the people of the Manor have been influenced by the Patroon".[35]

Benjamin Gilbert was elected town supervisor in 1803 to succeed Samuel Griffin, holding this office until 1809 and then again from 1812 to 1816. Griffin, however, was not finished with his political career. In 1814 he was appointed to a judgeship in Otsego County. As for Gilbert, it is not known if Clarke exerted any of his considerable influence to have his friend elected, but, given the contemporary dynamics of rural power and persuasion, it is not beyond the realm of speculation. From 1810 to 1812 the office of supervisor was held by John Bowers, son of the land owner Henry Bowers of Bowerstown. John relocated from New York City and built Lakelands, the great Federal mansion on the edge of Otsego Lake, in about 1805.[36] Gilbert did not seek election as town supervisor in 1810 due to his election to the New York State Assembly.

This was to be his final term in that body; thereafter he devoted himself entirely to furthering his fortune, bettering his community, and to setting his children up in the world.

As early as 1804 Gilbert had started exerting himself to further his fortune as many men on the frontier did: he used land as a vehicle to make money. In that year he loaned to Abijah Boughton of Middlefield the sum of £215 19s. 1.5d. at interest. This loan was backed by a mortgage Gilbert took on 102 1/2 acres owned by Boughton. When Boughton defaulted on the debt in 1812, Gilbert took recourse and had the property sold at public auction. In another example of Gilbert using land as a speculative vehicle, he, along with Silas Crippen of the town of Worcester and G. W. Prevost of the village of Cooperstown, had surveyed "a few thousand acres" in 1814 and had it divided into farms. They offered these farms for sale and promised that "every reasonable credit will be given—from seven to fourteen years."[37] Gilbert was not destined to end his days as a humble farmer and these two examples illustrate how he sought to gain wealth and gentility. He would revel in styling himself Benjamin Gilbert, Esquire.

Understanding Gilbert's predilection for gentility coupled with his prominent and influential position in both the town and county, it is logical that Gilbert sought to foster greater civility and culture in this wilderness. There is no doubt that he would have known the tavern keeper Pinney, a man also bent on cutting a position of prominence for himself in his new surroundings. In all likelihood Gilbert and Pinney would have encouraged the missionary Elder Benjamin Sawin when he came to Clarksville and preached the first sermon in 1806. Sawin received such encouragement that he returned often to the hamlet.[38]

The following year, Pinney established the first school in the hamlet. To the north of his tavern there rose a knoll overlooking the hamlet. This spot was marked out for the school. The spot is across from the present Baptist church and is next to the old Baptist burying ground. That same year a conference was formed as a branch of the (East) Worcester Baptist Church. The town of Worcester had organized a Baptist Society in 1799. This is a relatively early date in light of the fact that by 1795 there was only one church building in Otsego County; that being a Presbyterian church in Cherry Valley. That community, being much older, had already seen multiple Christian denominations take root. One sect, the Episcopalians, who organized in 1797 and incorporated in 1803 as Trinity Episcopal Church, saw Benjamin Gilbert elected as a Vestryman in that first year. The more cosmopolitan Cooperstown did not have a church building until 1805 when another Presbyterian church was built. The core of the Middlefield Baptists was Pomeroy Wright, F. Hodgson, L. Pitts, N. Wickham, H. Belknapp, P. Boyce, T. Pitts, B. Pitts, Wickham, and Metsey L. Eggleston.[39]

Under Elder Sawin, ordained a pastor in 1808, the Baptists used this school building for their worship for about twenty years, Sawin having taken up residence in Middlefield. For their regular monthly organizational meetings they used either the school building or met at the Pinney Tavern. They used the Cherry Valley Creek for Baptisms. By 1810, the church records show that there were forty Baptists in the town and by 1821 there were 142 members.[40] By comparison, the much larger village of Cooperstown had 98 Presbyterian church members by 1810. Thus, in the course of one remarkable year the hamlet of Clarkesville saw the erection of its first school and the founding of the First Baptist Society in Middlefield; both events happening under the direction of men of inspired vision. As was seen in the population and wealth trends, socially the town of Middlefield was one of the more progressive areas of this frontier county as well.

Very early in its existence, the Baptists found themselves wrestling with the issue of intemperance on the frontier, an issue destined to haunt rural America throughout much of this period. It was not uncommon to see members expelled, or having the hand of fellowship withdrawn, for appearing intoxicated in public. Such was the case with Jesse How in 1811. In April of that year, at its regular congregational meeting, the Baptist Society took testimony relative to How's use of liquor. Among those present was Polly Pinney, wife of the tavern keeper, who "testified that she saw him one evening when she thought he was too much in liquor and she said it was observed by others." A motion was immediately made and passed to withdraw the hand of fellowship from this man. Nor was this an isolated incident. In May 1813, "Brothers Wood, Hoskins, North and Pinney testified to the drunkenness of Brother Amos Jones". He suffered the same fate as How and saw the hand of fellowship withdrawn.[41]

This early congregation also had to address the issue of non-attendance, which was viewed as a serious infraction. On 20 June 1812 a committee was formed composed of Daniel Hoskins, Thomas Hodgson, and Joshua L. Pinney, whose charge it was to "attend to the temperal concerns of Elder Sawin." Repeatedly, this committee met with those who had been remiss in their attendance at church and reported back to the congregation. In some cases, such as that of Brother Wickham, reconciliation with the church congregation was achieved; with others such as with Betsey Pitts, this was not the case. Still in other cases, as with Gilbert Pinney, who confessed to the congregation in 1821 "that he had been forward to commune with people of other orders", fellowship was necessarily withdrawn.[42]

Such was the growth and fervency of this group of Baptists that in 1816 a group in Worcester contacted the Middlefield Baptist Society when they wanted to organize into a church. The Middlefield congregation appointed Elder Sawin, Thomas Hodgson, Edward Wright, Samuel Shepherd, and Joshua Pinney to attend this council. A similar request was received in 1821 from the town of Sharon in nearby Schoharie County. In this case Elder Sawin, B. North, J. L. Pinney, Elijah Spafford, and Thomas Bates were appointed to attend. This shows in a very striking way the leadership role the residents of Clarkesville were taking in the county.[43]

Concurrent with the founding of the school and the Baptist Society, was the establishment of a library in the town in 1810. This library, like others in Otsego County at this time, was organized by local residents. Members met once a year and paid dues which were used for the purchase of books. Circulation was only to members and these members were usually among the more enlightened in the town. Membership could be paid quarterly at a rate of seventy-five cents. The driving force behind this library was Henry Guy, who had settled in the hamlet on the west side of the Long Patent Road. He tended to the management of circulation and finances for the library; a position he held well into the 1820s.[44]

It was shortly after these events transpired that a remarkable physician came to Clarkesville. Dr. Sumner Ely arrived from Lyme, Connecticut in 1810 at the age of 23. He quickly developed a wide-ranging practice in the area and was very active in the Otsego County Medical Society from 1817 until his death in 1857. The Society had been organized in 1806. In later life he became a president of the American Medical Association.[45] Ely built his house in the hamlet a short distance from the Pinney Tavern on the same side of the Long Patent Road. It stands as a fine example of Federal architecture, following the Palladian three-part plan according to the sixteenth century Italian architect's design books.[46] Palladio's designs had become popular in America during the late Federal period. The front-facing gable was divided by three fluted pilasters, and located in the center of the gable was a most delicately carved fan. It has gained the status of folklore that Freemasons along the frontier would have fans installed in their house gables or above their doors as a sign to other Freemasons that one of their fold lived in the house. However, even though it is known that Ely was a Freemason, it is more likely that this association is more coincidental than intentional. Carved fans were merely architectural features of elegant, late Federal houses. The house had two balanced wings framing its central block with dental molding running under the eaves.[47] It was a most impressive house suiting the doctor's position in society.

When Ely decided to build his house in Clarkesville, he leased the land from Joshua Pinney. Pinney had taken a bond and mortgage from Clarke on 1 March 1814 to purchase the two acres and one rood of land for $425. Interest on this mortgage was due annually and the principle became due in 1824.[48] The fact that Pinney had to pay for the house that served as his tavern leaves no doubt that Clarke had built the house prior to Pinney's arrival in Clarkesville. Tenants were not required to purchase improvements they had made to land when they took mortgages for lands they had previously rented. Generally, only the land was assessed in the purchase price because the tenant had paid to construct the improvements. It was five years later when Ely purchased the parcel with his house from Pinney for $75.[49] The disparity in prices between what Pinney paid Clarke in 1814 and what Ely paid Pinney in 1819 has less to do with the amount of land each person bought and more to do with the fact that Pinney was purchasing land on which a very large house had been built prior to his arrival, and that Ely was buying land which had been vacant before he constructed his house.

As the first quarter of the nineteenth century headed for its close, Pinney rented other parts of his land to early settlers to Clarkesville as well, namely, Clark D. Parshall and Daniel A. Cummings. The paucity of extant documents from many of these early settlers requires that this rental arrangement be concluded based on logical deductions. Using the Ely house as an example, a reading of the relevant deeds make it clear that Ely did not take ownership to his house and parcel until 1819 even though he arrived in Clarksville in 1810 and married in 1816. The lack of any evidence of him taking up residence at any other site points to a construction date for his house as being prior to 1819. Further, an architectural review of the house indicates a construction date prior to 1819 rather than after 1819 as well. Its exterior ornamentation too closely ties the house to the Federal period since it lacks any sign of the Greek Revival influences then coming into vogue and being widely used in the architecture of the period. Taken together, it must be assumed that Ely took possession of and made improvements to his parcel prior to the 1819 purchase date. An additional dynamic of this arrangement points to the astuteness of Pinney as a business man. His primary financial concern at this time certainly was his tavern, however, he recognized an opportunity to profit from placing the mantle of landlord upon his shoulders.

The other piece of evidence that helps to establish the construction date of this house seems to place that date as 1816. In that year Ely married Hannah Gilbert and they received, as a wedding gift from Hannah's father, Benjamin Gilbert, $400. When the Freemasons in Cooperstown built the house that served as their lodge hall in 1797, it was at a cost of $300. It is reasonable to deduce that Ely could, therefore, have built his house on the Long Patent Road with the money from this wedding gift. Certainly the amount was sufficient and the timing, coinciding with his wedding, seems logical.

It can never be known with certainty what induced this young physician, Ely, to relocate to the frontier. However, two factors, working in tandem, might explain the move. In 1801 he entered Yale and graduated with the class of 1804. Among his classmates was none other than James Fenimore Cooper, the author, and son of William Cooper of Cooperstown. No doubt Ely had spent many hours listening to tales of the Otsego frontier from the man who would later immortalize it in literature. The other force that would have acted to pull Ely to Otsego would have been his older sister. Tabitha Ely had married Jedediah Peck in Lyme, Connecticut in 1772 and with her husband had moved to Burlington, Otsego County in 1790.[50] No doubt Sumner and Jedediah were good friends, both sharing a love of the furtherance of education and both striving to help the poor through the course of their respective careers. The only known area of discord would have been Sumner's Masonic association and Jedediah's disdain for this group. Ely petitioned for membership in Otsego Lodge on 21 October 1817, along with Joshua Pinney. Their petitions were accepted at the following meeting on 18 November, and Ely served as the Lodge's junior warden two years later in 1819. It is probable that Ely was inclined to join the lodge due to the influence of Benjamin Gilbert, his father-in-law, as well as the knowledge that many of Otsego's leading men were members. It is probably more than coincidental that one of Benjamin Gilbert's other sons-in-law, Dunham Spaulding, joined the lodge a short time later in 1821, two years prior to marrying Gilbert's daughter Esther.[51]

Not only did Ely serve as the area's physician, he also held the office of town clerk under Benjamin Gilbert, a post he filled from 1813 until 1816. He was appointed to this position to take over from Gilbert's good friend Samuel Griffin, who had served as town clerk since 1808. Griffin's non-appointment in 1813 was a result of his election to the New York State Assembly, where he served two consecutive terms. With these close political and social ties to Gilbert, Ely would have seen Gilbert's daughter often. In 1816 the prominent physician married Hannah, the daughter of the well-connected Gilbert, bringing her to reside in their fine house on the Long Patent Road. They must have made a striking pair; Ely standing a full six feet one inch tall with an athletic build and Hannah being described as "a lady of rare accomplishments and great amiability of temper".[52]

This was a most advantageous match for Dr. Ely; beyond the feelings of love he felt for Hannah, this marriage also provided Ely immediate entry into the circle of the county's most prominent families. Gilbert by this time was not only highly influential, but quite wealthy. For her wedding, he gave Hannah a gift of $400. He repeated this practice when his daughters Elizabeth and Esther both married in 1823: Elizabeth to Benjamin D. North Jr., and Esther to Dunham Spaulding, both men of Clarkesville.[53] The next year Ely succeeded his father-in-law as supervisor, assisted by his brother-in-law, Daniel, as town clerk. Daniel had since moved from his father's mansion (as Benjamin Gilbert referred to his house in his will) near Middlefield Centre and was living in a house he built on the Cooperstown Road heading west just across the Cherry Valley Creek from the hamlet of Clarkesville. Ely remained supervisor until 1828.

Unbridled success and prosperity did not visit all residents of the hamlet equally. Reuben Rich, who purchased lands both in and out of the hamlet, found himself on the wrong side of a lawsuit in 1816. Prior to that date Joshua Pinney had added dry goods merchant to the list of business ventures under his mantle and had extended considerable credit to Rich, who was unable to pay the debt. This year, remembered as the "year without summer" because much of New York saw frost in every month, was exceedingly hard on many farmers. Reuben Rich only serves as one example. In a suit brought before the Court of Common Pleas, Pinney prevailed over Rich in the amount of $114.21 plus damages, interest and costs. Still unable to pay, Sheriff James Hawkes seized and auctioned Rich's properties on 7 December 1816. One property was a farm of "about one hundred acres" and the other parcel was in the Long Patent in the hamlet of Clarkesville. The properties were purchased by Elijah Rich for $138.00.[54]

Whatever may have been Reuben Rich's intent when he had purchased these parcels initially is impossible to discern. However, it is curious to note that shortly before his debt problems with Pinney came to a head, he entered into an agreement with Jared Jewell to rent eighteen acres and twelve perches of land for one shilling an acre plus taxes. This parcel was in Lot Number 19 of the Long Patent, which would have placed it considerably south of Clarkesville, much closer to the neighboring hamlet of Westville. Indeed, the parcel is described as being along Reuben Rich's mill yard.[55] One wonders if this was the same mill that Moses Rich had set up in that area and whether Reuben had become a partner in that mill.

This episode between Pinney and Rich is illustrative of the sometimes tenuous ability to hold land in free title in Otsego during this early period. One bad harvest year had taken from Reuben Rich his title to land and pushed him back to a situation where he had to rent land. This in spite of the fact that he was at least a partner in a mill; an enterprise that was considered to have some expectation of prosperity. Certainly if Rich, as a mill owner, could succumb to the economic unpredictability attendant to weather fluctuations, how much more uncertain would be the economic welfare of the innumerable farmers. Obviously, as an agrarian based society, these economic ripples caused by such things as weather phenomena had a direct impact on the ability of the average person to buy and hold land, rather than to rent it. The difference being that in most cases involving rents, a landlord would be more sympathetic to the plight of the tenant during times of economic upheaval. This was clearly not the case when a creditor was dealing with someone who held title to their land.

The parcel that Reuben Rich lost and Elijah Rich purchased in the hamlet at this sheriff's sale was along the Long Patent Road within sight of Dr. Sumner Ely's house and it was here that Elijah decided to build a house. Where Ely's house followed the Palladian three part design with its accompanying grand appearance and pretensions, Rich's house was built along a much more modest scale. One and a half stories high with side gables and a five bay façade, it followed the most common plan for northern houses at this time.[56] The floor plan consisted of two large front rooms and two smaller back rooms. From the exterior, signs of elegance and ostentation were apparent primarily in the front door surround with simple pilasters capped with a fine entablature complete with an elliptical shelf. The door surround and entablature bore a remarkable similarity to that of Judge Samuel Nelson's law office built years later in 1829, now at the Farmers' Museum in Cooperstown. The hardware for the house came from Judd's Iron Works of Cherry Valley, which was a thriving business at this time. The owner, Oliver Judd, immigrated to Cherry Valley from Connecticut in 1805[57] and is credited with patenting a unique interior door latch with a stationery knob above a latch mechanism housed in the door, as opposed to the more common latch mechanism which had no knob and the latch ran along the outside edge of the door.

The difference in these two houses, built so close together in time and proximity by these men has much to do with their respective backgrounds. Ely was considerably more cosmopolitan than Rich. He had grown up in Connecticut and attended Yale. It is not surprising that he would have known about and been comfortable with the more sophisticated Palladian style of Federal design. Rich came from a local farming family and lacked the level of formal education and relatively wide-ranging travel experiences Ely had. It is, therefore, not surprising that Ely would have built a more sophisticated house and Rich would have built a house more similar to those with which he was familiar in the Clarkesville area.

Reuben Rich was not the only person in Clarkesville to run into difficulties resulting from this "year without summer." As farmers saw their crops fail, so too did mill owners see their business drop off; with no grain from the farmers, there was no grist for the mills. Moses Rich, who has been mentioned as setting up the first grist mill in the neighboring hamlet of Westville in 1795, had seen his eldest son, also named Moses, set up a grist mill in Clarkesville. This mill was later augmented by the addition of a saw mill, much the way his father, the elder Moses Rich, had done. These mills in Clarkesville were located along the Cooperstown Road where it crossed the Cherry Valley Creek. As has been stressed, mills were vital components of both the hamlet and the farms in the surrounding area. The fourteen acres of land on which the younger Moses Rich built his mills was rented from George Clarke. In addition to this parcel, Moses also rented forty-seven acres of an adjacent parcel to the north.

The disastrous year of 1816 was more than the younger Moses Rich's finances could weather. The slump in business which resulted from so many ruined crops caused him to go into arrears on his rent. It was for these arrears, which totaled $86.93, that George Clarke brought a suit in the Court of Common Pleas against Moses Rich. On 31 May 1817 Sheriff James Hawkes seized these parcels and the mill equipment and auctioned them. Both parcels were purchased for $180 by Ambrose L. Jordan and Peter Besancon of the neighboring town of Otsego. It is presumed that Moses went back to Westville to live out his days.[58]

It is not entirely clear why Jordan and Besancon purchased this mill beyond the fact that mills were a very profitable business. In all likelihood, these two men probably worked together to bring different assets to their partnership. Besancon has left scant record of his existence. He settled in the nearby community of Butternuts in the late eighteenth century with his wife and young son. His occupation is unknown, but quite possibly he brought the ability to operate a mill to this partnership. In 1812 he affiliated with the Cooperstown Masonic lodge, probably coming to reside in Cooperstown in that year.[59] Jordan, about whom much is known, brought the actual money to purchase the mill. Jordan was a lawyer whose legal mentor had been Jacob Van Rensselaer of Claverack. He came to Cooperstown in 1812 as well, and was quickly noticed as an "extraordinarily charming, well-read, dashing, and handsome young man". He stood six feet tall and had a slight and graceful figure. His visage was marked by expressive blue eyes and his head was topped with brown curly hair. He established a profitable law business and at one point presided over the Cooperstown board of trustees. He, too, was a member of the Cooperstown Masonic lodge, joining in 1816. In the Masonic lodge he held successively the offices of senior warden in 1818, and master in 1819. He was very active politically, and he coupled this with towering ambitions. On 10 June 1818 he was appointed district attorney for Otsego County by the New York Council of Appointment. His purchase of a mill in Clarkesville was an opportunity to acquire a potentially profitable business at a public auction, which could be presumed to mean that the sale price would be below true market value. What remained was for Jordan to find an individual who could actually operate a mill. This he found in Peter Besancon whom he knew as a fellow member of the Masonic lodge.[60]

The first few decades of the nineteenth century brought great prosperity to some in Clarkesville, while the vagaries of fortune brought economic ruin to others. Although the hamlet was beginning to take on the trappings of a less rustic community than it had been, it was still closely tied to the farming community surrounding it. During times of bountiful harvests and high wheat prices, those in and out of the hamlet prospered. Even with a shortage of specie so typical on the frontier, the barter system served well enough. However, as has been seen, a bad harvest year not only affected the farmers on the periphery of the hamlet, it also had ripple effects on those within the hamlet. People faced confiscation and loss of property and businesses. Economically, as well as socially, the hamlet did not exist in isolation from those farming the soil around it even though it would come to take on a very different character.

Clarkesville, still a tiny, isolated hamlet on the frontier, was now something more than a few houses huddled together against the wilderness. A town government had formed made up of men capable enough to develop an acceptable road network and tend to other practical matters. Traffic along the Long Patent Road had become sufficient to sustain business opportunities for a tavern and a mill in Clarksville and Westville. A store had even been established to alleviate the need to travel for basic supplies. However, the same men who were capable enough to tend to the young hamlet's practical needs, were also enlightened enough to steer the community toward pursuits which were beyond the mere basics of survival. Privately, these were the men who established a school and founded a church congregation, as well as started a library. Although the hamlet was on the outskirts of the frontier, wild by any definition, it would be a gross misstatement to characterize these people as backward, uneducated and poor.

Indeed, by every measure, the leaders of this hamlet had proven themselves to be just the opposite. They were enlightened, educated and visionary. They displayed a high regard for fashion as seen in the tastefulness inherent in the architectural styles which they followed in building their houses. Additionally, some of them were amassing wealth far beyond the reach of the common farmer. All factors pointed to launching Clarkesville toward a prosperous future.

Chapter Three

PROSPERITY AND SOCIAL EPIPHANY

As the decade of the 1820s dawned on Otsego County, pockets of settlement and even prosperity, were apparent. These centers were still largely concentrated along the northern edge of the county, specifically Cooperstown, Middlefield and Cherry Valley. This was logical in that the flow of commerce and communication still followed the established roads from Cooperstown, at the foot of Otsego Lake, through Middlefield and Cherry Valley, to Canajoharie and the Mohawk River, and thence to Albany and the Hudson River. Land values had begun to stabilize after their precipitous drop at the end of the previous decade and residents felt secure enough to engage in activities that came with more settled and steady development. The stage was set for a great increase in economic activity, which would bring attractive business opportunities and considerable wealth to some while others would continue to struggle in subsistence.

It was at this time, as people became more relaxed in their surroundings, that they turned their attention to the social questions of the day. Issues that had already awakened the concern of people in more urban areas came to the fore of the minds of the people in Otsego. Not required to spend all their time tending to the chores of home life, they looked about them and focused on less mundane issues. Already there had been great strides taken in this direction in Cooperstown with the founding of an academy, multiple churches, the Masonic lodge, and a weekly newspaper. It was now time for the residents of Middlefield, and specifically, the hamlet of Clarkesville, to follow suit. By the time the 1820s closed, Clarkesville would join the ranks of its neighbors with its own academy of higher learning, its own well-constructed church as opposed to a plain meeting house, and its own Masonic lodge. Additionally, its citizens would raise their voices to address the two prominent social issues of the day: slavery and intemperance.

Throughout the 1820s the crossroads of the hamlet became dotted with houses. These structures, much like those already discussed, followed the architectural fashions then current on the frontier. The Federal style in architecture, quickly being supplanted by the Greek Revival style in more urban areas, still held sway in Clarkesville. The extant houses of the hamlet from this period all testify to this fact. As emigrants and members of established families chose to build homes in this crossroads it is clear that they looked to imitate what they knew and what was considered tasteful. Both their familiarity with Federal forms and the recognition of the tastefulness of this style secured its adherence in Otsego, but here and there Greek Revival embellishments were cropping up.

It is not surprising that one of the first homes built in this decade was of Federal form with only hints of Greek Revival ornamentation. It also represents a migration within the hamlet of the prosperous few who moved from their earlier, more humble houses, to more ambitious, larger houses as their fortunes improved. Daniel A. Cummings had arrived in the hamlet early in the first quarter of the century and first rented, then, purchased land from Joshua Pinney on the eastern side of his holdings next to lands Pinney was renting to, then sold to, Clark D. Parshall. Daniel had come to the hamlet with his brother Hosea, who had his house on the northern side of the Cooperstown Road on the opposite side of the crossroads from Daniel. Daniel set up a business in the hamlet as a wagon maker and achieved some degree of prosperity by the early 1820s.

In 1821 Daniel entered into an agreement with George Clarke to purchase "10 perches and 14 [rood] of land for $19." This land was on the western side of the Long Patent Road running out of the hamlet and was across from the house built by Elijah Rich. He would be able to take possession of the land after the expiration of the lease Clarke had with Moses Rich for the same tract of land.[1] Rich, who had met with so much misfortune following the "year without summer", had not been able to utilize this parcel as he probably had intended: to build a house for himself and family. It would remain for Cummings to develop this village lot.

In keeping with a pattern of development in these frontier hamlets, Cummings remained in the area where he found prosperity, but moved from his humble house into a much grander one he had built. This house was a two story house with a full five bay façade. Its floor plan followed a typical Federal one room deep design, having one primary room in the front of the house on either side of an entrance hall with much smaller rooms behind these front rooms. The entrance hall contained an open staircase made from curly maple, a choice wood used to highlight drawer fronts and inlay in fine Federal furniture. This is a noteworthy choice of wood for so large an item as a staircase. Clearly the expense to build this staircase must have been great compared to other woods more commonly used for the purpose. Peter Kalm, the Swedish naturalist, had even remarked as early as the 1740s that curly maple was "much used in all kinds of joiners' work, and the utensils made of this wood are preferable to those of any kind in this country and are much dearer than those made of wild cherry or black walnut."[2] Indeed, as testament to the ostentation of using curly maple for a staircase, George Clarke employed the same wood in building the back stairs in Hyde Hall, in Springfield. The occurrence of the use of curly maple in this way is a rarity in Otsego County. The front door surround of the Cummings house had sidelights on either side and a transom light above to light a hall which otherwise had no windows. Both the curly maple staircase and the front door surround, coupled with the size of the house, would have suited a successful businessman of the period. In later years a building would be moved and appended to the back of this house to be used as a full service wing for the kitchen and the privy. These were in unhealthy proximity by modern standards, but were considered great conveniences when constructed.

This house was firmly rooted in the style of the Federal period. However, it succeeded in showing Daniel Cummings' attempt at architectural sophistication, for it reflected the growing prevalence of the Greek Revival fashion. Not only were the front entrance sidelights and transom of more Greek Revival than Federal in design, but, more telling was the wide frieze board which ran along the eaves and the wide corner posts of the façade. The heaviness of the frieze and corner posts was at odds with the overall delicacy of Federal embellishment and marks this house as an architecturally transitional building. The house's roots were decidedly in the Federal past, but Cummings was at the very least giving a nod to the emerging Greek fashion.

It is apparent that by the 1820s the hamlet of Clarkesville had taken its approximate form. Settlement and construction had marked out where the hamlet would be and where it was distinct from the wilderness around it. Quantifying the number of residents at this time within the bounds of Clarkesville would be difficult at best. However, one factor points to the hamlet as being quite well settled by 1815. That is the establishment of the post office. The post office at this time was a very profitable endeavor for those appointed postmaster. Postage was paid by the addressee when they came to pick up their mail. This system was established because a postmaster's salary was a certain percentage of the post office's revenue, with a cap of $2,000 per quarter. Thus being a postmaster could be quite lucrative.[3]

The profit opportunities from running a post office was a sufficient inducement for settlers to petition the United States Postal Service to establish offices at the earliest possible date. Samuel Griffin managed to have himself appointed as the postmaster when the first office was established in Middlefield. He had relocated from Middlefield Centre to Clarkesville with the migrations that siphoned the population from that hamlet early in the first decade of the new century. On 1 July 1815 he opened the first post office, probably in his house as was a common practice. This was a premature move, as the population was not sufficient at this point to warrant a post office and the office was discontinued on 24 October 1816.[4]

It was not until 12 December 1819 that a post office was firmly established and able to maintain itself permanently under the management of Joshua Pinney, who remained postmaster until 11 March 1835. He had the office in one of the front rooms of his tavern until 1833 when he sold the tavern to Benjamin

D. North Jr. From 1833 to 1835 the post office was in the store which was still owned by Pinney, but being run by his son, Egbert. The store was located next to the Hosea Cummings house on the Cooperstown Road. It was a two-story stone building with a central door flanked by single windows. Above the entrance was an upper story door for loading in merchandise to the second floor. Having the post office at the tavern was not only convenient for Pinney, but served to help keep his tavern business as the center of activity in the hamlet. Individuals were expected to come to the office periodically to see if they had any mail and post masters were in the habit of annually publishing a list of unclaimed letters in the local newspaper. They were induced to shoulder this expense because of the revenue which could be generated for them as patrons paid for their postage upon pick up.[5]

The post office was named Middlefield for the town as a whole since there was no other post office until one was set up in the hamlet of Middlefield Centre on 17 May 1826. This naming decision by the United States Postal Service was necessitated so as to avoid confusion with the Clarksville post office in Albany County, New York. Common usage continued to refer to the hamlet as Clarkesville as it had been known since George Clarke built his house on the Long Patent Road and this reference continued until well into the twentieth century even on some land deeds and maps. However, by the 1820s people were beginning to use Clarkesville and Middlefield interchangeably. Further, common usage was dropping the 'e' from Clarkesville. Clearly, the hamlet was being considered the center of activity in the town.

With the establishment of a post office in Clarkesville, the postal administration had to set routes folding Clarkesville into its existing system. These routes, once set, were bid out to individuals annually. Until very late in the nineteenth century the route that covered Clarkesville went from Cooperstown to Middlefield to Westville to Schenevus. It was required that the successful bidder leave Cooperstown at 10:30 AM Monday, Wednesday and Friday and arrive in Schenevus by 2:30 PM, where he would remain over night. The return trip would be on Tuesdays, Thursdays and Saturdays with a required departure time of 11:30 AM so that he could arrive in Cooperstown not later that 3:30 PM.[6]

As important as the milestone of the establishment of a post office in Clarkesville was, it needs to be seen as an indicator of how far developed the hamlet was in terms of business and population. The population migrations from points both in and out of the town of Middlefield to the hamlet of Clarkesville and the attendant building of houses has already been discussed. However, there were also several flourishing businesses at this time. These were cataloged in 1824 and included "5 grist mills, 14 saw mills, 4 fulling mills, 2 carding machines, 1 cotton and woollen factory, 3 distilleries and 2 asheries."[7] Not all of these businesses were in Clarkesville, but as will be seen, that location proved to have a wide array of businesses, making it the primary hamlet in the town of Middlefield.

All of these businesses, with the exception of the distilleries, were crucial to the economy of the hamlet. They represented those industries that were directly related to the agricultural interests that were the foundation of the local economy. Notable for its absence from this catalog is the mention of a blacksmith shop, even though there surely would have been one in the hamlet, and the tannery that was established in Clarkesville. Tanning, although a smelly and dirty operation, was a vital component of these communities as it provided an outlet for the bark that was discarded in sawmilling. In keeping with the frugality of the times, nothing was wasted. For the community, a tannery provided leather, a staple on the frontier for a whole host of items ranging from shoes and boots to saddles and harnesses. John Hayden, who had land holdings north of the hamlet, acquired a small parcel very near the mill in order to set up his tannery. This building was sandwiched between the saw mill and the carding machine. Hayden cut a prosperous and respectable figure in town. In 1820 he purchased a village lot in the hamlet from George Clarke for seventy-five dollars, on which he had built a house. He was destined to marry Eliza, the daughter of Joshua Pinney, and eventually, he became a deacon in the Baptist church.[8]

These enterprising and frugal people of this early period often found it necessary to start ancillary businesses to support the operation of their primary interests. Joshua Pinney found that in order to support his flourishing tavern, it was wise for him to set up a distillery to produce the liquors that he needed.[9] This gave him the ability to produce his own spirits for sale at his tavern, thereby increasing his profits by becoming both the producer and retailer of these intoxicating beverages. However, there were other considerations, not least of which was Pinney's desire to ensure that he had a steady supply of liquor when roads became impassable during inclement weather. As attentive to the roads as the highway commissioners were, there was still the very real concern that communication could be choked off for long periods of time, especially in winter. Another consideration may have been to market his liquors to other tavern owners in the area, although it is not known if he pursued this course. He located this distillery behind his tavern on the road leading from Clarkesville to the neighboring town of Westford so that it would be a convenient and short distance from his tavern.

Several other settlers of the hamlet took advantage of the myriad business opportunities available in the young, growing community in different ways. In many cases, either due to a lack of sufficient capital or expertise individually or for some other reasons, these people chose to partner with others. Dr. Ely, for example, although a fine physician, was not content to miss out on an opportunity he saw in Clarkesville. His brother-in-law, Daniel Gilbert, had moved into the hamlet after his marriage in 1809. These two men saw a tantalizing opportunity when Ambrose Jordan and Peter Besancon were prepared to sell the mill they had acquired in 1817 in a Sheriff sale that took that mill from Moses Rich. The exact nature of the partnership between Gilbert and Ely is unclear. The mill deed indicates only that Daniel Gilbert paid the $100 purchase price to Jordan and Besancon. However, subsequent maps and deeds, which use the property as a point of reference, uniformly refer to it as the "Gilbert and Ely Mills." The money for this purchase probably came from part of the $900 Daniel's father, Benjamin, gave to him upon his marriage to Abigail.[10] This mill property, situated along the Cherry Valley Creek where it was bridged by the Cooperstown Road leading out of Clarkesville, was probably from the beginning a somewhat unlikely place to put a mill. There were no natural rapids in the creek to provide sufficient water power to drive a mill so a dam had to be constructed to harness the water power. What was more important in determining the placement of this mill for Moses Rich, and the reason Gilbert and Ely saw such an opportunity here, was the mill's close proximity to the growing hamlet which assured a ready market for milled wood, but was also a convenient location for the surrounding farmers to bring their grain for grinding.

The other dynamic to this relationship is the same that drove so many other partnerships both then and now: capital. Neither man had the financial wherewithal to incur the cost and risk of purchasing and running a mill, but neither wanted to miss out on an opportunity with so much potential when Jordan and Besancon were ready to sell it. By pooling their resources and sharing the risk as well as the profit both men were able to take part in this venture. Indeed, Daniel Gilbert proved himself quite adept at forming profitable partnerships. He tied himself to Daniel North to open a store near the mill property as well.[11]

Daniel North and Daniel Gilbert had probably known each other for some time since they had been raised in the same community. North was destined to become a key person in Clarkesville; indeed the influence of the North family would last for generations. He was the son of Benjamin D. North, who has been mentioned as having come to Middlefield at the end of the Revolutionary War and rented a farm from George Clarke. The farm was located north of the hamlet. Daniel, born 17 January 1777, was his third son, after Robert and Benjamin Jr. About Robert very little is known, but Benjamin Jr. deserves some note. He was a well-respected man; in 1814 he, along with Joshua Pinney, was appointed as a justice of the peace by the New York State Council of Appointment. He purchased the only brick house in Middlefield in 1800. This house was located on the road near the western most end of the farm owned by his father. This was a very stately house and bore remarkable similarities to the house Clarke had built in Clarkesville which Joshua Pinney was operating as a tavern. It is worthy of note that Benjamin also operated his house as a tavern. As a testament to the honorable and profitable nature of tavern keeping, Daniel's second son, also named Benjamin D. North Jr. would follow in that same line of business. The bricks from which the house had been built were actually fashioned in a brickyard on the North farm along the Cherry Valley Creek.[12] It is to be expected that a brickyard would be near to the site of construction of any brick house during this period owing to the extreme difficulty in transporting something as heavy as bricks any great distance. Clearly Daniel came from a hard-working family, one not likely to miss a good business opportunity.

Partnerships were seen in this period as a natural way of pooling resources and mitigating individual risk. A further dynamic of these partnership relationships had to do with the varying levels of involvement each man had in these businesses. With regard to the partnership Ely formed, it is probable that Gilbert was responsible for the bulk of the daily operation of the mill. However, in all likelihood Ely acted in more than merely an absentee fashion. First of all, he would have wanted to be involved to some degree in ventures where his capital was so directly at risk and which were operating in such close proximity to his house. Secondly, and more to the point, his medical practice, although successful and far-reaching, probably did not consume all of his time. The idea of the rural doctor doing nothing but traveling the countryside to tend to his patients is a romanticized vision. The abundance of home remedies coupled with the distances and traveling times and general distrust of doctors, led many people to call for a doctor only as a last resort. These two facts of Ely's life would have allowed him the time and inclination to be very involved in the business of the mill. So too in the case of the store, with Gilbert tending to the daily operation of the mill, it probably fell to North to tend to the daily operation of the store. The location of the store was both logical in the fact that Gilbert already owned property on which to build it, and convenient in that it allowed Gilbert to be involved to some degree without leaving the mill for great lengths of time.

Business partnerships of this nature must not be viewed as a fleeting phenomenon. For the same reasons that they occurred in the early 1820s, they continued to be formed and became a staple of the business development of these rural hamlets. Thus, through the enterprise of men either individually or in concert, Clarkesville had come to possess a tavern, multiple stores, mill, and distillery, as well as having the town's first post office and a resident physician. Further, the hamlet likely had other businesses which have gone undocumented, such as a blacksmith shop. The level of comfort that came with this degree of settlement allowed the hamlet's residents to focus on their quality of life. This quality of life issue was closely intertwined with the religious ardor of the age, since, in some quarters, this earthly life was seen by some as mere prelude to a more divine state. The Baptist congregation had coalesced around Elder Benjamin Sawin in the first decade of the century and stood as the only well-organized group until the mid-1820s when the society of the hamlet was ripe to form other groups.

The first of these groups to take root was the Freemasons. Freemasonry had, since the mid-eighteenth century, served as a cement binding the various political, business and social leaders of the colonies together. Indeed, quite often these were all the same men. The fraternity spread rapidly in the colonies until the Revolution briefly checked its spread. With the conclusion of hostilities and the peaceful existence that ensued in the new Republic, there was a resurgence in interest in this group. Freemasonry was seen as uniquely able to forge a new hierarchy in the new Republic; a hierarchy based, not on class and social position, but on personal merit and honor.[13] It sought to bind men by their belief in one "universal creator" without espousing a particular religion. It paid homage to the ideas of the Enlightenment by looking at men without regard to their social rank or position. In this way it sought to break with the old colonial system of patronage and harkened to the true tenets of the new nation: tolerance and personal worth. This egalitarian doctrine resonated well both in more urban areas and on the frontier. It was very common for a community to seek a charter from the grand lodge of their state once they attained a modicum of comfort. As has been seen, in 1795 the Freemasons had been the first real non-religious social group to take shape in Cooperstown, with several members coming from Clarkesville specifically and Middlefield in general.

The men of Clarkesville now sought to establish their own Masonic lodge. Viewing their petition from the stance of the men making the request, this is a clear indication that they felt their community had "come of age" and was forging its own identity rather than existing in the shadow of its neighbor on Lake Otsego. On 23 December 1823, the men who were clearly the leaders of Clarkesville sent a formal request to the Grand Lodge of Free and Accepted Masons of the State of New York asking for a dispensation to form a lodge in Middlefield. Among the men who signed this letter were Joshua L. Pinney, Sumner Ely, John Hayden, Dunham Spaulding, and Benjamin Gilbert Jr. These men, in particular, form an interesting group in that they were all tied by marriage and/or business. Sumner Ely and Dunham Spaulding were both married to sisters of Benjamin Gilbert Jr. and John Hayden was destined to become a son-in-law to Joshua Pinney.[14]

In sending their petition to the Grand Lodge, they noted the proposed name of the lodge as "The Widow's Son," a reference of some significance within Freemasonry. Along with the petition, the following men were recommended to serve as officers: John J. Crandall, master, Bela Kaple, senior warden, and Benjamin Gilbert Jr. as junior warden. To bolster their petition, the signers of this letter were able to obtain the support of their brethren from Otsego Lodge, who, on 13 January 1824, officially recommended that Grand Lodge grant this dispensation. It is unknown what debate would have been carried on in Otsego Lodge over the granting of this recommendation, but it certainly was more than a rubber stamp. The neighboring communities that had previously asked Otsego Lodge for such recommendations received mixed results. Although these men had recommended that the Grand Lodge grant a dispensation to a group of Freemasons wanting to form a lodge in Cherry Valley in 1806 (this recommendation was again approved in 1816, necessitated by the fact that the Grand Lodge had not approved the petition of 1806) and Butternuts in 1808, they did not approve recommending a charter for Milford in 1812 or

1816, or Oaksville in 1823 or 1824. Both of these recommendations finally passed Otsego Lodge in 1826 and 1825 respectively. This indicated that Otsego Lodge took this business very seriously and was not prepared to routinely approve to recommend the granting of charters to all who wished to have one.[15]

Accordingly, the Grand Lodge issued a charter to the Widow's Son Lodge of Middlefield on 4 June 1824 allocating it as lodge number 391 in New York. Membership in this lodge grew rapidly, reaching thirty-nine by the end of 1825. Among the men joining the lodge were Daniel Gilbert, Nathan Bailey, Benjamin D. North, Angus Griffin, and Moses Rich Jr. All of these men were well on the way to making names for themselves in this hamlet. As with other lodges on the frontier, its membership came to resemble a business directory of the community. This was a common pattern. As these lodges formed in their community they tended to pull members from the surrounding open areas, but they were very much dominated by those in the heart of the community. As the first officers of this lodge were leaders of Clarkesville, when new officers were elected in 1825 they, too, were men of similar caliber: Benjamin Gilbert Jr. was elected master, Elihu Cone, senior warden, and Smith Murphy, junior warden.[16]

These Freemasons set up their lodge room on the third floor of Joshua Pinney's tavern. It was very common for lodges to meet at such public buildings. However, as these men were setting up their fraternity in Clarkesville, Freemasonry, as a secret fraternity, was coming under fire due to what has been labeled as the Morgan Affair. In 1826 Captain William Morgan was preparing to publish an exposé on the fraternity, revealing many of its secrets. Men from Batavia, LeRoy and Rochester, who were rumored to have been Freemasons, kidnapped Morgan and purportedly drowned him in Lake Ontario. Morgan's body was never found and the men in question, Nicholas G. Cheseboro, Colonel Edward Sawyer, Loton Lawson, and John Sheldon, were only charged with kidnapping.[17] The pressure that came to bear down on Freemasons across the state led many lodges to burn their minute books and other papers to prevent their proceedings from being exposed. Further, many lodges only met once a year and in secret to transact such business as was absolutely necessary while hiding the fact that a Masonic lodge existed in the community. In 1832 the Grand Lodge of New York ordered that all lodges in its jurisdiction send all of their minute books and other documents to New York for safe keeping. Those lodges that did not comply would have their charters declared forfeit.

The Morgan Affair had a profound effect on Freemasonry in New York. In the mid-1820s there were roughly 500 Masonic lodges throughout the state. However, by 1835 there were only 75 lodges in the state that could muster representatives to attend the proceedings of the Grand Lodge in New York City; in 1837 that number dropped to 26 lodges. Otsego Lodge, in response to this anti-Masonic crisis engendered by the Morgan Affair, did not meet from 1828 to 1846, except once a year to elect officers. When they sought to reconstitute in 1846, only nine members could be found within three miles of Cooperstown.

These men met and began discussion with Grand Lodge to have their charter restored. This was done in 1847 with the lodge being renumbered from 41 to 138.[18] However, Widow's Son Lodge did not follow such a course. In June 1834, their charter was declared forfeited by Grand Lodge and they never officially reconstituted. The last membership return for this lodge was dated June 1828. Virtually all documents relating to this lodge, as with so many others at this time, were destroyed.[19]

As these men were forming their Masonic lodge, many of them were also fostering their religious institution in the hamlet. Religious fervor was on the ascendant on the frontier and the Baptist community in Clarkesville was a benefactor of this resurgence. It was at this time that the small knot of Baptists determined that their needs would best be served by having a meeting house solely devoted to worship, and not used in concert with the school and other secular groups, such as the town government. New England citizenry had already come to the conclusion that religious and secular groups could no longer share the same building.[20] No doubt the Yankees flooding into Otsego brought those same notions with them. Thus, in 1825 the Middlefield Baptists organized themselves into a corporation. At their first meeting, held on 24 January 1825, with Benjamin North and Alexander Cummings presiding and Amos Thayer as clerk, the following trustees were elected by the congregation: Joshua L. Pinney, Daniel Gilbert, Benjamin North Jr., John J. Crandall, James Parshall Jr., and Silas Devol. These men immediately elected Benjamin North Jr. as their president, Daniel Gilbert as their clerk, Joshua Pinney as their collector, and Silas Devol as their treasurer.[21]

The first order of business was the building of a meeting house to be used exclusively for the Baptists. An understanding was established at this time between the trustees and George Clarke, now living his baronial lifestyle in Hyde Hall, the house he had built on Mount Wellington overlooking Lake Otsego, to allow the construction of their meetinghouse on Clarke lands across from their current meetinghouse. It would not be for another two years before Clarke would give a deed to this parcel, containing two acres two roods and twenty perches of land, for one dollar and "for the better maintenance and support of the Christian religion and its ordinances." There was, however, one condition to this grant of land. George Clarke made it clear in the deed that should members of the Protestant Episcopal Church incorporate as a congregation in Middlefield, then the Baptists would have to give them half of the land Clarke was granting. It was also specified that should the Baptists dissolve and there not be any Protestant Episcopal Church in Middlefield to claim the property, then it would revert back to Clarke or his heirs.[22]

The early spring was spent clearing the land on which the meetinghouse would be constructed. By April this chore was completed and the trustees appointed John J. Crandall, Esq. to superintend the building. Up to this point, the trustees determined, men would be paid $0.50 for each day worked and $1.00

for each day they worked with a team; from April forward they would be paid four shillings for each day a man worked and five shillings if he had a team.[23] Colonial currency was still widely accepted in America so when the Baptists ran out of American specie they reverted to the colonial currency they had available on the frontier. This change in payment method would not have caused any ill will as both forms of money were widely and interchangeably used.

In choosing a design for their meetinghouse, the Baptists relied on *The Country Builder's Assistant*, a pattern book by the architect Asher Benjamin. Born in Greenfield, Massachusetts in 1772, Benjamin started out in life as a carpenter, but soon turned his attention to design. In 1797 his first book appeared in which plate 27 was a "Design for a Church." This church featured a shallow entrance porch with three doors and three windows above, the center one being a Palladian window. All was topped with a square tower with a railing and urns above which was the belfry. This was the first published American architectural design book and with its appearance this church design swept across New England. Probably the first church built on Benjamin's design was in Lee, Massachusetts in 1800 (no longer extant). Soon thereafter, in 1803, another church following the Benjamin pattern was built in Lenox, Massachusetts.[24] This church so closely resembled the church the Baptist trustees had built in Clarkesville that it cannot be ascribed to mere coincidence; one of the trustees, most likely Crandall, since he was appointed to superintend the building, must have known about this Lenox church.

The Clarkesville Baptists did not slavishly follow the Benjamin design, though. One of the principle areas where their meetinghouse differed from the pattern book was in the gallery floor. Benjamin's design called for a sloped floor from the walls toward the center. After much discussion, it was determined that Ebeneezer Tucker and Angus Griffin would build the gallery floor on a horizontal plane, not an inclined plane. This is further, clear evidence that the Baptists were directly consulting Benjamin's design. There is no other reason for the minute books to be so specific about this discussion. The reason for this change from the design plan is unclear. However, it was likely a variation which suggested itself as a way to save money. Building a sloped gallery would entail more time and money than a horizontally planed gallery would. It is likely that the trustees saw no reason to expend the extra money in light of their positioning of the pulpit. Since the pulpit of the church was situated above the entrance door with its back to the Palladian window, it would be on a plane midway between the ground floor and the gallery. Building an inclined gallery would not facilitate viewing the minister any more that a horizontal plane would, so there was no need to spend the additional money to follow the Benjamin design in this detail. These men may have been building a very grand church for their frontier community, but they certainly did not lose sight of their frugal roots. At this same meeting Joshua Pinney and John J. Crandall were called on to buy the glass for the meetinghouse.[25]

The new meetinghouse was ready for use by January 1826. There had been an impressive dedication ceremony when the cornerstone had been laid. This ceremony must surely have been under the direction of the leading men of the hamlet, Joshua Pinney, Daniel Gilbert, Sumner Ely, Daniel North and Benjamin North Jr., who were coincidentally all Freemasons. This was a period when Freemasons were frequently called upon to lay cornerstones at public buildings. They had, after all, taken part in the laying of the cornerstone at the nation's capitol and the state capitol, and they had taken prominent parts in such public occasions as the opening of the Erie Canal. The cornerstone was carved with the following Biblical verse:

> *God so loved the*
> *World, that he*
> *gave his only*
> *begotten Son*
> *that whosoever*
> *believeth in*
> *him should*
> *not perish*
> *but be granted*
> *life*
>
> *Founded*
> *June 16ᵗʰ*
> *AL 5825*

However, the Freemasons also saw to it that this stone was adorned with Masonic symbols as a tribute to their fraternity and its roots as stone masons and builders. Among the symbols on the stone were the ladder leading to heaven and the square and compasses. More striking, though, is that the date was written in Masonic fashion. Instead of the customary AD (*Anno Domini*), for "Year of Our Lord," which commences with the birth year of Christ, this stone was marked AL (*Anno Lucius*), for "Year of Light," which commences with Archbishop Ussher's (or possibly Sir Isaac Newton's) dating of the Creation being 4000 years before the birth of Christ. This is a telling indication of the sway the Freemasons held in Clarkesville as a result of all of the prominent men being members of the fraternity.

When the church was ready for occupancy, it was decided to publicly auction the slips, or pews, to raise money to cover the building costs already incurred. The pews were divided into five classes, with the first class of twelve pews not to sell for less than $60.00 and so on down the line until the fifth class were to be sold for not less than $20.00. Those purchasing pews would have until 1 February 1827 to settle their account. Joshua Pinney and Silas Devol were chosen to bring refreshments to the auction. The auction results (see Appendix 5) are helpful in determining the comparative prosperity of those living in Clarkesville. Of the twelve pews in the first class, eleven exceeded the desired price of over $60.00. Most of those who purchased slips in this class are men about whom much is known: Joshua Pinney, Daniel North, Daniel Gilbert, Sumner Ely, Benjamin North Jr., and John J. Crandall. It is not surprising that the highest figures realized for pews was paid by Joshua Pinney and Daniel North, the preeminent businessmen in the hamlet, who paid $103.00 and $100.00 respectively. These were all entrepreneurs and leading citizens of the hamlet.

The other men who purchased pews in this class have left scant record of themselves. Ebenezar Tucker, who paid $90.00 for his pew, for example, is only known to posterity as one of the men who took a leading role in building the church and who figured so prominently in the debate on whether the gallery floor should be sloped or level. James Pitts and James Murphy are both known to have been very successful farmers and founded families which lived and thrived in the town of Middlefield for at least the next hundred years. However, historical records are nearly mute on Elias Ismond and Benjamin Lawson who paid $62.50 and $62.00 respectively for their pews.

The sale of pews in this first class is only part of the picture of prosperity in the hamlet, though. After all, even though there were twelve pews in this class, only eleven actually sold for over $60.00. Affluence was uneven at best in Clarkesville. There were ten pews that sold in the fifth class for not less than $20.00 and there were four pews that sold for less than $20.00 (there is no price recorded for one pew, that purchased by Salmon Coats). A further variable is that there were several pews that were broken and sold in halves and quarters. John Manzer and James Cummings split a pew, each paying $12.50 for a half. Chester Wetmore paid $6.25 for a quarter and David Blair paid $13.00 for half of the same pew, the disposition of the remaining quarter is not recorded. There are several other pews that fit into this group as well. Finally, there is the inexplicable purchase by Joshua Pinney of two additional pews; one for $46.00 and one for $35.00.

Of the sixty pews auctioned it is significant that sixteen, or 26%, sold for over $50.00. This was not a trifling figure. It leads to the conclusion that there was a large proportion of the hamlet's population with the affluence to devote great resources to their church. Although, in all likelihood, one could surmise that there was a combination of competition and expectation in the higher bids. Certainly it was no coincidence that the two most successful entrepreneurs in the hamlet, Joshua Pinney and Daniel North bid within $3.00 of each other. Further, it is also no coincidence that Sumner Ely and Benjamin North Jr., who were brothers-in-law, bid to within $3.00 of each other as well. At the other end of the spectrum, there were fourteen pews, or 23%, which sold for under $30.00. However, when split pews are factored in, there were thirty-three individuals who paid less than $30.00 out of the seventy-two individuals who purchased pews. This represents 46% of the people who purchased pews. This was only one indication of the uneven distribution of wealth which was accumulating in the hands of the industrious, and was leaving a noticeable disparity among the residents.

To understand more fully where Clarkesville stood in terms of prosperity and wealth comparative to other communities in Otsego County at this time it is helpful to look at a hamlet approximately ten miles west. In 1819 the hamlet of Noblesville in the town of New Lisbon purchased land for $60.00 on which to build a Congregational church. The members of this community also used plans drawn by Asher Benjamin in the same source book, testifying to how wide the distribution of this pattern book was throughout central New York. They erected their church in 1820 at a cost of $1,130.00; comprised of $600.00 for supplies and materials and $500.00 for labor payable to Horatio McGeorge and Ithamar Hitchcock. To raise this sum the congregation asked for pledges. These pledges, or signments, from forty-nine people, ranged from $120.00, pledged by Israel Chapin, to less than $24.00. Through this means they collected $989.00 of which $36.00 was never collected and considered "bad debt."[26] The average pledge was $23.24, but looking more closely at the breakdown reveals a similar, although less pronounced, uneven distribution of wealth in this community as seen in Clarkesville. Only nine of the forty-nine pledges, or 18% were over $50.00. However, thirty-one pledges, or fully 63%, were for amounts less than $25.00.

These pledges in Noblesville only tell part of this financial picture. This community also found it necessary to auction the pews for this church. Through this means, the congregation raised an additional $667.75 by auctioning thirty-four of thirty-six available pews (two pews seem not to have sold). The average pew bid was $19.64, with only four pews, or 12% selling for over $35.00. Included in those four pews were two that sold for $50.00, one of which sold to Israel Chapin. Significantly, though, is the case of Asaph Buck, who pledged $100.00 to the church's initial drive for money, but only bid $20.00 for his pew.[27] Indeed, twenty-four of the thirty-four pews, or 70.5%, sold for less than $24.00. One man, Israel Chapin, who seemed significantly wealthier than anyone in Clarkesville, being able to pledge to the church a total of $170.00, but his was an extreme and isolated example. Both Clarkesville and Noblesville were experiencing a similarly uneven distribution of wealth. However, the case of Clarkesville seems to point to a community where there were not only more people (more overall numbers of people bidding on church pews), but where the gulf between the wealthiest and the poorest was more pronounced.

In the case of Clarkesville however, bids at auction do not tell the whole story. It would remain problematic for some time after the auction to induce people to make good on their bids. The simplest explanation for this is that some people had bid beyond their means. Although that may have been true, it is probable that other forces were at work as well. It was certainly not unexpected that it would take time for bidders to accumulate enough cash to make good on their bids. This explains why bidders were given from January 1826 until February 1827 to pay their bids. Another factor was the scarcity of specie. Specie was still a very limited commodity on the frontier. As a result merchants were in the habit of issuing script for use at their stores. Should an individual wish to sell goods, usually produce, to a merchant, the merchant was quite likely to issue script in return which could be redeemed at his store. As early as 1816 Joshua Pinney was known to have been issuing such script and this was a practice that continued in Clarkesville into the 1860s. The store owned by Sayles and Antisdel was issuing script to alleviate the problem of shortage of specie during the Civil War.[28]

One of the other factors contributing to the length of time needed to collect these monies for bids was that many people, particularly farmers, had to wait for influxes of cash at specific times of the year, namely the sale of the harvest. As a result of these factors, the trustees found it necessary to obtain payment by other means. In November 1826 it was made known that Joshua Pinney would accept beef cattle at his store from people wishing to settle these obligations. Certainly, this bartering idea seemed aimed at alleviating a shortage of specie which was still apparent on the frontier, but by bartering beef cattle for pews it seems the trustees had identified farmers as the single largest group of people delinquent in paying their bids. This would be the same group that would have felt the lack of specie the most, only getting large amounts when their crops were sold. As these obligations were paid it became possible in 1828 for the Baptist trustees to pay their debt to John J. Crandall for forty dollars and to Joshua Pinney for ten dollars for unspecified services they had rendered since 1826. Further the demand against Ephraim Olds for five dollars payable in blacksmith work was sold to Benjamin North for four dollars. It was at that time that the trustees elected to sell their old meetinghouse and its clock to the highest bidder.[29] Unfortunately, they did not record the identity of the purchaser.

The Baptists were not alone in their inability to collect on debts owed them due to a shortage of specie on the frontier. Joshua Pinney found himself unable to meet some of his own obligations as this shortage impaired his ability to take in cash from his own customers and thereby pay those to whom he owed money. On 10 January 1825 he found it necessary to write to his creditors at the firm of J. & J. Townsend, merchants of Albany, to ask for an additional thirty to sixty days to settle his balance owing to them. Three years later, on 11 February 1828, Pinney again asked for an accounting of debits and credits from the firm of J. & J. Townsend in order to settle his account with them as well as the account of Pinney & Andrews when Simon J. Andrews, Pinney's business partner, died that January.[30] The shortage of specie among farmers on the frontier had ripple effects throughout the entire community. Although the bartering system worked well within the bounds of these frontier communities, it was not sufficient to settle accounts when firms and creditors from outside the community were involved.

While the Baptists were literally and figuratively getting their house in order, the residents of Clarkesville were also attending to the education of their children. As has already been discussed, Joshua Pinney was instrumental in setting up a school in 1807 in the Baptist Meeting House on the northern edge of the hamlet. By 1824 there were thirteen schools operating within the Town of Middlefield.[31] It was shortly after this point, when the Baptist Society began planning for the construction of a more elaborate building which would serve solely as a house of worship, that the residents began building a structure to be used principally as a school. This building was located on the southern edge of the hamlet, just past the houses that Elijah Rich and Daniel Cummings had built in 1816 and 1821 respectively. The new school was on the same side of the Long Patent Road as Rich's house. It was a small, stone building situated back from the road, consisting of only one story. The use of stone for this schoolhouse is an interesting choice in light of the fact that most schoolhouses on the frontier were only of wood frame construction. Their selection of building material conveyed the sense of settlement and permanence that was pervading the hamlet.

As in previous schools on the Otsego frontier, and as noted by Henry Clarke Wright and Levi Beardsley, two men who wrote highly detailed memoirs of this period in Otsego County, only the basics were taught: spelling, reading, writing and arithmetic. For most of the inhabitants along the frontier these basic skills constituted all the learning that was necessary in life. However, even as early as the 1790s people with higher intellectual and social aspirations had come together to form academies where higher learning was taught. It has been mentioned that Benjamin Gilbert sat on the board of trustees of the Otsego Academy and in all likelihood his sons Daniel, Benjamin and John attended this school. There was also an academy set up in Cherry Valley by the early part of the nineteenth century. It should be noted that, although the norm was to tend to the education of boys and young men, not all academies were for boys. There were some academies being set up by the 1820s which were solely for the education of girls, and a very few which were for both sexes.[32] This latter arrangement was a rather radical notion. It was not a widely accepted idea that adolescent boys and girls could be educated properly in the same building, particularly as they developed intellectually beyond the level of basic education as described above by Beardsley and Wright. This was based primarily on the notion that boys and girls had different educational needs, especially girls from families in middle- and upper-class families where it was expected that girls would need to learn more "elegant accomplishments." The advertisement by Angelica Gilbert for a Cooperstown Boarding School for Young Ladies was typical of these female academies. Here she promised to teach the "higher branches" of education as well as the "elegant accomplishments" which these girls and young ladies would need to learn. Female academies and boarding schools were not universally approved by mothers and grandmothers though. Indeed, some of these members of older generations were hostile to the idea of girls spending long amounts of time away from home as an intrusion into family life even though they recognized the value of educating girls. This was an age marked by ambivalence to female education. Female literacy was encouraged but female intellectuals were not.[33]

Of great significance regarding the residents of the hamlet of Clarkesville was their desire to reach further in educating their children, both boys and girls, than just their frontier school would provide. This was in emulation of the residents of the more settled and prosperous neighboring communities of Cooperstown and Cherry Valley. The families who were moving into the hamlet were indeed finding prosperity and a sense of comfort that translated into a desire to see that their children received an education which would secure for them admittance into the higher social circles then forming in the communities of northern Otsego County. To this end they banded together to help found an academic school in 1827. As Pinney had been a force behind establishing the first school in 1807, so was he now a prime force in establishing the academic school. This school was built just east of the crossroads, on the road heading out of the hamlet toward the community of Westford. It was situated on Pinney's land just a short distance before his distillery.[34] It was of Federal design with the requisite delicate moldings and fine pilasters running up along the entrance doors. The gable facing the road had a door on the right and left separated by a window. Above each door was an entablature crowned with a shelf very much like that on the house Elijah Rich had constructed in 1816. The beauty and simple elegance of its appearance were very much in keeping with the other structures springing up in Clarkesville.

To a large degree the residents and patrons of the school allowed the trustees to attend to setting a curriculum and finding a teacher. Daniel Gilbert, Silas Devol, and Nathan Bailey were elected trustees. Much light has already been shed on Gilbert and Devol. Nathan Bailey, though, has not left much of a record. He owned an extensive and profitable farm to the east of the hamlet at the top of the hill leading to the neighboring community of Westford. The rest of his career, however, has been lost to posterity.

The curriculum devised by the trustees was based largely on the ideals of the Enlightenment, which animated all forms of higher learning in Europe and America: Greek, Latin, rhetoric, history, English composition, the art of speaking, English grammar, penmanship, reading, and English pronunciation. This curriculum was comparable to the curricula of other area academic schools. Luther Saxton advertised one such school in Cooperstown which offered Greek, Latin, mathematics, geography, grammar, arithmetic, astronomy, natural and moral philosophy, rhetoric, history, logic and music. He was not alone in this course offering in Cooperstown, though. Franklin Lusk had a nearly identical curriculum at his school as well, with this difference: he promised that "The strictest attention will be paid to the Instruction of Pupils, and their morals scrupulously superintended".[35]   Schools, like families and churches, were thought to be appropriate places to instill in children a fine sense of moral conduct. It is indicative of this norm that Lusk saw fit to mention that he would attend to his pupils' moral education as well.

As much as this curriculum paid homage to the enlightenment, it had a more immediate link to colonial New England, from whence so many of Clarkesville's, and indeed Otsego County's, early residents had come. In 1647 the Massachusetts Bay Colony passed their monumental School Law. This law was soon emulated across New England. By this statute, towns with fifty or more families had to provide instruction in reading and writing, and towns with one hundred or more families had to provide instruction in Latin grammar as well. The need for schools to teach reading and writing in even the smallest New England communities was born out of the Puritan ideal that each individual must have the ability to read the Bible. The stress on Latin instruction was rooted in the English Tudor educational reforms, copied in New England and, then New York. The logic was that a teacher versed in Latin would have a better grasp of the English language and requisite grammatical curriculum.[36] The American Revolution interrupted this practice from its gradual adoption in rural New York. However, by the 1820s, even after the law had begun to lose adherents in New England, those New England settlers to Otsego sought to recreate what they remembered as cultured and necessary, even though it no longer had a basis in actual law.

These settlers were the driving force behind founding most such academies and they were willing to reach into their pockets to pay for it. The teacher for the Clarkesville school was to be paid a total of $58.15 for each term of fourteen weeks, which equated to $16.50 a month, plus board. The school was taught under the authority of District Number 1 so that it could be allocated public money. In the bill for the second term, $11.98 is noted as coming from public money. In its second term, this academic school counted seventy-eight students and included both boys and girls, rather than just boys, which was more common. Parents had the option of enrolling their children in any or all of the courses offered, at a cost of $0.015 per day, or $1.05 per quarter which was counted as the full fourteen week term. The relative importance the parents considered each course may be inferred from the enrollment numbers. All seventy-eight students were enrolled in reading, which was the class with the most pupils. On the other end of the spectrum there was only one student taking Greek and one taking History. Penmanship was obviously considered crucial to a child's development since that course was the second most enrolled class with forty-eight students. The importance of penmanship to a person's overall education during the nineteenth century must be stressed. Even as late as mid-century it was not uncommon to see notices in newspapers advertising courses in this discipline for those "who wish to improve their style of Penmanship".[37]

The enrollment cost of this academic school can be used to give a glimpse of the relative level of prosperity among the residents of the hamlet of Clarkesville as compared to the residents of the much more prosperous village of Cooperstown at the foot of Lake Otsego. Obviously, the methodology used by the trustees to determine tuition costs would have much to do with what they considered within the means of the people to pay, while at the same time being set high enough to make the hiring of a teacher and the cost of running a school financially viable. Using this data it is clear that, although Clarkesville had achieved a sufficient level of affluence to be able to support the establishment of an academic school, at a cost of $1.05 per quarter per student, these people's financial means paled in comparison to that of the people of Cooperstown. Considering the two Cooperstown academic schools already mentioned, that of Luther Saxton and that of Franklin Lusk, it is clear that that village had a basis of wealth far surpassing that of Clarkesville. Tuition at Saxton's school ranged from $3.00 per quarter, if the child was enrolled in geography, grammar, and arithmetic, to $5.00 per quarter, if the child took Greek, Latin, and mathematics. Taking music would raise the tuition to $8.00 per quarter. Whereas for Lusk's school the cost ranged from $3.00 per quarter for English grammar and arithmetic, to $4.00 per quarter for languages and mathematics.[38] As developed and populous as Clarkesville was, its inhabitants, generally, were incapable of expending the lavish amounts of money that the neighboring residents of the village of Cooperstown could.

A closer comparison to Clarkesville is made by comparing a select school in the town of Exeter with the academic school in the hamlet of Clarkesville. Exeter, located about ten miles northwest of Cooperstown, by 1824 could boast of having one Baptist meeting house, nine schoolhouses, one grist mill, four saw mills, three carding machines, two fulling mills, and one distillery. Its population in 1820 stood at 1,430. The whole town represented a small area of about 5.25 square miles with a small, but concentrated population of prosperous businessmen. In 1826 John S. Mitchell advertised that his school was recommencing on 17 April and that tuition would be $2.50 per quarter.[39] Although this tuition was more than twice that of Clarkesville, it can be assumed that the two centers were on a par in terms of economic development. Exeter's school as a select school would have been considered private, whereas Clarkesville's academic school was taught under the auspices of School District Number 1, hence public. As already mentioned, this fact made the school eligible to receive public money. With regard to tuition, public money made a considerable difference. The effect would have been that the cost of tuition would have logically been less than at a private school which would have received no public money to operate. There is an unknown variable as well with regard to enrollment. Clarkesville's school had seventy-eight students, but it is not known how many attended Mitchell's school. If enrollment in the latter was significantly less than the former, that would help explain the difference in tuition cost in terms of economic viability. It can be safely concluded that the Clarkesville academy points to the community as having been well settled, prosperous, and relaxed in its sur-roundings rather than a crude or rustic group of people fending off the wilds of the all encompassing wilderness.

Beyond the cost of tuition, there were other economic driving factors in de-termining enrollment to classes. Parents had to make a conscious decision per-taining to how much education they thought their children needed. Indeed, they had to consider how valuable education in general was on the frontier. Part of this decision was tied to how many children they had to educate. Daniel Gilbert, who was a leading resident and owned the mill and a store, had seven children enrolled in the school who cumulatively attended 307 days at a cost of $4.63. He was closely followed by Joshua Pinney, the tavern keeper, with six children enrolled who cumulatively attended 285.5 days at a cost of $4.31. Surprisingly, the two children of Dr. Ely attended for a total of 109.5 days at a cost of $1.65. This meant that Ely's children averaged an attendance of 54.75 days each, whereas Pinney's attended 47.5 days each and Gilbert's attended a mere 43.8 days each. Ely's children, by far, spent more time at this school than any of the other scholars. However, as these men were the business and social leaders of the community, they saw fit that their children were to be well educated. This academic school did not just count the wealthy as its patrons, though. The wid-ow Mary Ann Cornwall sent her one child to attend for nine days at a cost of $0.14.[40] Clearly, this school, even with voluntary enrollment, was widely sup-ported and education, in general, was thought to be both beneficial and neces-sary.

To fill the position of teacher, the trustees were able to induce a man named George Washington Johnson, from Easton, Massachusetts, to come to Clarkesville. He was assisted by Albert Sawin, son of Benjamin Sawin. Both men were renowned for their learning and it was, no doubt, felt that having a local man of intellectual talent at the school would help induce the inhabitants to be more trusting of the school's unknown teacher, even though he came with excellent credentials. This probably contributed to the school being so well sup-ported, as well. It is unclear how initial contact was made with Johnson, or who initiated it; what is known is that Johnson had been teaching a school for more than a year in Dutchess County, New York and came to Clarkesville with a good reference.

> *This certifies that the Bearer, Mr. George Washington Johnson, has resided in this town more than a year past, and sustained an unblemished moral character and correct exemplary habits, and discharged the duties of a school teacher with reputable ability and success.*
>
> *Phillip Hart*
> *Washington, Dutchess County*[41]

When he arrived in the hamlet, Johnson was 26 years old, having been born 5 January 1801. His father had died in 1816, a financial calamity which left his family nearly penniless. Shortly before he came to Clarkesville his mother had dissolved her home and sold the family farm. She took up residence with her other son, Jesse, in Easton, Massachusetts. Jesse, who was employed as a miller, was seven years older than George and had married Elisabeth Noyes the prior year. No doubt having his mother on hand was a great help since Jesse and Elisabeth were expecting their first child. Louisa Loraine was born to this couple in April of 1827. George had recently attended Dartmouth College and although he had not received his degree, having only attended for the years 1821 to 1824, this did not seem to impair his teaching credentials.[42] This young man was making his way to the western part of the state of New York with intentions of reading for law. He obviously had a sense that great opportunities awaited a young lawyer on the virgin lands to the west. He paused on his trek to teach at schools for a year or so as his financial needs required.

In many ways Johnson was typical of the type of teacher trustees in general sought for these academies. It was thought best to hire someone with a fine record of academic achievement as only graduation from a well-respected institution could provide. Johnson's attendance at Dartmouth College would certainly have recommended him well to the trustees in Clarkesville because it would have given some degree of immediate prestige to their academy. The trustees of the academy in Cherry Valley tried to capitalize on their teacher in the same way in 1821 when they advertised that "Alfred E. Campbell, late a graduate of Union College" would be teaching their upcoming term. It is interesting to note that the trustees of the Gilbertsville Academy and Collegiate Institution found it necessary to try to cover its teachers' lack of credentials in their advertisements by merely saying that "Skillful and experienced Teachers are employed in the various departments . . ."[43] The practical side of this desire for credentialed teachers from fine colleges was that it would better entice people to send their children to the academy and pay the relatively large sums of money necessary to support the institution, thereby ensuring the school's success.

Johnson's skill and patience as a teacher were well known to the trustees since he not only secured the testimonial quoted above, but on completion of his first term in Clarkesville he was presented with a similar testimonial by the trustees of the academic school.

Yesterday Mr. Daniel Gilbert, Mr. Silas Devol, and Mr. Nathan Bailey, Trustees, presented me with the following testimonial:

> *"This certifies that George Washington Johnson has instructed a public school in our village for three months past with distinguished ability and success, to the entire satisfaction of every individual therein; that his habits have been at all times correct and exemplary, and his deportment pleasing and gentlemanly; this testimonial we give him with equal truth and pleasure."*
>
> *Clarksville, Otsego Co.,*
> *Oct. 30th, 1827*[44]

Johnson took great pride in these testimonials as a reflection on his personal character and a public show of faith people reposed in him. In addition to teaching at the academic school, he also assisted in instructing the Bible class at church as another way of endearing himself to the residents. However, his journal reveals a different side to his character. With regard to church and Bible class, he wrote:

> *I am generally at meeting, at least half the day, Sundays and sometimes assist in instructing a Bible class, though both go much against the grain, but I do so, out of civility, to please those I have a desire to compliment in this way, at a sacrifice.*[45]

Further, his love and respect for the residents of Clarkesville was measured and circumscribed by his contempt for their petty flaws.

> *Middlefield, Otsego Co., N. Y.*
> *The villagers are mostly of New England blood, and have the characteristic New England intelligence, enterprise, and industry, but they have also the usual village jealousies and rivalries, religious and secular. The leading men are Dr. Sumner Ely, Daniel Gilbert, Joshua L. Pinney and Rev. Benjamin Sawin.*[46]

The character of individuals can be very complex, more so when they are viewed after the lapse of time. Intervening years can make it difficult to discern nuances, motives, and personal agendas. Johnson's diary gives rare insight into his character. On one hand he heartily despised the bulk of the people in the village, wanting only to please and impress those he considered important. This quality seemed to only be measured through the prism of who could further his interests. However, on the other hand, he had a genuine respect for education and talent. He recognized that in his assessment of the villagers and his descriptions of people. Dr. Ely, whom he admired greatly, he described as probably "college educated", a "free-thinker", and "skillful". He saw fit to mention, as well, that Ely was "anxious for the education of his children," two of whom, Adriel and Theodore, were enrolled in the academic school. It can be assumed, that as candid as Johnson's diary is, he had no intention of it being read by anyone other than himself, which seems to be very different from so many of his contemporary's diaries. Therefore, it is logical that his assessments of people were honest. Thus, as flatteringly as he describes Ely, it is equally telling that he saw fit to mention that the doctor was "well-off" and had a "neat house and office." His description of Ely shows both sides of Johnson's character, the respect for an intellectual equal and the sycophantic desire to impress those who could further his own career.

Johnson's character was found to be impeachable by some residents on other scores as well. He was prone to singing the praises of the beautiful ladies in the village in his diary. It is a question how obvious he made his infatuations in and around the hamlet known. For example, in reference to Ely's wife, Hannah, he said she had "delicate form and features - is sensitive - amiable - gentle - intelligent - ladylike - is very civil to me and I esteem her highly".[47] It would be easy to construe these words as having a more than innocent intention. Hannah was not the only woman in town of whom Johnson became enamored. He was very attracted to Charlotte Pinney, Joshua's daughter. He spent a lot of time with her on outings, picnics, and dances. However, his reputation with the ladies was too promiscuous for Polly Pinney, Charlotte's mother.

Polly Pinney has left a picture as an upright figure who was most devout in her religious observances and was quickly coming to abhor the many vices around her on the frontier. She became very involved in the religious revival in the area and was a driving force in the Baptist church. In referring to the establishment of that church she stated, "It was God's work; the instrumentality employed was of the weakest kind, and yet the result was marvelous."[48] As she saw life around her, she became deeply concerned with the use of alcohol. She obviously would have witnessed some of the greatest excesses of alcohol in the tavern Joshua Pinney operated. Polly Pinney would eventually, with her husband, become a renowned figure in the temperance movement.

In May of 1828, when Johnson was changing lodgings from the Pinney residence, he made the following notation in his journal:

> *As I was about to leave, my friend Mrs. P.[inney] conversed with me about the flirtation going on between me and her eldest daughter, Charlotte. She did not approve of courtship that looked not to marriage. Frank and right. I tried to be, in turn, frank, but, taken by surprise, I was hardly intelligible.*[49]

No doubt Johnson's poor reputation with the ladies was fostered by his dandified appearance on the frontier. Although Clarkesville was certainly a prosperous village with its residents dressing in fine apparel, Johnson would have stood out for his ostentatious attire. He ran accounts with many of the merchants in the hamlet, settling those accounts at the end of each term. In October of 1827 he settled his tailoring account for $6.62½ with William Campbell and purchased an umbrella from Silas Devol for $2.12. All totaled, for the time he spent in Clarkesville, he records $55.00 as having been spent on clothing plus $16.25 for a watch.[50] This was excessive by early Otsego standards even in the more genteel areas of Cooperstown. Certainly, it would not have gone without notice or comment that their school teacher was spending more than was deemed appropriate for one of his station on clothing.

For all of his faults, though, George Washington Johnson was respected in Clarkesville for the talent and abilities he brought to the academic school. This was so much the case that in March of 1828 Dr. Ely organized a select, or private, academic school for Johnson to teach. This school was a closer parallel to the school John S. Mitchell was running in Exeter. The course offering was to include languages, rhetoric, composition, logic, mathematics, and speaking.

Further, whereas the Exeter school charged $2.50 per quarter, the patrons of this school in Clarkesville were required to pay $3.00 per quarter. There were only seven students who attended this school: Sumner Ely's three children, Jane Howard's child, two of Daniel Gilbert's children, and one of Joshua Pinney's children. The select school only seems to have lasted for one quarter, that is, until Johnson left Clarkesville. It was taught at the "old school house," which presumably was the school building that was across from the Baptist church which Pinney had helped establish in 1807.[51] In referring to it as the "old school house," the residents must have been differentiating it from the newer school building on the southern end of the Long Patent Road.

As a young man, filled with hope, promise, and intellectual talent, Johnson became good friends with Sumner Ely, a man now in his forties and probably the most educated man in Clarkesville. Johnson frequently spent evenings with the doctor and his wife, Hannah, discussing the important questions of the day. He was impressed with Ely enough to comment in his diary that Ely "appeared to be a man of college education." Apparently, Ely never told him that he had attended Yale, certainly a strange omission and could point to Ely as having been a humble man. Among the engaging topics Ely and Johnson may have discussed, no doubt the issue of slavery would have been among them. New York State began passing legislation from 1785 to 1799 which led to the gradual abolition of slavery on 5 July 1827. However, by 1820 there were still reported to be 10,088 slaves held in the state. The number of slaves held in Otsego County for that year was minimal. It is known that in 1824 there were 235 free blacks in the county along with 16 slaves. The census records indicate that in 1830 there were 146 African-Americans living in the county. Of that number, twelve were living in Middlefield in two households; one household was headed by Peter Knox with three family members, the other was headed by Hayden Watters with seven family members.[52]

It is difficult to know exactly what Ely and Johnson's thoughts were on the slavery issue. It is comforting to assume that the Northern intelligentsia was universally opposed to this abomination. Indeed, Johnson's diary indicates that by the late 1830s, as a member of the Liberty Party, while living again in Massachusetts, he was an abolitionist. He even stood as that party's candidate for governor of Massachusetts in 1840. These anti-slavery activities were continued upon his return to Buffalo, New York later in 1840.[53] From Ely's activities in the 1830s it may be assumed that he was in agreement with the views that Abraham Lincoln would enunciate at a later date, specifically that it would be better to halt the spread of slavery and let it die out in its own course as its lack of economic sustainability became apparent. This was perceived as a better alternative to completely disrupting the union of states by antagonizing the slave holding states, which would be the effect of proposing emancipation. In 1835, Ely, along with many other notables in Otsego County gave notice of a public meeting to discuss this issue.

The undersigned, citizens of Otsego County, feeling that the measures pursued by the advocates of the immediate abolition of Slavery, are prejudicial to the peace and quiet of the American Union, and tend directly to a dissolution of the Confederacy of the States composing it, deem it important that an expression of public sentiment should be had upon the subject in this County . . .[54]

In addition to Ely, other men from Middlefield who signed this notice included E. B. Morehouse, George W. Stillman, William Temple, Samuel M. Ingalls, and Evander Williams. Additionally, there are other names of men who had recently moved from Middlefield to neighboring towns: Benoni H. Marks, now living in Burlington (his body would be removed back to Clarkesville for burial in the Baptist cemetery when he died in 1864[55]), and Erastus Belknap now living in Westford. These names were joined by other notables in the county such as James Fenimore Cooper, George Pomeroy, Ambrose W. Clark, George Starkweather, Elihu Phinney, and Jacob Morris. In total 141 of the leading men of the county signed this notice.

In light of the stance these men took, it is less likely that they were repulsed by the brutality of slavery as they were unconvinced of the economic profitability and, hence, long term viability, of slave labor. These educated men, however, certainly would have had their views challenged when Hiram Powers unveiled his famous statue, *The Greek Slave*. In pure white marble, this piece did more to change the focus of the slave debate by showing a white woman in bondage.[56] By changing the appearance of slavery and showing that it had affected the white race as well, and a Greek, no less, when Americans were in love with the ancient Greek world, the debate was pushed along from the simple economics of slavery and toward the inhumanity and brutality of the institution. This simple change in the appearance of slavery did more than the numerous articles which were printed in newspapers to highlight the misery of the slaves and the miserable business that was the slave trade. A typical example was the article which appeared in *The Freeman's Journal* in 1826 entitled "The Horrors of the Slave Trade." This article recounted the arrival of a slave ship in Trinity, Martinique. Readers were informed about how 100 slaves had died from starvation on the trip, how those that survived the voyage were terribly malnourished and naked, and how they were all purchased by the commandant of the port for his plantation.[57]

There was a gradual evolution in the debate on slavery occurring. Men like Ely, Morehouse, Cooper, Starkweather, and Phinney who opposed slavery based on its limited economic value were being pressured by other forces. The people being swept up in the religious revival occurring on the frontier were raising their voices against slavery and founding their opposition on a different premise. People like William Lloyd Garrison would raise a more militant voice from a different quarter. Garrison was an associate of the abolitionist Benjamin Lundy and in 1831 began publishing his anti-slavery sheet *The Liberator*. These new voices tied their sentiments to the religious revival by opposing slavery because it was anathema to the teachings of Christ: all men were brothers and created in God's image.[58] A man could not morally hold his brother in bondage. It was a compelling argument, stirring the community deeply.

This abolitionist wave was especially prominent in Clarkesville among the Baptists, a sect that generally seemed to abhor slavery. They found the basic premise that all people were equal in God's eyes particularly compelling. This sentiment moved them to integrate Clarkesville's Baptist congregation as early as 1819. In that year they admitted Dinah Ann Vincent, "a woman of color," to their congregation. It must have been a moving scene when she related her life's experiences and requested baptism. On the next day, 18 September, she was submerged in the Cherry Valley Creek to be baptized by Elder Sawin.[59]

Against this background was held a major anti-slavery rally on the fourth of July in the year slavery was abolished, 1827. Hayden Watters, of Middlefield, along with Thomas Mann of Cooperstown, organized this rally as a celebration of the abolition of slavery in New York. However, he used the occasion to take a stance against the entire institution of slavery. Held in Cooperstown with about sixty people of color in attendance, the group marched to the Presbyterian Church where Watters delivered an address. In his speech, he gave advice, that "if practiced, would prove a blessing to the African race, as it inculcated the necessity of sobriety, honesty, and industry, together with a proper regard to the education of their children". This demonstration, complete with music and banners, caught the attention of many white citizens who took part as observers. The entire event was aimed at not only celebrating their liberation in New York, but also showing that these recently freed peoples were prepared to become positive contributing members of the community. The call was for equality and integration. Watters and Mann would go on to work to establish a self-help society, and in September 1827 Watters would lead a discussion at the Cooperstown courthouse on the "merits and demerits of the African Colonization Society."[60]

Aside from the obvious statements about the general populace's feelings toward slavery, there is a larger context in which to place this rally. Cooperstown stood as one of a very few villages in rural New York to have such rallies. This is most obviously an indication of the progressive views of the populace, but, by implication, it points to the level of prosperity in northern Otsego County. When thoughts are consumed with the mundane chores of survival on an isolated frontier, it is not possible to consider much of the larger world. However, as prosperity frees a people from the banal, it is possible to consider the monumental questions which can consume society. Slavery in America was one such question and the people of northern Otsego County were prepared to raise their voices against it. It was certainly no coincidence that as the 1820s had brought a considerable level of prosperity to the area, so too was it the time that so many stunning social developments were occurring. The same enlightened spirit that led a free black man from Middlefield to organize such a momentous rally was the same spirit that animated the people who integrated their Baptist congregation in 1819 and that drove the men who set up first the academic school, and then the select school, in Clarkesville. They were people who found themselves freed from the drudging chores of survival to be able to consider larger and more profound thoughts.

Parallel to the issue of slavery, and considered an equal bane on society by the people of rural New York was drunkenness. The burgeoning middle class on the frontier had seen the building of distilleries and taverns long before the establishment of churches in many of their communities. William Cooper, of Cooperstown, had built a distillery several years before he gave land for the building of the Presbyterian and Episcopal churches. In Clarkesville, Pinney had set up a tavern as perhaps the first business in the hamlet, and, although it is true that taverns served many more needs than simply the selling of liquor, that was one of a tavern's primary sources of revenue. Indeed, due to the fact that in many ways taverns were the focal point in a community such as Clarkesville, they fostered the tendency to inebriation that was so ubiquitous in rural New York at this time. Pinney's tavern not only provided lodgings for travelers and served meals, but until 1833, it also served as the post office. Further, it was the meeting place of the Masonic lodge and occasionally the Baptist congregation when they attended to business. Filling these roles as it did, it is not surprising that it was the center of activity. Coupling this with its sale of liquor and it becomes apparent how pervasive liquor was. Buttressing his tavern business was Pinney's role in the distillery which, as has been noted, served to supply his tavern with a cheap source of alcohol.

As strong as this role of the tavern was in catering to the indulgence of alcohol was the opposing role of a middle class morality which had grown out of the American Revolution. In many ways the heroes of the Revolution had been transformed in people's minds to be more like the towering heroes of the ancient world. Americans of all walks of life had come to admire the ancient world of Greece, endeavoring to model their new republic on that example. It was this infatuation which led to the Greek Revival taste in architecture, but it ran much deeper than the art of architecture. The Greek language was taught at academies, as is evidenced by its being offered at the academy in Clarkesville, and people studied the heroes and philosophers of both the Greek and Roman world. Temperance having been one of Cicero's four cardinal virtues was not a fact lost on this growing middle class.

Such a blight was drunkenness that the people across New York banded together in their communities to form temperance societies. These societies railed against the evils of drunkenness and how that vice disrupted a peaceful social order. As early as 1808 Elihu Phinney had published in Cooperstown a sermon by Seth Williston which enumerated the evils of inebriation; among these evils was that it made a man unfit for his duty and unfit to do good. Further, he reasoned, that drunkenness led to poverty. However, the greatest evil caused by drunkenness was that it led to "loving and serving the creature more than the Creator."[61] These sentiments were echoed in a much later poem composed in 1874 by Harriet E. Tucker, of Maine, New York, in which she preserved the rationale for the righteousness of the temperance cause:

> *We are a peaceable people and live by hard labor,*
> *Each man is as good, every whit, as his neighbor,*
> *Unless he gets drunk, and then he's to blame*
> *And ought not to bear a very good name.*
> *Here, my good friends, pray let me digress*
> *And say I hope the number is less,*
> *Let us work with a will to get them all in*
> *To the Good Templar's fold, where they'll drink no more gin,*
> *And then what a happy people we'll be*
> *When nothing is drunk stronger than tea.*[62]

The characterization of a society made up of equals, as voiced in the poem, resonated well on the frontier. This sense of equality, coupled with the Masonic belief in a hierarchy based on merit and honor, was destined to have far-reaching effects on the social fabric of the frontier, grounded as it had been for so long on a quasi-aristocratic arrangement as personified by the Van Rensselaers, Philipses, Livingstons, and, locally, the Clarkes and Coopers. It is, therefore, clear that the temperance movement had tapped into many different threads which ran through society, and although this particular movement sought only one outcome, the abolition of intoxication, its rationale would come to be co-opted by other groups. It would be wrong to underestimate the sincerity of the people advocating temperance, even though many of them seemed to advance ideals which, through their irony, were almost comic. This irony was palpable in people such as Pinney who were deriving their livelihood from the sale of alcohol, but who became deeply involved in the temperance movement, even going so far as to market a cure for intemperance while running a tavern. A case in point demonstrating the sincerity of the cause was L. C. Turner of Cooperstown who took the cause so seriously that he obtained copies of the "Report of the American Temperance Society and the Report of the Buffalo Temperance Convention, sufficient for every family in the County" in 1835. He requested that the towns in the county send for their copies to distribute.[63] This was an attempt to disseminate information on the evils of drink to every family in Otsego County.

The residents of Clarkesville, like so many other small hamlets, had come to see the dangers of inebriation on the frontier. In this decade they banded together and formed a local chapter of the Sons of Temperance. Forming as it did in the late 1820s, it predates a similar group that formed in the neighboring hamlet of Middlefield Centre in 1848. The Middlefield Centre group reputedly failed because too many of its members indulged in liquor. The Clarkesville group was fraught with irony from its inception as well. The most glaring irony was that the group met at the home of Joshua and Polly Pinney, who were tavern keepers, and were obviously accumulating a portion of their wealth from the distillation and sale of liquor. Although some of these groups had a very short existence, the cause of temperance was one that took on the appearance of a crusade throughout the nineteenth century. In 1846 large temperance conventions were held in the nearby communities of Milford Center and Oneonta, and Cooperstown had an active temperance group as late as 1878.[64]

Very little is known about the Sons of Temperance, but it does shed further light on the double character of Joshua Pinney. The tavern keeper was not only supporting a group working to foster sobriety, he was also marketing a cure for intemperance. At this time there were several purported cures for intemperance, the two most notable in rural New York were Dr. Brown's cure and Dr. Chambers' cure. Pinney was marketing Dr. Brown's cure at a cost of three dollars per dose. One dose was supposed to be sufficient to cure "the most inveterate propensity for spirituous, intoxicating liquors, by which many individuals are rendered worse than useless to community, to their families, and to themselves, who, otherwise, would be valuable and respectable citizens."[65] The wording of Pinney's advertisement is interesting in that it separates the "illness" from the person. He was making it clear that these people would be valuable and respectable if only they were sober. His approach was very like the approach Tucker took in her poem, when she characterized people as all being equal were it not for the blight of alcohol. Further, it served as an unambiguous play on the desire of the men of Clarkesville to be respectable, catering, as advertising invariably does, to what people want to be and how they wish to appear.

Working toward the same ends as the Sons of Temperance were the Baptist congregation and the Masonic lodge in Clarkesville. In 1811 and 1813 the Baptist Congregation had voted to "withdraw the hand of fellowship" from two men; Jesse How in 1811 and Amos Jones in 1813. In the case of Jesse How, Polly Pinney "testified that she saw him one evening when she thought he was too much in liquor and she said it was observed by others . . ." As for the case in 1813, "Brothers Wood, Hoskins, North, and Pinney testified to the drunkenness of Brother Amos Jones".[66] It is interesting to note that in both cases one of the Pinneys was testifying against the man in question. One wonders if these incidences of intoxication occurred at Pinney's tavern. It also serves to show that Pinney's evolution from tavernkeeper and distiller to temperance advocate was a long, slow journey commencing more than twenty years prior to his finally divesting himself of these businesses. Later in life, Pinney stated that he became convinced of the merits of temperance because of what he saw as an innkeeper.

The Freemasons, as has been noted, distinguished people by merit and honor, thus it was felt that drunkenness was not conducive to either of these virtues. In a resolution dated 18 May 1826 and signed by Secretary Daniel Gilbert:

Nathan Howard - a vagrant - a person guilty of all the vices that degrade human nature - habitual intoxication - and his wife has procured a Bill of divorce from his adulterous habits (recently) the said Howard being cited to appear before the Lodge to show cause why he should not be expelled conducted himself in a disorderly and ____ manner - and gave no satisfaction to said Lodge - it was therefore unanimously Resolved that the said Nathan Howard ought to be expelled from the ancient and honourable order of Freemasonry . . .[67]

It was no coincidence that when these men accused Howard of "all the vices that degrade human nature" they saw fit to list intoxication as the first vice, making clear how horrible they viewed public drunkenness to be. As their resolution noted, Howard's adulterous behavior had also led his wife, Hannah, to obtain a divorce from him. This is significant in that during this period divorces were extremely unusual. It was much more common for two people to stay married, even in such situations, perhaps even going so far as to live separately, rather than divorce. What may have prompted Hannah's action was Nathan's flagrant transgressions against the sanctity of marriage. By Nathan's carrying on an adulterous affair openly (as opposed to clandestinely), Hannah would be able to break the bond of marriage and have the support of her family and the local community in so doing. Had Nathan been less open and flagrant in his affair, Hannah would not have been assured of support from family and friends in breaking the supreme family bond, marriage.

This expulsion of Nathan Howard from the Masonic lodge was not an isolated occurrence. On 17 August 1826 they suspended Jesse C. Smith for one year for "unmasonic conduct" as well. Nor was Widow's Son Lodge unique in this course of action. Otsego Lodge had a record of taking similar action as early as 1808 when they expelled a member for unmasonic conduct and ordered that a notice to that effect be published in the newspaper.[68] How these lodges were defining "unmasonic conduct" is a mystery that even their minutes do not reveal. Since no legal actions were found to have been taken against the men in question, it seems likely that these suspensions and expulsions were meant to punish them for socially unacceptable behavior rather than actual illegal acts. Within that context, it seems likely that the reprehensible conduct was very possibly inebriation.

The inherent contradiction the Pinneys felt in the advocacy of the cause of temperance and the ownership of the tavern and distillery could not be reconciled. The result was their endeavor to divest themselves of these businesses. The first step in this divestiture was the sale, on 1 October 1831, of Pinney's interest in the distillery to his long time friend and another fellow Freemason, Sumner Ely, who purchased it with Erastus L. Sterling, his partner in this venture. Sterling was seventeen years junior to Ely, having been born in 1804. Similar to Ely's partnership in the mill with Daniel Gilbert, Sterling, not Ely, probably tended to the daily operation of the distillery. Pinney sold this property and business for $650, granting to Ely and Sterling all the water rights on the property with the exception that Pinney would be allowed sufficient water for his use. A further covenant was that Ely and Sterling could not construct a dwelling house on this parcel without the consent of George Clarke. This was, no doubt, tied to a condition of Pinney's original purchase of the property.[69]

In 1833 the tavern was sold for $2,400 to Pinney's friend, fellow Freemason and church leader, Benjamin D. North Jr., the son of Daniel North.[70] It is no small coincidence that North's uncle, also named Benjamin D. North Jr., operated a tavern a short distance from the hamlet. No doubt the younger Benjamin D. North Jr. had been able to see first hand the profits to be made in owning a well-run tavern. Concurrent with the sale of the tavern was the moving of the location of the post office. Pinney still owned the store located in the stone building near the crossroads which he was running with his son Egbert and he still retained his position as postmaster. This store now became the new location for the post office. Thus was completed Pinney's trek from tavern keeper and distiller to temperance advocate. Upon his death in 1855 he was remembered as "one of the most active temperance men," and the Rose of Sharon Lodge No. 1, Independent Order of Good Templars, published a resolution mourning his passing. His obituary noted that he had been "extensively engaged in distilling" and that he had kept a public house until reading *The Genius of Temperance*, at which point "he abandoned both branches of that mischievous business".[71]

The tavern, as purchased by North and his wife Elizabeth, was still very much as it had been when George Clarke had it constructed in about 1791. However, the Norths saw fit to make some dramatic alterations to this already impressive edifice as a way of making it clear to the residents of Clarkesville that they were ushering in a new era to the burgeoning hamlet. Clarkesville's most impressive building was not destined to sit as an image of the past, stuck as a Federal style structure while the fashionable world was indulging in the beauties of the Greek Revival. Accordingly, a monumental Greek Revival portico was added to the front of the tavern. This portico ran the entire length of the façade, a full forty-two feet, and was supported by four towering columns cut from single tree trunks rising to the eaves of the second story. They had to be fabricated by draw shaving them down rather than turning them on a lathe because there was no lathe large enough in the vicinity to accommodate such massive timbers. These columns rested on stone slabs supported by foundations formed from rough stone, brick and rubble held in mortar. The ceiling of the portico was of plaster over wood forming a vaulted canopy sweeping from the front to meet the building.

On the face of it, the addition of this portico did what no other alterations could have done. For those who came to socialize at the tavern, it provided a spacious place outdoors to relax and converse, lined, as it no doubt was, with chairs and tables. It also immediately showed the wealth, prestige, and tastefulness of the proprietor to even the most casual passerby. Wealth and prestige were apparent in the fact that only someone of great prosperity could have such an awe-inspiring structure added to an already impressive building. Tastefulness was made clear in that the addition was in the most modern, Greek Revival style. Finally, the new owner of the tavern used this portico to show his knowledge of the cosmopolitan trends emanating from the resorts along the Hudson River. By the 1820s that region had developed a standard plan for a hotel which included a three story structure with a long piazza or portico.[72] In this change to the tavern, North may very well have hoped to change people's view of his establishment from being just a tavern to be more of a fashionable hotel like those springing up along the Hudson River.

Once inside the tavern, the guest would notice another stunning addition which the Norths made. During this period in America, scenic wallpapers, engraved on wood blocks, most frequently in France, were being used in more metropolitan areas to decorate walls. These were printed on numbered sheets to be assembled using a chart and were intended to cover all the walls of a room. Owing to their expense, such wallpapers only appeared in affluent areas of Otsego County during the 1830s, most notably Cooperstown. One striking *trompe l'oeil* wallpaper has been found in the entrance hall of Willow Hill, a fine house on the outskirts of Cherry Valley. These scenic papers were normally positioned above the chair rail or dado in a room.

People living in communities in central New York, being a great distance from more metropolitan centers and without the means to afford such wallpapers, often did not have access to this decorative finery so itinerant artists provided a substitute. The Norths employed the talents of such an artist in the parlor to the right of the entrance hall of their tavern. To this room was added a mural attributed to the itinerant painter William Price. This mural covered all four walls of the parlor and was above the chair rail, much in the style of these French papers. Although no signature has been found on this mural, it bears striking similarities to a mural signed by Price in the Carroll House in Springfield, New York, just fifteen miles north of Clarkesville.[73] The murals of the Carroll House are signed under the window sill, if Price signed the murals in Clarkesville in the same place, that signature would have been lost when subsequent owners of this tavern removed the original windows in a later renovation of this room. This full surround mural, painted in it's charming yet naive manner, follows the style similar to that of the Hudson River School then blossoming under the leadership of men such as Thomas Cole and Asher B. Durand. The scene depicts images of what could be the hills surrounding the hamlet enlivened with jagged rocks and romantic castles. The mural would inspire and awe the guest with the majesty of nature around the hamlet just as the guest had been awed by the majesty of the portico and building around themselves.

Both of these enhancements, the portico and the wall mural, may have caused the third striking alteration the Norths made seem almost anti-climatic. Another parlor was added to the southern corner of the tavern, adjacent to the painted parlor. This room, being the largest in the entire building, greatly increased the spaciousness of the whole. Resplendent with an exceptionally high ceiling and elegant cornice molding, then a rarity in northern Otsego County, would have marked this room as being a fitting tribute to wealth and prestige. North was obviously determined to build for himself a position of prominence in the hamlet and equally determined to see to it that his tavern retained its position as the center of social gatherings.

It is easy to see how North would have wanted to make his own imprint on the tavern and create an atmosphere which would keep his business as the hamlet's focal point. However, his alterations clearly seem excessive to accomplish that purpose. It is possible that another force was at work. Specifically, was there a competing tavern in such close proximity that North felt a need to differentiate his tavern so much so as to transform it into something closer to the elegant resort hotels on the Hudson River. There is certainly tantalizing evidence to suppose that this was the case.

It has been mentioned that Daniel Cummings' brother Hosea lived in a house on the northern side of the Cooperstown Road. It is not clear when he came to Clarkesville or when he built this house. It was a purely Federal style two story house with a five bay façade and a centered front door. The windows of this house were striking since they were the only windows in the hamlet known to have elaborate entablatures above them. The floor plan was almost identical to the plan of the house Daniel had built on the Long Patent Road. However, this house of Hosea's seems to date to a much earlier period. It made no acknowledgment of the Greek Revival fashion and certainly could have been built as early as the first decade of the nineteenth century.

Hosea lived in this house and rented the land from George Clarke for some time before he purchased it in 1822 for $27. The purchase price clearly indicates that Cummings was not buying the house from Clarke, but only a village lot. Cummings' impetus to purchase the parcel was so that he could sell the property to Hannah Howard. Further evidence that Cummings had built the house long before he purchased the property is seen in the fact that the deed recording his sale to Howard occured on the same day on which he bought the property from Clarke. The difference is that where Cummings paid $27 to Clarke for the property on 8 April 1822, Howard paid $400 to Cummings for the house and property on the same day.[74]

Hannah Howard was the wife of Nathan Howard whom the Freemasons expelled from their lodge on 18 May 1826 for drunkenness and adultery at the same time that Hannah was procuring a divorce from him for the same reasons. Divorce was a very extreme and unusual step for a woman to take in this period. Clearly, Nathan's transgressions must have been both intolerable and apparent to all in the community. Only under such circumstances would divorce not have carried social stigma and would have been supported by family and friends. After this point Nathan Howard does not seem to have stayed in Clarkesville. In this position Hannah Howard would have had few options of supporting herself on the frontier, and in most cases women in similar circumstances would have relied on family members for support. Since she retained ownership of this house until 1845, when she sold it to Nathan Watson for $220, it is obvious that this unmarried woman found some means of supporting herself.[75] It is compelling to conclude that she, at the very least, took in lodgers for income. This conclusion is further supported by the fact that this house was referred to in contemporary documents as Pinney & Howard, as stated earlier. This must certainly refer to a business name. It may have been the presence of this other tavern in the hamlet that led Benjamin North to make so many renovations to his tavern. This would be his way of stating that his tavern was not simply a boarding house, but was a much more elegant establishment.

North was unwittingly marking a watershed in the development of Clarkesville. His grandfather had come to the frontier when it was a wild land. This man had carved out a farm from a forest, but he had also seen younger men of enterprise follow his lead. Men like Joshua Pinney and Sumner Ely who came from the more settled areas of Albany, New York and Connecticut, were joined in Clarkesville by men such as Daniel Gilbert and Clark D. Parshall whose families had already settled in the Otsego region. Together these men recognized that their hamlet was on a crossroads literally and figuratively. As George Clarke had noted in his travel journal in 1791, this convergence of four roads was a good spot for a tavern or store, and so it was that business took root and flourished. Prosperity came as it inevitably does with a hard-working frugal people, and the hamlet grew exponentially. Social groups coalesced and in the span of a very few years businesses of every nature were joined by a church congregation, an academy, and a Masonic lodge.

The leaders in the business community tended to be the same leaders of the social and religious groups. This is partly explained by the relatively small number of people on the frontier. There were a limited number of people to take the reins of leadership in social groups. However, business partners and associates tended to help each further their social standing in the community, and alternately, people jealously vied with each other for social prominence. It is difficult to discern someone's motives, but that is not finally the point. The point is that regardless of motive, these people had pulled the hamlet from its infantile stage to a level of maturity where it was attaining some degree of self-sufficiency. The need for the bulk of the residents to travel long distances was lessening as most supplies one would need were becoming readily available in Clarksville.

Taken as a whole, these business and social developments propelled this village crossroads to a historical crossroads. The level of maturity in the community, coupled with the education level of some and the cosmopolitan tastes of others led the residents of this hamlet to look at some of the great social issues of the day. As issues of great importance gripped New York, these people were able to take note of their world and register their opinions on the issues of slavery and intemperance. It is noteworthy that as temperance societies were forming across New York, Clarksville joined the ranks of villages and hamlets with such societies. Further, it is indicative of a mature community that the Baptists of Clarksville were sufficiently tolerant to integrate their congregation, and more so, that an African-American from the area was able to organize an abolitionist rally in an amicable environment. These were all the signs of the budding middle class morality that was becoming pervasive in the Northern states.

The degree of social and moral sophistication apparent in the hamlet found expression in such tangible manifestations as the elegant additions North made to his tavern. This was a sophistication which had come to Clarkesville in a relatively short space of years. Clearly prosperity had been uneven, but it had been such that its effects were wide-spread. People of all stations took part in the social fabric of the hamlet. Classes based on economic success were clear, but allowances were made so that participation in society could be nearly universal. When the Baptist church auctioned pews they were divided in classes based on cost. However, a sense of equality had led to ingenious ways of making sure that all who wanted a pew could be included either by purchasing less expensive pews or by purchasing sections of a pew. It could be argued alternately that this indicated that the ideal of a classless society had not taken hold or that clever ways had been found to be inclusive: was the glass half empty or half full? Whatever the case, the direction of the hamlet had been set and although there were disruptive forces on the horizon, Clarkesville was clearly headed toward steady habits which would lead to a steady prosperity.

A bird's eye view of the hamlet of Middlefield, looking northeast. Photographic post card, c. 1910. Collection of Dominick J. Reisen.

A second bird's eye view of the hamlet, this time facing southwest. Note the poles for supporting hop vines, running along the center of the photograph. Photographic post card, c.1910. Collection of Dominick J. Reisen.

The four corners of the hamlet of Middlefield looking south along the Long Patent Road. Two of the three stores that graced these corners are clearly seen. Photographic post card, c.1910. Collection of Dominick J. Reisen.

The hamlet of Middlefield looking west along the Cooperstown Road showing the Manning and Mortimer Gilbert store on the left. Past the store can be seen the house built by Manning and Mortimer Gilbert in the 1840s, and then the American Hotel. On the right is the Central Hotel which had been run by Hannah Howard. Photographic post card, c.1910. Courtesy of Rodney and Jeanne Johnson.

The Parshall store as it appeared in the early twentieth century. The Baptist church can be seen in the background. Photographic post card. Courtesy of Rodney and Jeanne Johnson.

The saw mill in the hamlet of Middlefield as it appeared in the early twentieth century, with its contemporary feed store at right. Photographic post card. Courtesy of Rodney and Jeanne Johnson.

The Middlefield Baptist church and cemetery. This beautiful church was constructed according to a design by the architect Asher Benjamin. The Palladian window on the front façade added an elegant, cosmopolitan appearance to this rural building. Photographic post card. Collection of Dominick J. Reisen.

The Methodist church as it was when completed around 1832, before the alterations made around 1910, when the belfry and entrance were moved to the eastern (left) façade. The parsonage is at left. Photographic post card. Courtesy of Rodney and Jeanne Johnson.

Above: The American Hotel. In the 1840s the imposing structure in the fore-ground was added to the smaller section in the background. Photographic post card, c. 1910. Courtesy of Rodney and Jeanne Johnson.
Below: The home of Harrison North, shortly after it was erected in 1859, built in the hamlet of Middlefield by William O. Ashley of nearby Westford. Photograph of an original tin type. Courtesy of Rodney and Jeanne Johnson.

The house built by George Clarke c. 1791 in the hamlet of Middlefield. First Joshua Pinney, and then Benjamin North, operated a tavern here. Also the site of the Masonic lodge and the first post office, it was later the home of the Metcalf family. Photograph by Dominick J. Reisen.

Dr. Azel Metcalf (left) and his son, George Washington Metcalf, in his Civil War uniform. Courtesy of Vieve Metcalfe.

Chapter Four

THE CHANGING OF THE GUARD

Surveying the landscape of Clarkesville while it was being transformed by the whirlwind changes of the 1820s would reveal a place completely unrecognizable from the little cluster settlement where the first town meeting occurred in 1797. That first meeting was a gathering of the leaders of the community. Such prominent men as Samuel Griffin, Moses Rich and Benjamin Gilbert assumed the mantle of responsibility for establishing the town government. They also grafted onto the wilderness the trappings of civilization which would make their community not unlike the places from whence they came. This would tend to make their community more inviting to the influx of settlers coming to Otsego County. This graft flourished in the virgin soil and from it grew a new crop of leaders. These new men carried the torch as it was passed from a generation which had labored and grown tired. As has been seen, this new generation, like the previous one, married their economic prosperity to their assumed role as social leaders. However, more than that, in the admirable ethic that grew a republic of united states out of a wilderness, these men felt obligated to serve the community that had given them their good fortune.

In exploring this other phase of the development of Clarkesville, and indeed Middlefield township as a whole, it is necessary to look at different aspects of the careers of personages who have become familiar. Among this new generation of leaders are the recognizable names of Dr. Sumner Ely, Benjamin D. North Jr. and Daniel Gilbert. So much has already been said about their business and social records, but that only gives part of the picture. To this list will be added such names as John Hayden, Erastus Sterling and Eben B. Morehouse. The influence these men exerted over the development of the hamlet, and the town in general, was enormous in as much as they were involved in so many of the economic, political and social facets of the community. However, there were external forces coming to bear on the hamlet over which these men had no control. Of these external forces, the one of paramount importance was a change in the transportation network most often associated with the construction of the Erie Canal. This, coupled with alterations in the flow of traffic in Middlefield which began to bypass Clarkesville, slowly changed the face of the hamlet. This change was so gradual as to be nearly imperceptible to the inhabitants at the time. The force of change hit from other quarters as well. The death of George Clarke at Hyde Hall brought to the fore his son. The Clarke land holdings throughout Middlefield were extensive and this younger Clarke took a greater interest in the activities of his tenant farmers. Over time this contributed to a sea change in the agricultural base of the county of Otsego, and obviously, on the foundation of Clarkesville's prosperity.

The ways in which the new leaders of Clarkesville dealt with these changes reveal people who displayed good judgment in coping with the brunt of external forces. However, skill was combined with a fair amount of luck. These men could not understand and foresee the full effects of what was happening to their community. Their reactions to the changes they did see on their horizon were prompted in many instances by the instinct to preserve their business interests and personal prosperity. Although that at first glance may appear to be a completely self-centered approach, the result was quite different. Their efforts helped lay the groundwork for the hamlet to settle into a comfortable and steady prosperity which took it through the nineteenth century. The paradox of working to preserve one's business interests is that to do so often means making one's community a better place in which to live, thereby attracting more consumers. Indeed this is what these men, like those before them, recognized. As the first generation had sought to make Clarkesville an inviting haven in the wilderness, this new generation sought to preserve and improve that haven in order to combat the forces which were acting to siphon off its population and disrupt its economic base with tantalizing prospects in other regions.

The beginnings of changes that hit the political landscape of Middlefield can be traced back to 1817. It was in that year that Dr. Sumner Ely was elected town supervisor. As a young and enterprising man making his way in the world as a physician, he first entered the political arena in 1813 as town clerk at the age of twenty-six. This step should certainly have marked this man out for a long history of community and political involvement in light of the fact that he had only recently arrived in Clarkesville from Connecticut. As town clerk he served under his future father-in-law, Benjamin Gilbert, a man whose career, as has been seen, had played such an important role in the town and county. However, the year that Ely was elected supervisor was one of pivotal change for the town. Benjamin Gilbert went to his home near the hamlet of Middlefield Centre to enjoy his well-deserved retirement from political affairs, and as Ely assumed the duties of supervisor, his brother-in-law, Daniel Gilbert, at the young age of twenty-nine, joined him in the governing circle as town clerk.

This smooth transition is more symbolic through hindsight than it was at the time. In the early nineteenth century it was simply the peaceable transfer of power mirrored on the local level that the citizens of the new republic had envisioned happening on the federal level when they established their new government in the late eighteenth century. The ideal of this new form of governance was that it would be free from the influence of a privileged class. Idealism, though, is often not quite played out by actual events. The late eighteenth century political and, to a lesser extent, social landscape of Otsego County had been dominated by such quasi-aristocratic personages as William Cooper and Jacob Morris. As the early nineteenth century unfolded George Clarke added his name to this list. The basis of this influence rested on the vast tracts of land these men controlled on this frontier. In that regard their influence was similar to that which was wielded in the Hudson and Mohawk River valleys by such families as the Livingstons, Van Rensselaers, and Philipses. Ironically, this was the same basis of power of the European aristocracy which the ideals of the Revolution had found so repugnant. However, the very foundation of this authority was being challenged by the evolution of two natural occurrences: the purchase of land by a greater number of people and the rise of a prosperous, business-oriented middle class.

In the hamlet of Clarkesville, it has been shown that George Clarke was not averse to selling his land to the inhabitants. After relatively short periods in which this land was leased to the residents he showed a willingness to sell these village parcels outright. This leasing period could be viewed as the requisite "breathing space" allowing the new settlers to use their resources and capital to build their houses and establish their livelihood. At the end of such a time, these residents of the hamlet often did buy their parcels. Joshua Pinney is an excellent example; leasing his house and land for some years, establishing his tavern business, and then purchasing the parcel from Clarke. Other examples include Moses Rich Jr. (the mill owner) and Daniel Cummings (the wagon maker.) Men such as Pinney would later break up their larger parcels to sell bits to later settlers. Pinney did this both for Clark D. Parshall and Sumner Ely when they came to settle in Clarkesville. This selling off of land by Clarke was not a universal offering to all settlers. Although he was willing to sell village lots within the hamlet of Clarkesville, he showed a decided reluctance to sell his farm parcels to his tenant farmers. Clearly, he recognized that the basis of his wealth was in the rental income he received from his tenant farmers, not his village tenants. This was a mentality much in keeping with his genteel English roots. It was destined to have far-reaching effects on the future course of Middlefield township when his son George Hyde Clarke came into his inheritance.

As more people became landowners and established prosperous enterprises another subtle shift occurred The power and influence of Cooper, Morris, Clarke, *et al.*, was based not *ipso facto* on their vast land holdings. Instead land served as the basis of wealth and power, the vehicle to fortune, and this wealth was the true foundation of power and influence, both politically and socially, on this frontier. With the growth and success of other business ventures, other avenues to prosperity and wealth, a middle class formed. This social and economic stratification in society empowered the enfranchised many which were created after the Revolution to break the monopolistic influence of the quasi-aristocracy which had begun to coalesce in the colonial period. In short, the power and influence of the large landowners began to dissolve and give way to a wider, more inclusive democracy. This allowed for a greater influence by the middle class as this class turned their attention to inclusion in political affairs. There was a challenge to the landed elite by the rising business class. The politics of deference was not dead, though, it was merely altered in its focus.

Sumner Ely's rise in the political arena of Middlefield is illustrative of this phenomenon of a prosperous middle class challenge to, and assumption of, authority. Indeed, he is only one of many in this new middle class who began to exert influence in Middlefield in the 1820s. This political influence, though, was a natural corollary to the social influence already discussed at length. His election as town supervisor in 1817 was, no doubt, a result of the deference the town's people held for their resident physician who was also a prosperous businessman. This election was followed in 1818 by an appointment as a commissioner for Otsego County, conferred by the New York State Council of Appointment.[1] Both of these honors may have been aided by his close tie to the very prominent Gilbert family. Although there was a mounting challenge to the authority of the landed class, power was still conferred by the laboring many based, to some degree, on economic and social deference. Ely served as town supervisor for eleven years until 1828 when he started taking a greater interest in the affairs of the county. He would ultimately be rewarded by the electorate with a seat in the New York State Senate in 1840.

Ely's participation in county-wide affairs was focused on two main projects: the Otsego County Medical Society and the founding of the Otsego County Poor House. Involvement in both of these institutions is very revealing to his character. Ely was the quintessential rural doctor who took great pride in his ability to help people. In many ways he must have been a true philanthropist at heart. He had been active in the medical society as early as 1817 and at their annual meeting in 1820 he assumed the position of censor along with doctors Delos White, Theodore Pomeroy, N. Buckingham, and Anson Tuttle.[2]

Early in the nineteenth century the medical professionals in Otsego realized that they needed to take steps to ensure that those practicing medicine in the county possessed an adequate degree of training. The formation of a medical society was seen as a way of accomplishing this goal. Under the able leadership of Joseph White, M. D. of Cherry Valley, a well-respected physician and former member of the New York State Senate from 1796 to 1799, a group of doctors from the county came together in 1806 to form the Otsego County Medical Society. Membership in the society would only be available to those who passed the examination of the censors, an examination based on uniform standards. This was seen as a way of guarding against quacks and other unsuitable persons from harming the reputation of the medical profession as a whole. However, more than that, it was seen as a way of helping the public at large to discern in whom they could repose medical trust and their care.[3] It is logical to see Ely's name prominently figured with this group in light of his desire to see excellent medical care available to the people of the county.

The early frontier had seen a plethora of home medical and dental remedies flourish. Part of the reason for this is explained by the need to do something for a suffering person when doctors were scarce. Often a family member would take matters into his own hands. In his memoirs, Levi Beardsley recounts the time when his father extracted his uncle's tooth by using a piece of wood as a punch and knocking the tooth out with a hammer. This was because, "there was no turn screw or other instrument for drawing teeth in the neighborhood . . ."[4]

With the multitude of household remedies in the wilderness, some of which worked, some of which merely masked the condition, and some of which did actual harm, there rose up quacks and charlatans who eagerly peddled "cures." Along with these frauds were people with little or no medical training proclaiming themselves doctors. This dismayed the growing number of properly trained physicians on the frontier across New York State. It was believed that county medical societies and the imposition of uniform examination standards would best ensure the integrity of their profession. This would have the added benefit of aiding the public in choosing a doctor. The year 1806 was a watershed in central New York with the founding of many county societies including Otsego County's neighbors Delaware and Broome counties. This culminated in the organization of the Medical Society of New York State in 1807.

By 1827 Ely was ready to assume greater duties within the society. At their annual meeting in that year they elected Dr. Caleb Richardson as their president and Dr. Anson Tuttle as vice president. Dr. Thomas Fuller served as treasurer. The fourth of the officers of this organization and accepting election as secretary was Dr. Sumner Ely. In addition to holding this post, he also served, along with doctors Delos White, Horace Manly, and Ariel Spafford, as censor. In this capacity he was charged with examining all those wishing to obtain membership in the society. He held these positions for two years, until 1829, when he was selected to represent Otsego County as a delegate to the New York State Medical Society. He later served as president of the Otsego County Medical Society from 1830 to 1831.[5]

The other county level project that occupied Ely's philanthropic energies during this period was the establishment and founding of the Otsego County Poor House. This institution had the express purpose of housing paupers in the county until they were able to find productive and profitable employment. Ely and other like-minded men in Otsego realized that the vagaries of the agricultural and business sectors did not visit all with prosperity and that some people, through no fault of their own, fell on hard times and needed temporary assistance. The reality of the situation was not hard to grasp, people who flocked to this wilderness came with great hopes and dreams of making a better life for themselves and their families. However, the stark reality, gauged by the large number of forced sales of real estate by the sheriff, indicates that many had their dreams dashed to the ground and ended up penniless. It was thought best to provide for the feeding and sheltering of these people as a way of maintaining order and peace in society. Left to their own devices and pushed to desperation, it was feared these paupers might turn to criminal or other unsavory means of support. Turning to their English roots for a guide and looking as far back as the Tudor period, these men realized a dual obligation to assist the down-trodden and to protect the social order.[6] A relatively small expenditure on the part of each town, and thus indirectly on all men, to support the county's paupers was seen as both a decent thing to do for these people, and for society at large it meant the maintenance of order. The poor house as an institution would ultimately allow for the assurance that these paupers received the rudiments of education and a firm moral compass.

The first step on the laudable path of establishing a place of shelter for the poor and destitute in the county was taken with the purchase by the Otsego County Board of Supervisors of 132 acres in Middlefield township from William Temple for $3,000 on 13 November 1826. Temple was born to a family which had migrated from Massachusetts. He remained a farmer his entire life and attained some degree of prosperity as such. In 1827 he became a member of the Otsego Masonic lodge. He eventually became active in politics. He was elected Middlefield town supervisor from 1837 through 1839. He would later serve as a justice of the peace and ultimately he would sit for two terms in the New York State legislature. In an ironic twist, his son, William, who was born in 1823, would one day be appointed for three years as Superintendent of the Poor for Otsego County.[7]

The board of supervisors also established a board of superintendents of the poor house. This board included General George Morell, Levi Gray, James Phinney, Henry Phinney, and Dr. Sumner Ely.[8] These men were charged with erecting and supervising the operation of a poor house. At their first meeting held on 13 December 1826 this board selected General Morell as their chairman and Henry Phinney as secretary and treasurer. It was also determined that Morell would visit the poor houses of Rensselaer, Albany, and Columbia counties to investigate the best way to build a poor house. He presented a plan for the construction of the Otsego County Poor House at a board meeting held on 8 February 1827. His plan was adopted at this meeting and two months later he was appointed to superintend the building of the poor house. This was a handsome stone building rising two and one half stories with two gable quarter-round windows in either end. This simple, balanced fenestration was also being used locally in the early cotton mills being built in Otsego County at this time. In November of 1827 the Otsego County Poor House was opened to receive paupers.[9]

In addition to feeding and sheltering these paupers, the board of superintendents was required to tend to their health needs. To this end Dr. Sumner Ely was appointed on 14 March 1828 as the physician for the poor house. He was contracted at a rate of $70 per year. In this capacity it was mandated that he visit the poor house once each week or as necessary. In December of that year he was re-appointed to this position at a rate of $118 annually, plus obstetrics and surgical operations. When he assumed the position of chairman of the board of superintendents on 25 November 1829, he relinquished his position as physician for the poor house. Dr. John Ingraham was contracted to fill Ely's former position as physician. As chairman of the board, Ely had his long-time friend Elihu Phinney assisting him as secretary and treasurer.[10]

Beyond seeing that these vital health needs were filled, the board also sought to care for the paupers' educational and moral well being. Particular attention was paid to the children who were residents. William Wendell was boarded at the poor house to instruct the children for six hours each day and on 9 May 1829 the Keeper of the Poor, Evan Coats, was directed by the board to procure books for a Bible class and to send the children to the district school in Middlefield. Further, in January of 1830 the board decided to forbid the residents having "spirituous" liquors "except as deemed necessary by a physician."[11] It was felt that the consumption of alcohol was not conducive to building good moral character nor was it felt that the temptation to drunkenness would assist these paupers in obtaining profitable employment. It was a rule formulated from the paternalistic mindset still prevalent in America. The clear goal was not to allow residence at the poor house to be anything other than temporary.

Although the county and towns paid to support the operation of the poor house, the paupers were expected to work to support the establishment as well. In February of 1829 the board of superintendents printed indentures for boarding out resident children. Through indenturing these children it was thought that they would learn a trade and thus be prevented from falling prey to poverty and slovenly ways. Adult residents were also required to earn their keep. On 14 June 1828 the board authorized the purchase of 200 pounds of wool, eight hogs, and "no more that thirty sheep." The stated goal was for the paupers to raise farm produce to sell to contribute to the support of the poor house operation.[12] Indeed, in their annual report for 1830 the board of superintendents reported that the produce of the poor house farm was valued at $693.27 (see Table 3, next page).

After helping to establish this institution of relief, Sumner Ely continued on the board of superintendents until 13 November 1835 with the exception of a brief period from November 1831 to November 1832. That year saw a completely new board assume supervision of the poor house. Included on the new board were Silas Devol and John Russell. Russell was a man of substance who had been appointed as a judge for Otsego County as early as 1814.[13] Devol has been mentioned already as a man of growing importance in Clarkesville. He came from Chatham, Columbia County, to Otsego County in 1818 when he bought property in Cherry Valley. Three months after purchasing the property he sold it inexplicably at a steep loss and relocated to Clarkesville, where he rented a house. He was a merchant who had served on the board of the academic school, which both of his daughters, Sally and Caroline, attended. Further, he had been elected as a trustee of the Baptist Society in Middlefield and was very involved in the building of the Baptist church in the hamlet. When the slips were auctioned for the church, he purchased his family's pew for $45.50.[14] Devol is another example of a member of the prosperous business class who began taking his position as a community leader, replacing the older, landed class.

TABLE 3: VALUE OF PRODUCE, OTSEGO COUNTY POOR HOUSE

AMOUNT	PRODUCE	VALUE ($)
400 bushels	rye	200.00
200 bushels	corn	100.00
230 bushels	oats	57.50
6.5 bushels	beans	4.88
2.5 bushels	flax seed	1.75
350 bushels	potatoes	65.63
150 bushels	turnips	18.75
30 bushels	onions	15.00
30 bushels	beets	7.50
2000	cabbages	60.00
200 lbs	flax	16.00
90 lbs	wool	22.50
30 tons	hay	120.00
10 bushels	carrots	1.88
10 bushels	parsnips	1.88
Total		$693.27

Source: Annual Report for 1830, Records of Superintendent of the Poor, 1826-1911, New York State Historical Association, Cooperstown.

During that year from November 1831 to November 1832 there seems to have been some upheaval which led the entire board of superintendents to resign on 29 November 1831. The exact cause of this mass board overhaul and upheaval is unclear, but was probably tied to the conduct of Evan Coats. One week after assuming its duties, the new board met with Coats on the charge of intemperance. In what must have been a fiery meeting, Coats' only remarks and defense, in light of the board's desire to replace him, was that he had been contracted by the previous board to continue as keeper until 9 April 1832.

This meeting led to a fair amount of wrangling which came to a head on 12 February 1832. At a meeting held at Sherman's Tavern in Cooperstown between board members John Russell, Stephen Gregory, and Silas Devol it was decided that Gregory would notify Coats to quit his position on 22 February 1832. How this drama ultimately played out is unclear and it is not known if Coats resigned or served out his term. However, this new Board of Superintendents of the Poor was replaced on 21 November 1832 by yet another board comprised of Sumner Ely, Amos Winsor, George Holland, George Stillman, and George Pomeroy.[15] It is interesting to note that not only was George Pomeroy the son-in-law of William Cooper, but Sumner Ely, George Stillman, and George Pomeroy were close personal friends. It seems more than coincidental that the result of this internal struggle led to Sumner Ely assuming control of the board again and getting some of his close friends on the board to serve with him. No doubt he did not want to lose control of his board again.

His service to the county in establishing and superintending the poor house from 1826 to 1835 showed Sumner Ely to be deeply concerned with the welfare of those less fortunate. To a lesser extent this was evident in his involvement with the Otsego County Medical Society. In both instances his efforts were focused on assisting large numbers of people; helping people in ways that they could not do themselves. However, he also had a reputation in the community of befriending and helping his neighbors on a more individual basis. This was evident in his friendship with George Washington Johnson, the teacher of the academy in Clarkesville. Not only was he a primary supporter of this school, he went further by leading a drive to have Johnson teach a select school in the hamlet. This was a vote of confidence in Johnson's abilities that was Ely's way of furthering the career of this young and ambitious teacher.

Throughout his life, Ely had a deep love of learning and was very concerned with education, especially the education of members of his family. This helps explain his drive to have Johnson teach a select school in the hamlet where Ely's children could further their education. As a well-educated man himself and a graduate of Yale, Ely had a facile ability to quote the classics of literature. In letters to family members he was known to not only quote Milton and Shakespeare with ease, but also the Bible extensively. This love of education and this care for his family led Ely, in the 1830's, to take in his nephew William, who came to live with him and his wife, Hannah, and their four sons, Adriel Gilbert, Theodore Dwight, Sumner Stow, and Benjamin Cornwall. As he tended to the education of his own children, so he tended to the education of his nephew. When writing to William's mother, Lydia in 1838 he noted, "I understand you propose to give him (William) a liberal education I have no doubt he will make such use of the advantage you give him as will do honor to the name he has and show that the fond hopes of a mother have not been misplaced." [16]

Ely took similar care in tending to the education of people outside his family when he saw promise in their abilities. When the ambitious young man Azel E. Metcalf came to Clarkesville, he too was befriended by Ely. As with the case of George Washington Johnson, Ely showed a penchant for intelligent and enterprising people. Metcalf arrived in Westford, Otsego County in the early 1820s when his mother, Bethia, married James B. Roe. He moved to the hamlet of Clarkesville in 1824 at the age of 16. The reasons for this move to the hamlet are not clear. However, his obituary written in 1882 refers to his desire to become a doctor and his means of training. "Thrown on his own resources at an early age, by virtue of untiring and dauntless perseverance, he fitted himself for the profession, which through an active life he adorned and dignified."[17] This statement notwithstanding, it is possible that he came to Clarkesville seeking to study under Ely. The reference to being "thrown on his own resources" could mean that it was on his own that he sought out Ely as a mentor. In light of the far-reaching reputation Ely was developing, even in the early 1820s, it certainly would be logical for a perspective medical student living so close to Clarkesville to seek out Ely as his teacher.

Certainly the study of medicine was grueling. In addition to the obvious knowledge of anatomy and physiology was the study of mathematics. Doctors had to have a firm understanding of this subject in order to prescribe drugs and herbal treatments to patients, especially since in most instances it was the doctor who prepared these medications. A firm grasp of proportions and ratios was vital. It can be seen from Doctor E. W. Spafford's practice book how important proficiency in mathematics was deemed. Spafford was studying to become a doctor in Cherry Valley in about 1834 to 1836 and page after page of his practice book is devoted to various mathematical formulas to gain proficiency. Azel Metcalf spent eight years of study under the watchful eye of Dr. Sumner Ely, who most likely took him under his wing and tended to his medical training in Clarkesville. This long course of study bore fruit with Metcalf's passage of his medical examination conducted by the Medical Society of Herkimer County. That was on 27 February 1832. It is unexplainable why he took his examination under the Herkimer County society and not the Otsego County Medical Society. That same year though, again no doubt shepherded by Ely, Metcalf was admitted to the Otsego County Medical Society.[18] As a further compliment to his former student and as a boost to Metcalf's blossoming career and prestige, Ely, as chairman of the Board of Superintendents of the Poor, helped to procure Metcalf's appointment as the physician for the Otsego County Poor House on 1 December 1832.[19]

Part of the ease with which Dr. Sumner Ely moved into the sphere of county affairs was no doubt due to the connections his father-in-law, Benjamin Gilbert, had forged during his long career. Gilbert's other son-in-law, Benjamin North Jr. very probably by his choice, never cut such a figure on the county scene. North would have received the same help from Gilbert that Ely had received had he possessed a desire to enter county affairs. Indeed, North, unlike Ely, would have been helped by his own family's reputation, as well as Gilbert's reputation. The esteem to which Benjamin North Sr. had been held and the trust reposed in his judgment was such that he had been called on to help arbitrate land claims by some pioneers. Further, the junior North's cousin, also named Benjamin North Jr. had been appointed, along with Joshua Pinney, as a justice by the New York State Council of Appointment.[20]

County-wide influence and politics, for whatever reason, did not capture the attention of Benjamin North Jr. Instead, he chose to focus his attention on affairs of business and it was in this realm that North experienced his meteoric rise. A great deal has already been said about his business and social rise, but it was in the 1830s that he truly came into his own and assumed a position of leadership in Clarkesville. He had purchased Pinney's tavern in 1833. Another very significant step in this direction occurred in 1835 when he, in partnership with John Hayden, the tannery owner, purchased the last of Joshua Pinney's business holdings, the store in the hamlet, for $550.[21] Pinney had long since given up his first hand operation of the business. For many years his son had been conducting this enterprise under the name of E. R. Pinney and Co. It is clear Pinney had over this time granted numerous people credit at his store. After the sale of the property, he took out an advertisement in the *Otsego Herald* informing those in debt to him that, "all demands now due must be PAID to C. D. Parshall (who is authorized to receive the same) by the first day of October next . . ."[22] Pinney, for his part was ready to move on.

The purchase of this store by North in combination with his ownership of the tavern created a solid foundation on which to build his fortune and all but assured his success. Both businesses, as has been discussed, were seen as key to any community. His ownership of this store, however, has given birth to one of the conundrums that has held the attention of the inquisitive. In the gable of this building is a stone engraved "BDN 1829." Obviously, the "BDN" refers to Benjamin D. North, but it is curious that there is no reference to his partner John Hayden. Further, the date of 1829 has no apparent significance for either North or the building itself. North did not own the building until 1835 and the building has the appearance of being of earlier vintage than 1829. This is truly one of the mysteries that continues to perplex the people of the hamlet.

His ownership of these key businesses probably would not have, in and of themselves, assured North's marked financial success although they may have been sufficient to provide a prosperous livelihood. In a time of change, he devised unique ways in which to attract people to Clarkesville in order to promote his enterprises. One such example was his deft ability to capitalize on local events and encourage itinerants to stop at his tavern. It has already been discussed how he had the itinerant painter William Price stay at the tavern. No doubt as Price was painting his murals in the tavern, many people came to the tavern to view the artist at work, and partake of North's food and drink. During this period as well the traveling circus started making its appearance across the New York landscape. North saw the value of prompting such shows to stop in Clarkesville. This would encourage both local and non-local traffic to his tavern and store. To attract audiences to these circuses, he hung large, flamboyant posters about the tavern.[23] The innovative aspect of these activities was in the fact that North was trying to promote an event in order to sell participants goods and services he had to offer. This is different from prior business advancing techniques which relied on selling to a local market based on that market's needs. Indeed, North was trying to create business activity through the artificial means of bringing people to the vicinity of his businesses for unrelated reasons, in these cases it was to view an itinerant painter and to take part in viewing a circus.

John Hayden, North's partner in the retail business, found his path to prosperity in his tannery operation. His tannery was located near Gilbert and Ely's saw mill along the Cherry Valley Creek. It was both logical and convenient to situate the tannery in such close proximity to the saw mill in light of the symbiotic relationship that existed between saw mills and tanneries. Logs felled as land was cleared were brought to the mill to be cut into lumber for the construction of houses, barns, out buildings, etc. In turn, the bark waste from the milling procedure was sold to tanneries. This bark waste, particularly from oak and hemlock, was an integral ingredient in the tanning procedure. The leather was made by soaking the animal hides in a solution of tannin which was extracted from bark. The process required large amounts of water. This was another reason to situate the tannery by the Cherry Valley Creek. Tanning was one of the core industries on the frontier. It was this industry which worked animal hides into the soft pliable leather used for making boots, belts, harnesses and saddles as well as things like book bindings, hats and stockings.[24] As vital as these accoutrements were to men on the frontier, it is not surprising that a good tannery operation could make significant money for its owner.

It is not known when Hayden first came to Middlefield. He had been among those men who had petitioned the Grand Lodge of Free and Accepted Masons of the State of New York for a warrant to form a lodge in Clarkesville in 1823 along with his father-in-law, Joshua Pinney. Further, he had been present at the auctioning of pews for the Baptist church and had paid $28.50 for half a pew for himself and his family.[25] By comparison with the other purchase prices for pews, this does not indicate that he was a man of great means at this point. However, by 1835, at the age of 40, he had attained a level of success through his tannery business such that he was able to lend his capital to a partnership with North to purchase a retail operation from Pinney. This was clearly the record of a man who was making his own fortune in the world one step at a time. He would later take his place as one of the political leaders in the community by serving as town clerk from 1840 to 1844.

The career of John Hayden exemplified what was becoming a normal progression in central New York: the financially successful business class was replacing the landed semi-aristocratic class as the political leaders on the frontier. Other men who followed similar paths were Daniel Gilbert, who served as town clerk from 1817 to 1820 under his brother-in-law, Sumner Ely, and was elected

town supervisor for 1831, and Erastus Sterling, who was elected town supervisor for 1834, at the age of 30. Sterling, as has been discussed, had tied his financial fortunes to the purchase, with his partner Sumner Ely, of the distillery
from Pinney in 1831. It was quickly becoming typical that these successful business owners would eventually take their turn heading the political structures in
the town and county. Indeed, some of these men even attained productive roles
in the state arena. The more established landed families saw their own power
and prestige pass to the business class.[26]   The glaring exception to this phenomenon was Benjamin D. North Jr., who, for all his leadership in business and
social circles, never assumed political office in the town or county.

To give the impression that these men were free from the petty cares and
concerns attendant to a society with people of varying degrees of moral fiber
and economic success is to give an overly benign view of early Otsego. Under-
neath this layer of economic prosperity, philanthropy, and civic-mindedness
were individuals who, for whatever reason, succumbed to a life of crime. Benjamin North Jr. fell prey to such felonious activity when he found that one of
his horses had been taken from its pasture. Although in the advertisement he
took out in *The Freeman's Journal* he ascribed the loss of his horse to either stray-
ing or theft, it is telling that he felt it necessary to suggest the idea of theft. This
would indicate that there was a level of crime in the area of which people had to
be wary. He went on to state that, "Whoever will give information of, or return,
said Mare (sic), will be liberally rewarded by the subscriber, at Clarkesville, Otsego County."[27]

This glimpse into the careers and personalities of these new leaders is helpful in illuminating what sort of people were coming to take control of the reins
of economic and political power in Clarkesville from that earlier crop of men
who had settled and organized the new hamlet and town. Clearly the business
class began identifying itself with and assuming control of the local government.
These men rose to the challenge of meeting the new demands placed on them
in a rapidly changing arena. Chief among these changes, and one upon which
these men had relatively little influence, was a transportation revolution which
would have far-reaching effects on the hamlet. The small streets that created the
crossroads around which Clarkesville had developed were typical rural roads.
However, the need for better and more reliable transportation means led to the
construction of superior roads in the form of turnpikes. Further, the need to re-
duce transportation costs for goods and increase the speed with which these
could get to market led to improvements that became marvels of the age.
Canals, led in importance by the Erie Canal, and later, railroads, altered traffic
flows and aided the development of communities along these canal and railroad
routes. These new routes had profound effects on Clarkesville, situated as it was
on neither a canal nor a railroad line.

During much of the early nineteenth century Middlefield township was
criss-crossed by typical rural roads, which were for the most part little more

than narrow paths through forests. The roads running through the hamlet of Clarkesville were no doubt wider and better maintained than those in the hinterland. However, even these roads could degenerate into muddy quagmires during wet periods in early spring and become dusty nightmares in the dry summer. To some degree these roads were best utilized when they were frozen in the dead of winter. That is, if snow was not so heavy as to make them impassable. This was the case throughout central New York for fairly obvious reasons. Rural communities simply did not have the labor pool or capital to expend on road construction. As the frontier was settled, the building of houses and barns was a much higher priority, and when the community did pull together for the building of public works it was usually for the erecting of a school or church. This notwithstanding, road building was viewed as a community task as well. Unfortunately, it was often viewed grudgingly by men who were working off their highway tax assessment under the supervision of highway overseers who had no real road engineering experience.[28]

As a result of these factors, roads were built sparingly even though they were vital for communication and trade. Main arteries of traffic would develop between hamlets and villages with only rugged connections to outlying farms. Often individual farmers would have to build connecting roads across their farmland to meet with the nearest main road. Difficulties arose when these farmers, out of necessity, had to ask other landowners for permission to build these minor roads across their land. The requesting of rights of way became a troublesome issue and there was no guarantee that such a request would be met with a favorable response. Such was the case when Joshua Phelon, Esq., asked Rufus Hibbard in 1847 for permission for a right of way to build a plank road through his land to connect with a main road via a route which would have been shorter than traversing entirely within Phelon's land. In this case, permission was withheld because the right of way was deemed to have little benefit to Hibbard. However, Hibbard proposed a solution to this impasse by stating that, "I should not be willing to have the road laid as you propose short of three hundred dollars at the loss."[29] This was an unfortunate response from the point of view of Phelon, who was required to find a different, less direct route to the main road or to pay a large sum of money for the privilege of a right of way.

Incidents such as this created major concerns for these men. A difficult route to the nearest village or hamlet acted as an impediment to trade, ultimately raising the price of goods as they reached markets. One of the earliest methods of improving the road network was through the creation of turnpikes. These turnpikes made their appearance in the late eighteenth century. They were chartered by the New York State legislature, which authorized the formation of turnpike authorities as well as planned the routes the turnpikes would take. Their construction was financed by the selling of shares to the public on the assurance that dividends would be paid back to these shareholders. The maintenance of these thoroughfares and the payment of dividends were derived from the tolls which were collected along these roads, with toll houses spaced approximately ten miles apart. The amount charged at tolls was regulated by the state in order to prevent gouging by local authorities and toll collectors. Toll rates were nearly identical throughout central New York. Table 4 shows a good example from the nearby town of Sharon.

TABLE 4: TURNPIKE TOLL RATES, TOWN OF SHARON

Each score of sheep or hogs	$0.05
Each score of cattle	$0.12
Horse and rider or led horse	$0.04
Sulky, chair or chaise with 1 horse	$0.12
Chariot, coach or phaeton	$0.25
Stage, wagon, or other wheeled vehicle drawn by two horses or oxen	$0.12
Additional horse or oxen	$0.02
Cart, sleigh or sled drawn by 2 horses or oxen	$0.06
Additional horse or ox	$0.02

By special enactment in 1808, the legislature exempted people from tolls going to and from church or to the grist mill for the purpose of grinding for the family.

Source: Sandra Manko, Katina Manko, and Jean Bakkom, eds., *Reflections on Sharon: 1797-1997 A Pictorial History* (Sharon Springs, 1997), 8.

William Cooper had successfully petitioned for a charter to have such a turnpike built to go through Cooperstown heading west, the so called Second Great Western Turnpike. This route would go west toward the town of Sherburne in neighboring Chenango County. He stood as the primary stockholder and president in the venture. It was very common to have a small number of very wealthy men owning the bulk of the turnpike shares with community members of lesser means owning the remainder. A smaller, feeder turnpike road, leading into the Great Western Turnpike, which ran through Cherry Valley, was established running from that village to the neighboring community of Roseboom. The turnpike section of this route terminated at Roseboom, although the road continued along a southerly course along the western side of the Cherry Valley Creek. This route ran in close proximity to but bypassed the hamlet of Clarkesville, located as it was on the eastern side of the Cherry Valley Creek. Ultimately, this would have far-reaching consequences for the hamlet as a more traveled road was situated on the other side of the waterway from the heart of the hamlet.

Turnpikes, unfortunately, were more successful in theory than they were in practice. The theory was that subscription shares would finance their construction and the collection of tolls would pay for maintenance, leaving enough of a surplus to pay handsome dividends to the shareholders who had subscribed to the construction. The financial success of these projects rested on a return on investment for the shareholders greater than could be gotten from other investments. So enticing was this idea that by 1821, 278 turnpike companies had been incorporated and approximately 6,000 miles of turnpike had been authorized by the legislature. Nearly 4,000 of those miles had been constructed by this date. The reality, however, was a bit different. Road construction costs were usually higher than anticipated and maintenance ate up nearly all of the revenue generated by tolls. This was compounded by the fact that travelers often found ways to bypass the toll house and thus not pay the tolls. This left very little, if any, money to be disbursed in the form of dividends to shareholders. Any returns on investments which were realized were usually quite meager. In January of 1830 such a paltry dividend was declared by the board of directors of the Third Great Western Turnpike Road Company of thirty-five cents on each share. The result of these pitiful returns on investment was the failure of many turnpike authorities. Consequently, by 1836 over half of the 4,000 miles of turnpikes had been abandoned by their respective turnpike companies because they were found to not be profitable.[30]

The turnpike boom that crested in the 1820s and died away quite suddenly in the 1830s had some very significant effects on travel and commerce in northern Otsego County. The opening of better built and maintained roads allowed for the introduction of stage coaches and freighting wagons which could run with more frequency and regularity. By 1830 J. Gates & Co. was running the Cooperstown & Utica Stage. There were scheduled departures on Mondays, Wednesdays and Fridays from Cooperstown to Utica. Return trips were made on Tuesdays, Thursdays and Saturdays.[31] Stage coaches shortened travel times by having the ability to change tired horses at set intervals, and were thus able to travel at higher speeds. Travelers no longer had to supply and care for their own horses on trips. Freighting wagons did for shipping what stage coaches did for passenger travel. The added benefit of freighting wagons was that the products of farms and home industries could be shipped in smaller quantities. A wagon could be filled with the produce of several farms, rather than having one individual waiting to make a lone trip with only his produce.

These benefits cannot be overstated. Improvements in the transportation network brought a more regular, steady contact with more distant communities, thus lessening the feeling of isolation on the frontier. It also was the beginning of the freeing of these communities from the degree of semi-subsistence to which they had become accustomed. Pioneers on the New York frontier had never been required to be self-sufficient. However, the communities in which they lived found it necessary to set up manufactures which could produce the bulk of the items necessary to exist. The ability to travel and ship goods in and out of the frontier with greater ease was deemed a primary goal of these turnpike companies. These turnpikes and the attendant development of stage coaches and freighting wagons also reduced the cost of travel and shipping, making the final sale price of goods more competitive once they reached market. Conversely, goods shipped into Otsego County became more affordable to the residents. These improvements to the core of the transportation network were among the most important goals of turnpikes and represented a true success for this road improvement system.

An additional advantage of this commerce with more distant parts of the state was that it helped to alleviate the lack of specie on the frontier. Trade in these isolated areas had always been hampered by the lack of cash. This had given way to a purchasing system based to a large degree on barter. It was a common practice for farmers who brought the excess produce of their farms to merchants to receive credit from these merchant store owners. This credit could be used to purchase items at these stores rather than farmers expending the small amounts of specie they were able to obtain. With the advent of more long distance trade facilitated by these stage coaches and freighting wagons, barter became less of an option. Middlemen in these distant cities had to pay these farmers in cash. The unintended result of these turnpikes, therefore, was that it led to a significant maturing of the frontier economy. Trading over longer distances with merchants not well-known to the seller propelled the frontier economy from a barter-based to a more cash-based system.

The successes of the turnpikes system notwithstanding, the simple financial fact was that as long as turnpikes did not return significant dividends to shareholders the system would be severely hampered and would fail. However, the death knell for turnpikes came with the advent of the canal building frenzy that hit New York in the 1820s, led first and foremost by the building of the Erie Canal. This mammoth enterprise was built as an act of faith with no guarantee that it could ever collect in tolls sufficient dollars to repay New York State for the huge expenditure that would be required to complete the project. Such a canal had been conceived of even before the War of Independence and as early as 1808 such a scheme had been put forth in Albert Gallatin's plan for internal improvements submitted to the United States Congress. William Cooper was no doubt familiar with Gallatin's internal improvements plan. Cooper was convinced not only of the viability of such a great canal, but also of its economic necessity if New York was to realize its full trading potential.

The trade of this vast country must be divided between Montreal and New York, and the half of it be thus lost to the United States, unless an inland communication can be formed from Lake Erie to the Hudson. This project, worthy of a nation's enterprise, has been for some time meditated by individuals. Of its practicality there can be no doubt, whilst the world has as yet produced no work so noble; nor has the universe such another situation to improve. Its obvious utility will hereafter challenge more attention; men of great minds will turn their thoughts and devote their energies to its accomplishment, and I doubt not that it will one day be achieved.[32]

The New York State legislature started giving serious consideration to the plan prior to the War of 1812 even though it was not long after this point that it became obvious that the federal government would offer no monetary assistance to build this waterway. However, those opposed to the construction of this canal pointed out the clear engineering difficulties of building a 364 mile canal into a scantily populated frontier when the longest canal then existing in the United States was not even twenty-eight miles long.[33]

The New York State legislature passed a bill in 1817 providing for the construction of the artificial river. This was over the objections of many skeptics who referred to the project derisively as "Clinton's Big Ditch" in recognition of the key role played by Governor DeWitt Clinton in shepherding the bill through the legislature. Naysayers pointed not only to the engineering hurdles to be overcome, but also to the fact that the entire state had a population of little more than a million people and most of these lived in the lower Hudson River valley. Many doubted the wisdom of building this canal through largely unsettled wilderness. However, these people were proved wrong after the canal opened in 1825. It was with no small amount of pride that Governor Clinton presided as the waters of Lake Erie were mingled with those of the Hudson River.

> *. . . cannon announced the completion [of the canal]; and the boats glided through the lock into the Hudson. Gov. Clinton was standing in the bow of the first boat; he was well dressed, and never appeared better. He no doubt exulted in his feelings, in the success of the great measure, on which he had for many years staked his reputation, and for which he had contended against fearful odds, and a determined opposition.*[34]

In its first year the Erie Canal and the Champlain Canal, a smaller, feeder canal to the Erie, collected almost $500,000 in tolls. The following year over $750,000 in tolls were collected. Additionally, special duties would add another $350,000 to that number. Against this total revenue would be deducted, for repairs, salaries, and interest on the canal debt, a figure of about $525,000. This would leave $575,000 to be applied to paying the canal debt. Further, tonnage on the Erie increased every year up until 1880. The Erie Canal was hailed a marvel of the modern world and proved to a skeptical world that the United States was indeed a special, new place. To those who had opposed its construction, it proved the wisdom and foresight of those who had advocated the project.[35]

The Erie Canal proved to be an unparalleled success in improving transportation along the Mohawk River corridor from Albany to Buffalo and thence down the Hudson River to New York City. Even before it was completed politicians, farmers and merchants started talking about ways to expand it. Additionally, plans were devised to build a network of feeder canals stretching north and south along the Erie. One such canal was built stretching down from the Erie through Chenango County to Binghamton. Not all canal plans were brought to fruition, though. A group of citizens petitioned the state to run an expanded Erie Canal through Schoharie and Greene counties, neighbors of Otsego County to the east, as Chenango was a neighbor to the west.[36] The Schoharie request came to naught as did a grand scheme to link the Erie Canal with Otsego Lake (the source of the Susquehanna River) and thence to Binghamton and the coal mines of Pennsylvania. This proposed waterway was dubbed the Susquehanna Canal.

The residents of Otsego County, particularly those along the Susquehanna River and the Cherry Valley Creek, recognized the value of building the Susquehanna Canal. Like so many other communities in New York, they too got caught up in the canal building frenzy with plans of their own. The effect of the Erie Canal had been to bring great prosperity to towns up to twelve miles away from the canal. After that point the benefits of decreased transportation costs and the speed of travel were hardly felt. Indeed, the prosperity that came with the Erie did not reach into areas very far from the canal which was what led to the drive to expand the network. In some respects the Erie Canal even had a negative effect on these outlying communities. Clarkesville, which had developed economic roots largely as a result of the high wheat yields coming from the Cherry Valley Creek valley and the accompanying strong prices being paid for wheat, suffered greatly as wheat prices collapsed with the opening of the canal. The Erie Canal reduced the price of shipping a ton of wheat from Buffalo to New York City from $100 to $10. Further, as the western New York and Ohio lands opened up to cultivation the sheer quantity of wheat coming from these regions eclipsed that coming from Otsego. By 1835, 86,000 barrels of flour and 95,000 bushels of wheat were being shipped from Buffalo down the canal. Within five years these numbers had increased to 633,000 barrels of flour and over 881,000 bushels of wheat.[37] The backbone of Clarkesville's agricultural economy was shattered. The residents of Otsego had to either join the canal network or re-orient their agricultural foundation.

The effects of the Erie Canal were not fully felt until years after the canal was opened. However, it must be borne in mind that with the canal opening in stages, the residents of Otsego had been able to see the proverbial writing on the wall. With the opening of the canal the residents of Cooperstown, like so many communities in New York State, celebrated this august event. They had a particular tie with the canal in that the man who had been most responsible for commencing the project, Governor DeWitt Clinton, was the son of General James Clinton who had dammed the outlet of Otsego Lake in order to create the flood which brought his bateaux down the Susquehanna River to Binghamton at the outset of the Sullivan-Clinton Campaign. This was the pivotal event that had secured the safety of Otsego from further large scale Indian attacks like that which had occurred at Cherry Valley during the Revolution. It was at this celebration in 1825 that the idea of the Susquehanna Canal was toasted lavishly. Henry Phinney, son of Elihu Phinney the founder of the *Otsego Herald*, toasted, "The contemplated Susquehanna River Canal" and Elisha Foote commended, "A speedy union of the pure waters of Otsego Lake with the Erie Canal."[38]

This Susquehanna Canal never came to fruition largely due to the fact that, as Levi Beardsley, then a member of the New York State Senate, stated in his memoirs, "The Otsego canal project was in a measure lost sight of, as that county had no backers from abroad . . ."[39] As a result, Otsego County suffered economically from its inability to get its farm produce to the Albany markets and thence to New York City cheaper than those regions along the canal network could ship their goods. This change in a once promising picture led to a siphoning off of population to areas in closer proximity to canals. The town of Middlefield saw its population decline by close to 300 persons in the period 1830 to 1840. This was the case in most of Otsego County with three quarters of its towns losing population in this period. The villages of Cooperstown and Oneonta were two communities which did not follow this downward trend. This overall reversal of previous trends of increasing population caused property values to drop precipitously as well. In 1819 real property and improvements in the county were valued at $5,771,082, but by 1824 this figure had declined by 17% to $4,799,753. This decline in value continued for the next decade so that in 1835 the figure stood at $4,788,285.[40] Nothing shows more graphically the effects of this population drain through both emigration from and lack of immigration to Otsego County than the fact that property in the county was falling in value so rapidly. There was more real estate for sale in the county than there were buyers.

Of the many people who left Middlefield to find greater fortunes along canal routes, one who must have been sorely missed was Joshua Pinney. The career of Pinney has already been discussed at length. It has been seen how, starting in the 1830s, he divested himself of all of his business holdings in Clarkesville. It was after reading *The Genius of Temperance* that he became convinced of the evils of alcohol. This led him to take up a staunch advocacy of the temperance cause. This, no doubt, was a very powerful factor weighing on him as he decided to sell his tavern and distillery. He then sold his store to the North and Hayden partnership. With the sale of all of his business holdings completed, he resigned his position as postmaster in Clarkesville, a position assumed by his friend, Dr. Ely. Pinney left Clarkesville with his family in June 1835 to relocate in Owego, New York This town was experiencing a great acceleration in business expansion with the construction of the Chenango Canal which passed through Binghamton to Owego before turning south into Pennsylvania. It was here that Pinney opened a drug store with his son Hammon. This business was later expanded and became known as the Owego Arcade, which was a drug and book store.[41]

Prospects of greater opportunity enticed others from Clarkesville to Owego as well. William A. Ely, the son of Dr. Sumner Ely, relocated to Owego where he purchased about two acres on Main Street. This parcel was later sold to Joshua Pinney in 1838 for $600.[42] These men were joined in this canal town by the young Dr. Azel Metcalf, who moved to Owego in 1837. Here he formed a medical partnership with Dr. Ezekiel Lovejoy. Lovejoy, at 33 years old, was five years older than Metcalf and had a medical degree from a college as opposed to being certified by a county medical society. When Metcalf left Clarkesville, though, he chose not to sell his property. He had purchased a house from Erek Bradford and Jane Howard on 16 August 1834 for $250. This house was located along the road heading east out of the hamlet toward the town of Westford next to Joseph Reynolds' house. It had been built by Henry Guy in the late 1820's and is probably the earliest house in the hamlet of Clarkesville to display the full flowering of the Greek Revival style in architecture. An asymmetrical façade consisted of a two story, three bay upright section with an off-center front door and a one story wing. Guy purchased the property from George Clarke in 1828 for $30 and resided there until 1830 when he sold the house to Jane Howard for $150.[43]

Jane Howard stands out in Middlefield history as a strikingly independent female figure. No doubt she learned much from her mother Hannah Howard, who purchased the property next to this house in 1822 to run as a hotel. Jane was raising a child on her own in 1826 and was actively having the child educated at the academic school under George Washington Johnson. During the second term for that year, her child attended school for 57.5 days at a cost of $0.86. She was also a subscriber to Johnson's select school in 1828. In 1833, Jane married Erek Bradford of Cooperstown. Prior to the marriage, Jane obtained a prenuptial agreement leaving her in control of "the real and personal property of every kind and description of which she is now owner." These were very bold actions for a woman to take at this time. It was only after Howard's death in 1834 that Bradford gained control of her house in Clarkesville and sold it to Metcalf.[44]

Metcalf did not sell this property when he moved to Owego. He may have kept this parcel because his mother and siblings still lived in the area and he may have anticipated a desire to return. An alternative idea is that with the steep drop in property values already discussed and the attendant lack of buyers in the area, he may just not have found a buyer for his property. Why these men chose to move to Owego of all the canal towns available is not known. It is likely that when Pinney moved he maintained correspondence with his friends in Clarkesville, particularly Dr. Ely. He may have convinced others from his former home of the fine prospects he had found which induced them to follow. Of these men, only Metcalf chose to return.

When it became obvious to the leaders of Middlefield, as it did to so many other leaders across central New York, that they would not reap enormous benefits from the canal network being developed in the state, they sought another solution to their dilemma. The basic problem in central New York was the lack of a well-constructed and maintained road network that would aid commerce. The concern was not only that the canals were not aiding the prosperity of their town, it was that they were actually having a detrimental effect on that prosperity. The answer to this problem came from an unlikely quarter. Around 1834 the idea of the plank road was introduced to Canada from Russia. This method of road construction ran planks about three or four inches thick by eight feet wide on stringers placed over a graded surface. The clear benefit was that this type of road provided for a smooth surface which was not susceptible to the hazards of mud and the annoyance of dust. Additionally, these roads were relatively inexpensive to build, costing approximately $1,000 to $1,500 per mile, which was considerably less than the cost of building canals or railroads when these started making their appearance.[45]

Plank roads made their appearance in central New York around 1844 where they quickly became very popular. When first introduced they seemed to answer the contemporary problems with the inland transportation network. So successful were they that between 1847 and 1854 more than 340 New York plank road companies had been chartered. By the latter date approximately 3,000 miles of plank road had been constructed in the state. In the spirit of turnpikes, private individuals would form these companies, have the roads built, and charge tolls to cover maintenance and pay dividends. Even though these roads would wear quickly under heavy traffic, it was reasoned that heavy traffic would produce more toll revenue and therefore not only cover maintenance costs but could pay handsome dividends to stock holders.[46]

These plank roads were typically short, going from villages or hamlets to smaller, outlying clusters of farms and residences.[47] The turnpike feeder which had run from Cherry Valley to Roseboom became the primary plank road thoroughfare in Middlefield. How far this plank surface extended beyond Roseboom heading south toward Clarkesville is unknown. What is clear is that a good, smooth road heading out of Cherry Valley on the west side of the Cherry Valley Creek would have the effect of routing traffic along that side of the water. Traffic going to and from Clarkesville had to cross the Cherry Valley Creek in order to hook up with this more traveled and better maintained road. It was not immediately recognized by the residents of Clarkesville that causing travelers to turn from the main plank road to enter the hamlet would hamper commerce in Clarkesville by virtue of this hamlet getting by-passed by the main road. This did have the effect of perpetuating the isolation of the hamlet even as other areas in Otsego County were becoming less isolated and more connected by a growing network of roads.

Plank roads were not without their problems, though. In wet weather the planks were typically very slippery. A slippery surface was an obvious hazard to horses which could lose their footing, fall, and break their legs. However, the bigger problem was the maintenance of these roads. Heavy traffic took its toll. Planking had been estimated to last between seven and ten years, but in actuality the planks had to be replaced with much greater frequency. As traffic and rot created holes in the surface, these roads posed another danger to horses. It was not uncommon to have to replace these planks after only five years.[48] Traffic on the road coming from Cherry Valley was certainly not sufficient to justify such constant and expensive maintenance. In many instances as sections of plank wore and rotted away they were simply not replaced.

These problems with developing a reliable and easy transportation network continued to have adverse effects on population in the area. It is a curious fact that Azel Metcalf, after migrating to the canal town of Owego, decided to return to Clarkesville. The draw of the canal towns, with their stupendous growth, has been written about extensively. No doubt the apparently greater opportunities there were a real inducement to migrate. Metcalf's return, though, illustrates a point often overlooked. Contemporaries, particularly the more gifted and ambitious, still found opportunity in Otsego County. However, the demographics of the county were beginning to change. The area around Otsego Lake, including Middlefield and Cherry Valley, which had seen their first settlers arrive in the middle of the eighteenth century, was relatively more densely populated than the southern area of the county near the growing town of Oneonta. Land was cheaper in this southern valley which was watered by the Susquehanna River and the Schenevus Creek, thus making it a very attractive area. Indeed, quite a bit of Otsego County migration was from the northern portion of the county to this southern portion. It was this demographic change which had a marked influence on the final major nineteenth century innovation in the transportation network in the county.

The last and greatest transportation innovation of the nineteenth century, and certainly the one that had the farthest reaching and longest lasting effects, was the introduction of the railroad. One of the first references to a railroad in America was made in 1811 in a proposal made to Robert Livingston of New York. The proposed railroad was made as an alternative to building a canal. Livingston dismissed the idea in his reply by stating, "I had before read of your very ingenious propositions as to railway communication. I fear, however, on mature reflection, that they will be liable to serious objection, and ultimately more expensive than a canal." These two modes of transport were in constant competition until the mid-nineteenth century with the triumph of railroads over canals. An early railroad enthusiast, John Stevens, had gone so far as to urge the construction of a railroad parallel to the Mohawk River instead of the construction of the Erie Canal. Even though he was on the losing side of that debate, the year after the Erie Canal opened in 1825 the first railroad charter was granted by the New York State legislature. As a member of the Assembly, Levi Beardsley made the curious statement that, "I know the bill [authorizing the charter] was advocated, and voted for, more to enable an experiment to be made, than from any belief that the [rail] road would be constructed." This novel idea had supporters but not believers. Railroads as an idea also had detractors; these were found primarily among the older citizens. Deborah Norris Logan, the widow of the prominent Pennsylvania politician and Jeffersonian Republican George Logan, in the late 1820s wrote about the "odious railroads."[49] This new technology with it myriad possibilities was not universally praised nor even thought to be within the realm of practicality.

These misgivings by rather progressive men of the age notwithstanding, railroads had clear advantages over canals. First and foremost a locomotive could run all year rather than only in warm weather. Canals on the other hand were inaccessible in winter when the water froze. Additionally, canals were dependent on water level to run efficiently and either floods or droughts could severely hamper canal traffic. Railroads quickly proved that they would be both more regular and dependable than canals. This was the primary reason that people came to favor railroads over canals. It is not surprising, therefore, that between 1827 and 1878 New York State had given over $1 million in subsidies through loans of credit to build railroads. This was in addition to the $37 million that municipalities had expended. By the year 1850 railroad mileage had surpassed canal mileage in New York by 606 miles, with 1,409 miles devoted to railroads and 803 miles devoted to canals. This disparity was in stark contrast to the situation in 1840 when canal mileage surpassed railroad mileage 640 miles to 453 miles. Railroad mileage continued to grow such that by 1860 the disparity was even more pronounced when railroad mileage totaled 2,682 and canal mileage had remained stagnant at its 1850 total of 803.[50]

When it became obvious to the residents of Otsego that there would be no canal linking them to the burgeoning canal network, they began to pin their hopes on a railroad network. One of the most forward thinking men in this regard was Jacob Dietz, a merchant from Oneonta. In 1827 he wrote a series of editorials extolling the virtues of railroads which were published in *The Freeman's Journal*. This was the Cooperstown newspaper that had been established when the Phinney brothers, who had taken over the Phinney publishing firm from their father, had moved from the area and ceased operating the *Otsego Herald*. In April 1828 a charter was granted to the Catskill and Ithaca Railroad Company. This was a milestone for Otsego because the proposed route of this line would bring it through Oneonta. However, natural barriers along the route coupled with engineering limitations of the time played a large role in preventing this line from materializing.

The failure of the Catskill and Ithaca line did not discourage the residents of Otsego. Undaunted, they thought of ways to combine the idea of canals and railroads. On 12 November 1828 Sherman Page, Jacob Dietz, Erastus Craft, William Campbell, Samuel Starkweather, Robert Campbell, T. R. Austin and Schuyler Crippen filed notice to construct a railroad from the Erie Canal to Otsego Lake. In this enterprise, Jacob Dietz, the wealthy merchant and railroad en-

thusiast from Oneonta, was being joined by Samuel Starkweather, the philanthropist who served on the Board of Superintendents of the Otsego County
Poor House, and Schuyler Crippen who would become a member of the New
York State Assembly in 1831. Their proposed railroad line, combined with improvements to the Susquehanna River to make it navigable, it was thought,
would create a link with Pennsylvania. This would greatly facilitate trade along a
route through the Otsego region. This scheme also came to naught as did various other plans to link Otsego Lake to the outside area.[51]

One of the most promising railroad schemes for northern Otsego County,
including Cooperstown and Middlefield, was a line stretching along the Susquehanna River from Otsego Lake to Colliersville. This was the community growing at the point where the Schenevus Creek met the Susquehanna River and was
a short distance east of Oneonta. On 14 December 1831 a meeting was held at
the home of Levi Hunt in Cooperstown to discuss this idea. Among those
present were Robert Campbell and General George Morell, who played such a
crucial role in the establishment of the Otsego County Poor House. Nothing
came of the proposed route until 26 April 1832 when the Otsego Railroad running from Cooperstown to Colliersville received its charter. It is not surprising
that the directors of this new company were the two maverick land owners at
either terminus of this line, Peter Collier and George Clarke. The business and
personal interests of George Clarke have been discussed at length. As for his
partner, it is worthy of note that Peter Collier, among other activities, had been
a member of the New York State Assembly in 1831. No doubt this played a
role in the ease with which their charter was granted. Together these men raised
capital totaling $200,000.[52] The logic of this route was that it could link with a
railroad line running through the river valley from Albany to Binghamton. This
latter route did not progress past the planning stage until 1851, though, when
money began being actively raised for its construction.

Without exception these extraordinary changes and innovations to the
transportation network had only marginal impact on Clarkesville. Indeed, the
hamlet would eventually suffer adverse effects from the improvements to the
transportation route developing along the opposite side of the Cherry Valley
Creek. This was not perceived by even the most forward-looking men of the
period. However, the new leaders of Middlefield recognized to some degree that
they needed to somehow get their town folded into this transportation network
to secure their future prosperity. To this end, three railroad companies were
chartered with proposed routes going through Middlefield. These companies included the Canajoharie and Binghamton, which was chartered in 1835, the
Cherry Valley and Susquehanna, which was chartered on 10 May 1836 with capital of $500,000, and the Cooperstown and Cherry Valley, which was chartered
on 15 May 1837 with capital of $150,000. As with the railroad companies
already mentioned, these were only "paper railroads," a term coined much later
and used to designate railroads that never progressed very far past the charter-

ing stage.[53]

It was not until 1851 that one of the first railroads to become reality began being planned for the Otsego region. The organizational meeting of the Albany and Susquehanna Railroad was held in Oneonta on 2 April 1851. This railroad was envisioned as running from Albany to Binghamton and would follow the southern border of Otsego County through Oneonta. Among the project's supporters were such men as Erastus Corning, Edward C. Delavan, Robert H. Pruyn, and Ezra P. Prentice. Prentice was the president of the New York State Agricultural Society and his support was garnered by the logic that this project would assist in lowering the cost of transporting Otsego County's wealth of agricultural products to Albany and New York City markets. Local merchants backed the projected railroad because it would also lower the cost of bringing finished goods to Otsego, thereby increasing their profits.[54]

It was not long before people in the northern end of Otsego County realized that this railroad could potentially isolate them. *The Freeman's Journal* noted in early 1854 that, "Oneonta is growing rapidly in population and business, and bids fair to become one of the largest – if not the largest village – in the county. It is already the residence of several very enterprising businessmen, who are prepared to make the most of the Susquehanna Railroad for the benefit of their village." Two years later this same paper had soured on the railroad project to such a degree that it referred to the directors of the A & S in the most unflattering of terms, referring to their efforts to sell shares of the railroad as a fleecing of the people cloaked in civic garb.[55]

The long-term ramifications of situating these new transportation routes such that they circumvented Clarkesville were to marginalize and isolate the hamlet even as much of the rest of Otsego County was becoming more closely tied together. As these routes were being formed the leaders of Middlefield had no way of fully appreciating those long-term consequences. What they did understand was that without folding their town and this hamlet into the improved transportation network other areas would prosper at the expense of their community. These facts notwithstanding, the 1820s and 1830s was a time of dramatic economic expansion and social maturation for the hamlet. While these men, as business owners and community leaders, were grappling with the issue of improved transportation, the residents of Clarkesville were coming together in many ways to improve the quality of life in the hamlet as best they knew how. By the late 1820s Clarkesville was home to a public school, an academy, a select school, a flourishing Baptist society and impressive church edifice, a Masonic lodge, and various business enterprises. Not to be left out, in 1828 the Methodist society took concrete steps to raise their house of worship, firmly joining the social fabric of the hamlet.

By the year 1828, the Methodists could reckon a history of over a quarter century of activity in Middlefield, having come together first in the area around the hamlet of Middlefield Centre. It was in 1802 that the Reverend William Colbert, who had been appointed the presiding elder of the Albany district on 19 March of that year, traveled to Otsego County. He preached a sermon in the town of Pittsfield and the village of Cooperstown, before riding to Daniel Mc-Collum's house in Middlefield Centre. It was here that perhaps the first Methodist sermon was preached in Middlefield. The McCollum house was a known place of regular prayer meetings. Although the Methodists were a strong and devoted group, they only enjoyed the services of traveling preachers at this early period.[56]

The following year the Reverend Colbert again traveled to Middlefield Centre. It was recorded that, "Thursday, 22," says he [Colbert], "We spent at Middlefield (Centre), and at night Samuel Budd preached, and I spoke after him. In this place there appears to be a very happy society." So strong and well-organized was this society that on 12 November 1803 the quarterly meeting for the Otsego Circuit was held in Middlefield Centre at the home of Isaac Green. Colbert records that the meeting was followed the next day by "a blessed love-feast and sacrament." Finally, in 1804 the Reverend Bidlack was stationed on the Otsego Circuit and ultimately settled in Middlefield Centre near Red Creek. He was a towering man, standing over six feet tall and, although he was not characterized by deep thinking, he was considered an effective preacher.[57]

It was some time after these foundations were laid in Middlefield Centre that a knot of Methodists started coalescing in Clarkesville. The core of this group included John Cook, Josiah Deyo, John Griffin and Elias Ismond. All of these men lived in the hamlet or within close proximity to it. They represented some of the earliest families to settle in the Clarkesville area. Of particular note are Josiah Deyo and Elias Ismond. Josiah Deyo, who was born in 1763, was the son of Christian Deyo. Christian came to Middlefield after the Revolutionary War at a relatively advanced age, having been born in 1732. The Deyo family lived in the hamlet and Christian, when he died in 1807, was buried in the Baptist burying ground which was located on the crest of land to the north, overlooking the hamlet next to the Baptist meeting house. Elias Ismond purchased his 100-acre farm, which was located about a mile north of the hamlet, in 1800 for $500.00. He came to Middlefield from Chatham, Columbia County, and was married to Betsey Pitts. As a true pioneer he had to endure great hardship when he first arrived in Otsego, living with the North family on their farm, which was very near Ismond's newly purchased farm, while he cleared his land and erected a crude log house for his family. By 1827 he had prospered sufficiently as a farmer to be able to expend $2.19 so that his children Pamelia, Polly and Levi could attend the second term at the academy in Clarkesville.[58]

These men were joined by other families surrounding the hamlet such as the Diefendorfs, who settled on a farm on what became known as Diefendorf Hill, the Galers, who christened their homestead Galer Hill, the Browns, and the Gilletts. Additionally, in testament to the fact that Clarkesville was considered a local center of activity, families from outside the town of Middlefield came to worship with the Methodists of Clarkesville. Of special note was the significant number of people who came from the hamlet of Hallesville (Pleasant Brook) in the town of Cherry Valley. One of the most dedicated of these men from Hallesville was Daniel Eldred, who, when he died in 1863, was remembered as having been "One of the pioneers of Methodism in Ots. Co. Fifty years in the service of the Lord. Fifty years an official member. A model Christian."[59]

These two groups of Methodists building congregations in the hamlets of Middlefield Centre and Clarkesville eventually joined forces and centered their activities in the latter location. As their group grew and matured, formal organizational structures were formed including a board of trustees. It was these trustees who, in 1828, successfully convinced George Clarke to donate two acres of land on the southern extreme of the hamlet for the erection of their church. This parcel was on a gentle rise leading out of the hamlet, described in the deed Clarke granted as being next to Daniel W. Rice's house lot. Although Daniel Rice had died fourteen years before the deed was granted and his son John was living in the house, this house was a well-known landmark to the people of Middlefield. Daniel had been born in Warwick, Rhode Island, in 1756 and came to Middlefield with his family in search of greater opportunities, along with so many others after the Revolution. His house was a humble, one and a half story dwelling befitting the modicum of prosperity he had found in Clarkesville. When he died in 1814, his family was able to display his good worldly fortunes by inscribing his gravestone with a lengthy verse which, ironically, spoke of the futility of man's life on earth.

> *All few and full of sorrow are the days*
> *Of miserable man his life decays*
> *Like that fruit flower which with the suns up rise*
> *Her bud unfolds and with the evening dies*
> *He like an empty shade glides away*
> *And all his life is but a winters day*[60]

As with the Baptists, Clarke made this donation "for the better maintenance and support of the Christian religion and its ordinances," but he also inserted a clause in the deed stating that "if it shall happen that any number of persons hereafter being members of the Protestant Episcopal Church shall establish themselves by incorporation as a congregation" then the Trustees of the Methodist Episcopal Society shall yield "one half of the premises hereby granted and their appurtenances excepting the improvements now made or hereafter made" by the trustees. Clarke placed two conditions on this donation. The first was that all water privileges on the land were excepted from the donation and not transferred to the Methodist trustees and the second was that the Methodists had to build a church for their congregation within five years.[61]

Immediately upon obtaining this grant of land, the Methodists banded together to raise the frame of their church. This went up on 21 June 1828, thereby setting them well on their way to meeting Clarke's second condition.[62] Through their concerted efforts the Methodist Episcopal Society succeeded in raising their church by 1832, within the five-year time frame laid out in their deed as specified by Clarke. This was a very different edifice than that which had been constructed by the Baptists in 1826. Where the Baptist church was based on designs drawn by Asher Benjamin in 1797 and was a fine example of Federal architecture, the Methodist church revealed the flowering of the Greek Revival style in architecture as it was developing in the rural communities of central New York.

This building had a front-facing gable surmounted by a belfry. The entire façade was characterized by broad, heavy moldings. The primary entrance accessed a level under the main floor with interior stairs leading up to the congregation's meeting room. This entrance was flanked by handsome windows with six over six paned sashes. The panes measured eight inches by ten inches, like those in the Baptist church. However, the Baptist church employed larger twelve over twelve paned sashes. These relatively larger windows in the Baptist church testified to the prominence of and grandeur of this building. It was a stylistic point of Greek Revival architecture to employ six over six, eight by ten inch paned windows. The fenestration illuminating the main floor of the Methodist church illustrated a real difference between these two churches. The windows here were broad and tall painted stained glass windows, comprised of double hung sash consisting of sixteen panes of seven by nine inch glass. They were capped with Gothic arched top sashes with muntins converging from the lower divisions and gracefully intersecting. This was in contrast to the earlier style windows in the Baptist church which were all clear glass and much less ornate. This newer church was an impressive building and was raised at a cost of $2,000.[63]

With their church completed, the Methodists proudly laid their stamp on the social fabric of the hamlet and town in a way more in keeping with the maturing nature of community life in Clarkesville. The Baptists at this time were also expanding their presence in the community. At a congregational meeting held on 5 June 1833, it was moved that the Baptist congregation purchase the house occupied by David Shepherd for $300 for use as a parsonage. This house was located on the opposite side of the road from their church, a little closer to the four corners of the hamlet. This seems to have been a hotly debated issue since as late as 1835 final action had still not been taken and the issue was debated anew. At a meeting held on 7 September of that year the congregation debated "the propriety for paying for the dwelling house occupied by David Shepherd." On this issue "a vote was taken and unanimously carried that the amount due from the society to William A. Walker" be paid to consummate this transaction. To help with this purchase, Daniel North pledged to a note of $200. Accordingly, the parsonage was purchased and remained in the possession of the trustees of the Baptist Society until after the conclusion of the Civil War.[64]

It is ironic that as this was occurring, other groups were fading out of the light and out of existence. One group fading from existence was the Freemasons, an organization which had formed with such strength and promise, having as its leaders Joshua Pinney, Daniel Gilbert, Sumner Ely and John Hayden. As has been, shown they were all men who were well respected in Clarkesville and who held, or would come to hold, leading social, political and business positions. The advent of the Morgan Affair, which has already been discussed, forced many Masonic lodges to hide from public view. It is likely that Clarkesville's Widow's Son Lodge took this course. It seems unlikely that the stature of the men who formed and were leading this lodge would allow for it to disassemble even though all documentary evidence of the lodge's existence ceases in the early 1830s. There is also the curious fact that the lodge room was still reported as being set up in 1957 when an inventory was taken for the estate of Mabel Folmesbee, then owner of the former Pinney Tavern, where the Masonic lodge had held its meetings. This lends credence to the hypothesis that Widow's Son Lodge met clandestinely long after it disappeared from the public eye.

The select school was another institution that fell victim to the changing life of the hamlet. This school had been formed largely through Sumner Ely's efforts, but it had been unable to sustain itself when George Washington Johnson left the hamlet in 1828. Thereafter, higher education for the residents meant sending their children to the academy. However, even the academy had difficulties. By the early 1830s this institution ceased to be a viable enterprise. This left the public grade school as the only educational institution in the hamlet. Parents who wished for their children to further their studies had to provide for them to leave the hamlet.

The building which had housed the academy, located next to David Belknap's house on the road leading to Westford, became the property of Benjamin and Elizabeth North when they purchased the Pinney Tavern and its property and buildings. Shortly after this purchase, North found a willing buyer for the academy building in Erastus Sterling. Sterling had been living in the hamlet for some time, probably as a tenant of George Clarke. In 1831 he, along with Sumner Ely, had purchased the distillery from Pinney. If Sterling had held intentions of erecting a dwelling on this parcel to be close to his business enterprise, he quickly found that project to be problematic. The deed for the distillery restricted his ability to build a house on the parcel. This restriction was tied to George Clarke's original ownership of the lot and stated that Sterling could not "erect or build a dwelling house upon the (distillery) premises without the consent of George Clarke the original lessor."[65]

As Sterling's fortunes grew with the distillery and as his political influence increased with his election as town supervisor in 1834, he no doubt chafed under his tenancy status and sought to purchase a house. In central New York in the nineteenth century there was a definite social distinction between those who owned their home and those who were tenants. Clearly Sterling had reached a point where his income could support owning a house. However, there was also the social expectation that one in his leadership position should own rather than rent his home. With the discontinuation of the academy, he purchased this handsome building for $85 from the Norths to serve as his house on 15 July 1834.[66]

Institutions and social organizations were not the only entities dropping off the Clarkesville landscape. People, some of whom had played important roles in the community were also leaving. Silas Devol was one such personage. Shortly after the death of his first wife, Jane, on 13 October 1832, he made plans to leave the hamlet. On 7 June 1835 he purchased seventy-five acres of land for $225 from Richard M. Kemball in the nearby town of Decatur.[67] He lived out his days on this far side of Otsego County, but when he died in 1846 his family brought his body back to Clarkesville for interment in the Middlefield Baptist cemetery next to his first wife. He had lived a religious life and was remembered as a good man. His family saw fit to have his gravestone inscribed thus:

> *In Christ alone I humbly trust*
> *To rise in judgement with the just*

Eventually, Martha, his mother, Annis, his second wife, and A. Wilson, his son, would all be interred in the family plot.

Sumner Ely's family also abandoned the hamlet as they grew. Adriel Gilbert Ely, who had been born in 1817 and had attended the academy in Clarkesville, followed in his father's footsteps to become a physician. He relocated to Girard, Pennsylvania. Adriel was later joined in Pennsylvania by his younger brother Benjamin Cornwall Ely, who also became a doctor. Their youngest brother, William Horace Ely removed to the town of East Worcester, Otsego County, much later when he married Ellen Caryl in 1855. William's father-in-law, Leonard Caryl, was a merchant and hotel owner from that town. Indeed, so successful was Caryl that in 1841 he had constructed a massive, three-story brick residence on Main Street which William and Ellen eventually inherited.[68] All of these children of Sumner and Hannah Ely became important social and business leaders in their adopted communities.

Emigration was not the only reason for Clarkesville and Middlefield to lose some of its finest leaders. This period saw death snatch away several of the first generation of men who had held the reins of authority in the town. One of the first of these was also one of the pioneers to come to the area. Benjamin Gilbert, whose career had been varied and illustrious, died on 19 January 1828. Like so many of America's Revolutionary War veterans, Gilbert's family commemorated his service in that war above all the other accomplishments of his life. On his monument, after his regimental service record, was inscribed:

Lexington - Bunker Hill - Saratoga

These were the three most pivotal battles of the war in which Gilbert had participated and it constituted a record of which his family was justifiably proud. Even his obituary spoke extensively of his Revolutionary War service and gave only a brief reference to his other accomplishments.

> *DIED - In Middlefield, on the 19th inst. Benjamin Gilbert, Esq. aged 72 years and 8 months. He entered the service of his country at the first commencement of hostilities by Great Britain, took part in the battle of Bunker Hill and various other engagements, and continued in the Army till its disbandment; was an officer in the corps commanded by La Fayette. Since the organization of the State Government, he has represented this County in the Legislature, and was for 11 years Sheriff of the County.*[69]

Several years later another of the early pioneers passed out of this world. The Reverend Benjamin Sawin, who had first come to Middlefield to preach and had stayed to become the Baptist minister, died in March of 1833.[70] As other men had come to the hamlet seeking material success and opportunity, the Reverend Sawin had sought to tend to their religious needs. This he did admirably. He survived largely through the generosity of his congregation, never amassing great worldly possessions for himself. In death as in life his congregation held him in very high regard.

The passing of these two men was universally mourned by the residents of the hamlet. However, in 1835 the death of George Clarke at Hyde Hall was greeted differently.[71] Although many residents had had good and honest dealings with Clarke and believed him to have been an upright man, many of his tenants had mixed feelings. This was tied to the growing disenchantment with the tenancy arrangements which had been devised to settle the frontier. This method of settlement, as has been discussed, relied on large landowners enticing a multitude of settlers to the frontier through the lure of easy lease terms. These lease terms were usually for extremely long periods. Therefore, these leases and the income they created for their landlords led many landlords to not wish to terminate the tenancy arrangements. This had the effect of making it very difficult for tenants to ultimately purchase the land. As a result, Clarke, as one such landlord, had encountered some opposition to his leases as early as 1811, being brought to court where he finally prevailed in having his landed rights confirmed. This did not dispel the ill will which had existed, in fact to some degree it probably fueled the fire. All considered, Levi Beardsley provided a balanced view in his memoir of the situation.

> *To do justice to his [George Clarke's] memory, I wish to state as the result of my honest and unbiased judgment, that had tenants treated him with respect and kindness, and paid him the rents honestly due to him, they would have had no good right to complain; but they dis-*

liked the relation of landlord and tenant, and hence he was frequently annoyed with insolent demands, which his high English notions of strict right would not allow him to concede.[72]

No doubt the mixed feelings of admiration for and contempt of Clarke was inextricably tied to both his position as a landlord and his heritage as an Englishman. The latter fact rankled many of the patriotic feelings of Americans in the new republic. These alternate emotions were difficult to reconcile in many people's minds even though Clarke often tried to demonstrate his devotion to his adopted country. Indeed, in 1826, at a celebration of America's fiftieth anniversary of independence, Clarke toasted "Rational liberty, that ennobles the mind, enlightens the understanding, mollifies the heart, and fits us for this world and the next."[73] These were sentiments in keeping with America's founders and would have naturally appealed to the sensibilities of those at the gathering. Given all these facts, it is understandable that upon his death, all eyes were turned to Hyde Hall during this time to get a sense of how George Clarke's son and heir, George Hyde Clarke, would behave toward his tenants. They were destined to find this man cut from quite a different cloth than his father had been.

Upon his death, Clarke left an extensive estate to be settled. This estate included vast land holdings in thirteen New York counties as well as Great Britain and Jamaica. His New York lands were located in Dutchess, Rensselaer, Washington, Greene, Delaware, Albany, Montgomery, Oneida, Schoharie, Saratoga, St. Lawrence, Franklin, and Otsego counties. The task of settling the American portion of this estate fell to his adopted son Alfred Clarke with the assistance of his good and trusted friends Richard F. Cooper, grandson of William Cooper and son of Richard Cooper who had been Clarke's wife's first husband, and Eben B. Morehouse.[74]

Of these men, it was perhaps Morehouse who had the most interesting career. He had been born in 1791 in Columbia County, New York. His early training had been in the field of medicine and in February 1812 he received his diploma from the New York State Medical Society to practice medicine. For a brief period he practiced medicine in Caughnawage in Montgomery County, New York. Sometime prior to 1815 his dislike of this profession led him to abandon his career as a physician. In September of that year he accepted an invitation from Ambrose Jordan, a long time friend who also came from Columbia County, to serve as a clerk in his law practice, Stranahan & Jordan, in Cooperstown.[75] It was with no small amount of wonder that the community watched the rapid rise in political influence of Morehouse. Shortly after his arrival in the village, Morehouse was introduced to George Clarke. Not much is known about his early acquaintance with Clarke, but by the late 1820s they had become good friends, with Morehouse being a frequent guest at Hyde Hall. It is hard to know whether or not it was partly due to Clarke's benign disposition to Morehouse that aided the latter's rise. Certainly as a man of wealth, privilege and landed authority, Clarke would have been able to assist any man of talent who caught his attention and in whose abilities he had confidence.

Morehouse was admitted to the New York bar in January 1818. As a young attorney, Morehouse gained his first influential appointment in 1829, by which time he was already a man of considerable wealth. In that year he was named district attorney. The following year he was one of the commissioners, along with John A. Dix, John H. Prentiss, Robert Campbell and George A. Stark-weather, who opened the subscription book for the newly created Otsego County Bank. This bank commenced operation on 9 November 1830 with dis-counted bills of $210.50 and deposits of $102.00. In light of Morehouse's close friendship with Clarke, it is perhaps not surprising to see Clarke as one of the first two customers of this bank (John C. Morris was the other).[76]

A few years later, in 1834, Morehouse purchased fifty acres from Anthony and Hannah Lynes for $450 in the town of Middlefield. This parcel was located in the Bowers Patent within sight of the Bowers family home, Lakelands.[77] This plot was directly across the Susquehanna River from the village of Cooper-stown. It was nestled at the foot of Mount Vision, at whose summit William Cooper had first looked down on the site of what became Cooperstown. On this plot, Morehouse constructed a house of imposing grandeur coupled with a quiet poise. Built of stone, this house was a monument to the Greek Revival ar-chitectural style then coming into vogue even while it retained certain details of pure Federal flavor. Two balanced one story wings flanked a two-story center block. The façade of this central section featured a front facing gable with heavy eaves and facia supported by a grand portico complete with four Doric columns rising the full two stories. The symmetry of the whole was broken by the off-center entrance, which was set on the right side of this central block.

Even the siting of Morehouse's home inspired awe, set as it was on a knoll at the end of Cooperstown's main street, looking down over the village. The house, like the owner, commanded attention. To approach the home, one had to pass through a gatehouse that served as a testament to the builder's know-ledge of newer picturesque architectural forms. The gatehouse was constructed in the Egyptian Revival style that crept into the American consciousness in the first quarter of the nineteenth century. It was of trapezoidal shape with the sides and the opening sloping inward from a wide base; the whole giving the impres-sion of a truncated pyramid. There was a simple Gothic style window above the opening to the gatehouse and the structure was capped by a very tasteful Cavetto cornice. All of these features were emblematic of this avant-garde archi-tectural phase.

Morehouse's career was on the ascendant with his appointment as district attorney. Following this appointment, he was elected to the New York State As-sembly in 1831 and in 1835 he was elected to succeed Erastus Sterling as super-visor of Middlefield. Among his social involvements was his membership in the Masonic lodge of Cooperstown. He became a Freemason in 1816, the same year that other notable Cooperstown attorney, Ambrose L. Jordan, joined the lodge. Ultimately his career would lead to his gaining a seat as a New York State Supreme Court Justice in 1847. However, before that event transpired, he suffered a catastrophic reversal of fortune which forced him to sell his beloved house, Woodside Hall, to Samuel Beall in 1836. The house and five acres and thirty-seven perches was sold for an impressive $12,000. Unofficially, it was rumored that he had lost the house to Beall in a card game at Hyde Hall. During his time of non-residence at Woodside Hall, it was observed that he would not look at the house while about the streets of Cooperstown. In due time, he was able to retake possession of Woodside Hall. In 1839 he purchased back from Beall the house and the five acres and thirty-seven perches of land for $5,000. To his joy, he was able to live out his days there until his death in 1849. Before that event, he had the honor of entertaining President Martin Van Buren at a reception at his house in 1839.[78]

This was certainly an impressive man who was being called on to assist in settling the large Clarke estate. Clarke's will made provisions for his family members, both in America and in Great Britain, and left bequests to numerous friends and dependents including each of his servants who received one month's wages. To his wife, Ann Low Cary Cooper Clarke, he left an annuity of $3,000 as well as use of a suite of rooms at Hyde Hall, and the estate was to provide her with a carriage, horses, a man-servant, and a maid-servant. To his adopted son, Alfred, he left an annuity of $1,000. The two other executors were also given bequests. Richard F. Cooper was given use of a dwelling house and law office in Cooperstown. Additionally, he and Morehouse were each given $500. The will explained this gift thus:

> I [George Clarke] request that they [Cooper and Morehouse] will each accept of the same [the $500 bequest] as a token of my esteem and as an acknowledgement for their care & trouble in the execution of the trusts of my Will.[79]

Upon Clarke's death, his son and heir to his American lands was only thirteen years old. During the time of the minority of this younger George Clarke, the executors of the will were to manage the estates in his best interests. This was a daunting task in light of the fact that the younger Clarke, by virtue of this bequest, had become the owner of the largest landed estate in New York. In Otsego County alone he owned approximately 16,000 acres, most of which was rented out to tenant farmers.[80] It would remain to be seen how this young man would treat his tenants and what interest he would take in this vast agricultural expanse. Until he reached the age of 21 though, this management chore rested with the executors of his father's estate.

This was a time of transition for Middlefield. The first generation of leaders had begun to pass away, to be replaced by a new set of leaders who proved themselves in many ways to be quite capable of taking the reins of power. However, they had presided over the social, economic and political life of the hamlet during a time that witnessed the closing and discontinuation of many of the social enterprises which had been started with such promise. Among these were the academy and select school. Additionally, they also oversaw the building of the Methodist church and the firm rooting of that congregation in the hamlet. Of the issues with which these men had to grapple, the most pressing and the one over which they had the least control was the development of new transportation networks. It was these shifting lines of commerce that led many of Clarkesville's residents to leave the hamlet for perceived better opportunities in other locations. That notwithstanding, it was also a time when many of the brightest stars in the hamlet chose to stay and were able to prosper. This proved that there was still significant opportunity in northern Otsego County for the ambitious, and this led to the return of men such as Dr. Metcalf who were able to carve out good lives for themselves.

These shifting nuances in the life of the hamlet were reflected in its architecture. The early 1820s had been characterized by a slow transition in styles, with houses such as that built by Daniel Cummings being designed according to the Federal style, and with only nods to the developing Greek Revival style. By the late 1820s this trend was reversed. This is seen best in the house that Ebenezer Pratt constructed on the west side of the Long Patent Road across from Dr. Ely's fine Federal style home. The Pratt house, which was built around 1829, was designed around a Greek Revival plan. It was asymmetrical in appearance with a two story main section complete with front-facing gable and a single, one story wing appended to the left of this main section. However, as the Cummings house had looked forward, the Pratt house looked backward. The entrance to this latter house featured a delicate triangular entablature and the overall moldings of the exterior were light in appearance. These traits were all much more characteristic of the Federal rather than the Greek Revival style.

Ebenezer Pratt had purchased the parcel on which he built this house from George Clarke on 1 July 1829 for $18. It consisted of nearly fourteen perches of land. Not much is known of Pratt. He was a relative of Rice Pratt who, in 1823, had been one of the original petitioners of the Grand Lodge of Free and Accepted Masons of the State of New York to allow for the establishment of a Masonic lodge in Clarkesville. Rice died in the neighboring town of Milford in 1859. Ebenezer is first mentioned in 1826 when he purchased his family's pew in the Baptist church. He paid $27 for this pew which does not indicate that he was a man of affluence. The house he constructed around 1829, though, certainly was a house fit for a man of considerable means. He only lived in this house for a short period, selling the house to Clark D. Parshall on 11 March 1835 for $500 before leaving the area. Parshall's deed was recorded by Joseph W. Reynolds, who lived around the corner on the road leading to Westford, next to the house owned by Azel Metcalf. Reynolds was a man of some influence in the community as a recorder of deeds during a time of rapid turnover in real estate. He was an idiosyncratic man who was known as the Squire Reynolds rather than the more common form of Joseph Reynolds, Esquire.[81]

Moving in tandem with this slow change in architecture, there was another, more subtle, transition occurring in Clarkesville, a change that would affect the identity of the hamlet. As has been noted, when the post office was established the name of the hamlet had been changed officially from Clarkesville to Middlefield. This was to avoid confusion with a previously established post office at Clarksville in Albany County. Despite that fact, most people still referred to the hamlet as Clarkesville, but concurrent with the name change was a growing inconsistency in spelling. George Clarke had generally been consistent in his spelling in his papers, referring to the hamlet as "Clarkesville," following his name. This spelling was used as late as 1839 in *The Freeman's Journal*, when Benjamin North had taken out an advertisement offering a reward for the return of his horse. On occasion, though, as in the case of the Methodist church deed, George Clarke did alter his spelling without explanation, and referred to "Clarks Ville." However, with greater frequency, people were beginning to drop the "e" from the name and spell it as "Clarksville." The relentless nature of the postal service was also pushing a change. This was leading to growing numbers of people referring to Middlefield and either meaning the town as a whole or the hamlet, depending on the context. The postal service notwithstanding, identity and long usage would lead people to refer to the hamlet by its former name of "Clarksville" in official and non-official parlance long into the twentieth century. This was despite the official postal name of the hamlet.

These changes and transitions in the hamlet's leadership, transportation networks, social organizations, architectural appearance and even in its name had profound effects on the life of the hamlet. The fact that the fifteen years from 1820 to 1835 were a period of such deep-seated and rapid change is a testament to both the nature of the times and the dynamic leadership qualities of the people of Clarkesville. Looking back over that time, its residents would remember a fledgling settlement where, by 1835, stood a bustling community. Clarkesville, as it was in the late 1830s, was the result of the growing influence of people who lived there and found opportunity and prosperity, but also of the changing world around the hamlet. No longer was it a semi-sufficient community, it had become deeply tied to the surrounding area and this would continue to pull at how the hamlet developed and the direction in which its businesses and social institutions grew.

Chapter Five

A Steady Prosperity

The development of hamlets across New York State in the early nineteenth century is the story of the growth of organic population centers. That is, the boundaries of hamlets were formed, expanded and contracted as the population, businesses, and social organizations grew and flourished or faded. This is in contrast to the demarcation of towns. Town boundaries were devised primarily as political units and may have encompassed one or more hamlets. As such, town borders were more arbitrary than hamlet borders; the latter could be very fluid during this period. As the nineteenth century progressed these hamlets became a microcosm of the larger economic and social world. To a great degree they started becoming even more self-sufficient than they had previously been. The inhabitants of hamlets created schools, built churches, founded businesses and social organizations. By the mid-nineteenth century within a hamlet could be found such a myriad number of businesses and social groups that most people found it necessary to travel far from the hamlet on only special occasions.

This nucleus of activity that grew in the hamlet did not develop in a vacuum. The rapid growth of business and prosperity in Clarksville had much to do with the success of the agricultural enterprise of the surrounding farm families. Indeed, to a large degree, agricultural success was due to the expanse of low-lying flat land around Clarksville that was flooded in the spring by the Cherry Valley Creek. It was these farm families, by virtue of their large numbers, that allowed business to flourish in the hamlet. They spent their money in Clarksville's stores and taverns and they brought their timber and grain to the mills in the hamlet. However, this relationship between farmers in the outlying areas and the businessmen of the hamlet was symbiotic. Stores in the hamlet bought produce such as eggs, butter, and cheese from these farmers and specific businesses grew in the hamlet to assist the farmers. A carding machine, for example, was brought to the hamlet to tend to the large quantities of wool being produced in the area. The foundation of Clarksville's prosperity rested on the farmers and agricultural produce of the area more so than on any other single entity.

The first pioneers to the Middlefield area had planted wheat, both summer and winter varieties, among the tree stumps left from clearing the land of the Cherry Valley Creek valley. This alluvial area was fertile and wheat grew exceptionally well. Indeed, as early as 1791 wheat was identified as one of the most valuable commodities of Otsego County. As more land came under cultivation additional grain crops were added to the farmers' output. By 1817 the newly formed Otsego County Agricultural Society identified not only wheat but also Indian corn, peas, and barley as crops of significant cultivation in the county. By 1830 the production of grains and other crops common in the county had grown to include rye, corn, oats, beans, flax seed, potatoes, turnips, onions, beets, cabbage, flax, hay, carrots, and parsnips. This increased diversity was made possible as more land came under cultivation. By 1820 Middlefield had 12,898 acres of improved lands supporting 589 farmers. Over the next forty-five years this figure nearly doubled to 25,612 acres of improved lands out of a total land area of 37,456 acres for the town of Middlefield.[1]

Throughout the first half of the nineteenth century Middlefield and the area around Clarksville, like much of Otsego County, developed a crop output characterized by its diversity. This was a result of the maturing of agriculture in the region. More land under cultivation gave farmers more options for planting different crops. As this cultivated land increased, farmers were often advised which crops might grow well on their lands. This advice was normally given by better educated, gentleman farmers and members of the local aristocracy such as Jacob Morris, a founder of the Otsego County Agricultural Society, and George Clarke. These men were typically more in tune with new farming practices than the common farmer. Local newspapers would often print this advice as a means of disseminating it to as many people as possible as in 1819 when the *Otsego Herald* printed an article extolling the virtues of planting summer wheat instead of winter wheat. Summer wheat was not only thought to be preferable to rye, but it also was not prone to winter kill in central New York as was the case with winter wheat.[2]

Part of the reason for this increased diversity, though, was the result of necessity. Different crops were grown to help feed the farmer's family and growing numbers of livestock, but also to support domestic manufacturing. For example, hay was grown to support the growing herds of sheep and cattle that farmers were creating. Flax, on the other hand, was grown to support the domestic cloth industry that engaged the time of many farm women and added to the farm family's income. In fact, so valuable was this domestic industry that spinning and weaving of cloth could be responsible for nearly half of a family's income.[3]

The increased number of crops that were grown as the nineteenth century progressed was only one source of the agricultural diversity shaping farm life in Middlefield. Animal husbandry was the other. This branch of agriculture had taken more time to develop in Otsego for two reasons. As pioneers ventured into the wilderness it was not practical to invest in cattle and sheep. The raising of animals did not promise such immediate cash returns as crops, which could lead to influxes of cash into a family's hands in a single year. Added to this concern was the danger of wild animals such as bears, wolves, and panthers that posed a real threat to domestic herds. By the 1820s, however, it had become possible and practical to start building small herds of sheep and cattle. Initially, these animals were held in such small numbers as to be only used to support the family's immediate needs for milk and wool.

In support of the recognition of the importance of agriculture to the general economy, on 1 January 1817, a group of men formed the Otsego County Agricultural Society, the first such society organized in New York State. It would not be for another two years before New York Governor DeWitt Clinton asked the state legislature to appropriate money in support of such societies. Clinton, like these men in Otsego, saw how crucial agricultural prosperity was to the general economy. It was also generally felt among educated men that farmers throughout the northeast employed backward methods of land cultivation and animal husbandry, especially compared to the farmers of England. Contemporaries in America gave great credit to the British Board of Agriculture for stimulating improvement in agriculture.[4] With the complimentary goals of improving agriculture and, thereby, improving the general economy, there grew a great effort among the upper classes to educate farmers in better agricultural practices.

It was these aims that spurred the formation of Otsego County's agricultural society. This group's organizational meeting was held at the residence of Colonel Henry of Cooperstown. At this meeting were Matthew Derbyshire, Samuel Coleman, Reverend John Smith, James Fenimore Cooper, Strang Hayden, and William Crandall. Within a month the society had a constitution and Jacob Morris was elected president with John H. Prentiss serving as vice president and James Fenimore Cooper as corresponding secretary. One of the provisions of this constitution was that there be a person from each town in the county appointed to serve on the three standing committees of tillage, domestic animals, and manufactures. Those representatives from Middlefield were Abner Dunham, Daniel Mason, and Joshua Pinney respectively. By October of that year the society held its first exhibition at the Presbyterian church in Cooperstown. Although the life of this society was relatively short-lived, ceasing operations in 1825 until resurrected in 1841, it did much to encourage good agricultural practices.[5]

In order to encourage sound agricultural practices and reward farmers who furthered the science of cultivation and animal husbandry, the Otsego County Agricultural Society gave monetary prizes at its exhibitions in various categories of tillage, manufacturing, and domestic animals. For its exhibition in 1820 the society gave premiums (prizes) in animal husbandry for the best stud horse, breed mare and colt, bull, cow, heifer, oxen, ram and ewe. Among the members of the judging committee for this category was Daniel North, who, in addition to being one of the leading businessmen of Clarksville, owned an exceptional farm outside of the hamlet. In fact, in the exhibition of 1820, he took the prize for best stud horse. He was joined in this prize-winners' circle by three other men from Middlefield: Zimri Palmer for best breed mare and colt, Mial Pierce for best one year old colt, and William A. Walker for best ram. North would continue to build on his horse breeding stock. In 1828 he advertised that he had acquired a new horse from Virginia, *Young Eagle*, which had an excellent blood-line and was available for stud.[6]

As the herds of livestock across the county were built by farmers, greater at-tention was paid to protecting these animals. Although the danger of wild beasts had subsided for the most part, there were other dangers. One specific danger was that of dogs. As a result, in 1826, the New York State legislature passed an act taxing dog owners for their dogs. This money was paid into a county fund to be used to remunerate owners of sheep, which were injured or killed by dogs. The other dangers to herds were theft and wandering. Quite often advertise-ments were taken out in the newspaper offering rewards for animals that had wandered or believed to have been stolen. Nehemiah Howe of Hartwick, Ot-sego County, offered a reward when his heifer wandered off in 1835 and Ben-jamin North of Clarksville did likewise when his mare wandered or was stolen in 1839.[7]

It was the particular danger to sheep that was of considerable importance. This was in testament to their enormous economic value. Wool production in Middlefield had become a very large concern as early as 1820 with 4,483 sheep reported in the town in that year, this compared to 106,527 sheep in the whole of Otsego County. This number swelled to 7,150 sheep in Middlefield fifteen years later. Over the next decades these flocks would grow considerably larger. In tandem with the increase in size of flocks of sheep was an effort to increase the quality of the breeds. In 1854 George Clarke was able to boast that he had shorn a fleece from a yearling French Merino lamb that weighed seventeen pounds.[8] He noted this as a challenge to surrounding farmers, particularly those on farms being leased from him. This was clearly his effort to introduce superi-or breeds and bloodlines to the area. It was also part of his effort to start influ-encing the activities of his tenant farmers.

By the year 1820, Middlefield produced 21,546 yards of cloth. This is indic-ative of the fact that home woolen manufacture had become such a significant segment of the New York economy by the early nineteenth century. The act set-ting up a fund to remunerate sheep owners for damage caused by dogs was not the first state foray into the woolen industry. The state government had expen-ded $23,000 between 1809 and 1819 to encourage home woolen manufacture in recognition of its contribution to the overall economy. So extensive had wool production in the area surrounding Clarksville become that a carding machine was set up along the Cherry Valley Creek in front of the bark mill and saw mill in the hamlet.[9] Carding was the process whereby wool was disentangled and combed out in preparation for spinning. In cases of limited home production of wool a farmer's wife or daughter could card the family wool, but as the size of individual sheep flocks grew it became too labor intensive and time consuming to do this work at home. Having a carding machine in the vicinity of one's farm was viewed as a great aid in woolen production and a great advancement in the settlement of Clarksville.

As woolen production increased, home manufacture could not keep pace with the demand for woolen cloth. The establishment of a carding machine in Clarksville had helped to increase production dramatically, but that ultimately proved insufficient to meet the demand for woolens. To satisfy this growing industry a cotton mill, which had been set up in 1815 in the hamlet of Phoenix Mills, at the southern extreme of Middlefield, was converted to a woolen mill around 1866 under the ownership of John F. Scott of Cooperstown. By 1872 the Phoenix Woolen Mill employed forty people and boasted an annual output of 100,000 pounds of wool. Ancillary to this woolen production were other businesses, which sprang up as the inhabitants of the county desired finer items. In 1826 one such business located in Oaksville, a hamlet north of Cooperstown, advertised "Fancy Dying, and Calico Printing" on silk, cotton or wool.[10]

Throughout much of the nineteenth century woolen production was one of the agricultural backbones of Middlefield. One of the other core agricultural industries that developed in Middlefield was dairying. Both of these pursuits were pushed to the fore in the 1820s. That decade saw the opening of the Erie Canal, which facilitated a flood of cheaper grains from the western farms of Ohio into New York. These western farms were built on fresh virgin soil that assured large yields that eastern New York farmers could no longer hope to match. The result was a precipitous drop in grain prices. The year that the Erie Canal opened witnessed the collapse of the market price of wheat. This threatened to ruin many farmers in Otsego unless they converted to animal husbandry, or some over agricultural commodity that had not yet developed in the west to any large degree. Sheep farming was one route, but this too was forced to change as western farms experimented in this area. As important as sheep farming was to Middlefield farmers, that too was pinched by western farms starting in the 1840s. By 1855 the number of sheep in Middlefield had dropped to 3,430 from the high point in 1835. This paved the way for the triumph of dairying by the 1850s.[11]

Dairy farming was well suited to the Middlefield landscape. Extensive cultivation by early pioneers coupled with a lack of soil preservation techniques ensured that the rich upper layer of humus and virgin soil had largely washed away by the 1820s. Further, although low laying land around areas like the Cherry Valley Creek were ideally suited to cultivation, much of Middlefield was hilly and did not lend itself well to the plow. This topographical feature, however, made excellent pasture land and lent itself well to hay fields. Both conditions were nicely fitted to a dairy industry. Farmers found another inducement to dairying. Steady milk production, primarily in the spring and summer months, meant a steadier stream of income. This was in contrast to large influxes of cash only when crops were harvested. Farm household income was augmented by the myriad products attendant to dairying other than milk, specifically, butter and cheese.

As cow herds increased and dairy farming took hold in Middlefield it quickly became the predominant agricultural pursuit of the early to mid-nineteenth century. Indeed, as early as 1813 the dairy products of the town had a high reputation and by 1820 the cattle herds in Middlefield numbered 2,266. This number grew to 3,692 cattle in 1835 and to 5,788 cattle in 1875. By the 1840s even the poorest of farm families were beginning to build cow herds both for domestic dairy produce and for sale.[12] With the advent of large scale dairy farming together with the different work needed to care for a dairy herd rather than field crops, there occurred an unexpected change in the division of labor on farms. When area farms were involved mostly in growing grain crops men were largely responsible for field work and women were mostly responsible for household work. In the barnyard men would typically care for horses and other large animals and women would tend to small animals such as chickens. Growth in dairy herds and the production of milk, cheese and butter altered this division of labor.

Caring for a cow herd was different from growing grain crops in that most of the work with a cow herd and the dairy operation was centered in the barnyard and home. This tended to blur the previous line of distinction between male and female work. Although men still cared for cattle and did most of the barn chores, women often joined men in milking. Furthermore, women usually skimmed cream and made butter for both the household and for sale. However, it was not uncommon for men to assist women in operations such as churning just as women might assist in the barn caring for the herd as necessary. In this way, farm life in Middlefield began to change from a clearly demarcated set of tasks between men and women into a more integrated effort among various family members of both sexes.[13]

The growth in the dairy industry and milk production naturally grew by leaps and bounds those other operations that were closely tied to milk, specifically butter and cheese making. Butter production was of particular importance to farm families because it tended to be very lucrative. Even poor families with only a few cows could hope to earn significant income through this avenue. It has been estimated that milking even as few as seven cows in the 1870s could lead to a butter production worth about $250.00 a year. Henry Hilton Wood, a farmer living on the western side of the town of Middlefield after the Civil War, reported that his ten cows allowed him to make about 800 pounds of butter during the summer months. Usually the butter from this home production was sold to local stores. The Manning and Mortimer Gilbert store in the hamlet of Clarksville was one such store that purchased butter from local farmers. On one occasion in 1860 Mrs. D. Gilbert sold this store $15.68 worth of butter. It is tantalizing to surmise the value of her annual butter output.[14]

The process of making butter through churning could be a hard, tedious task. That notwithstanding, the financial payoff made the labor worthwhile. Indeed it was because this operation was so important to the financial well being of the family that men were willing to assist in the production of butter. By 1865 Middlefield families were producing a total of 170,795 pounds of butter, or 6% of the total butter production of Otsego County, which stood at 2,811,199 pounds for that year. This butter was then packaged in fifty-pound tubs and sent, via local store merchants or agents, to more urban areas such as New York City for sale. Obviously only a small portion of this total production would have stayed in the county for local repurchase from these stores. In order to ensure proper credit, many farm families, store owners and agents either purchased or carved distinctive wooden stamps or prints to mark their tubs to avoid confusion with other farmers' butter. Indeed, E. & H. Cory of Cooperstown advertised butter prints as well as "all the articles attached to the DAIRY BUSINESS" for sale in their store.[15]

Cheese making was the other off shoot of the dairy farming industry growing in Middlefield. Farmers embraced this activity again because of the amount of money that could be made with relatively few cows. In 1845 it was estimated that one cow could produce 110 pounds of cheese and through improvements in the herd stock it was thought that 400 pounds per cow was a reasonable goal. It soon became apparent that cheese making as a home industry was not practical with this level of production. By 1849 dairy farmers across New York State were using about two billion pounds of milk in the production of cheese. By 1865 cheese production in Middlefield hit 22,485 pounds. This trend toward large-scale production had been apparent much earlier which led to the setting up of cheese factories across the region by the 1850s.[16] Middlefield had several cheese factories scattered through the town by the 1870s. In the hamlet of Clarksville one such factory was set up on the west side of the Cherry Valley Creek across the road from the saw mill and carding machine, next to the flour mill. Farmers would necessarily have to bring their milk to the cheese factory every day to prevent it from spoiling. Therefore, situated in this location, the cheese factory was well placed to accommodate farmers as they came to town for lumber or with raw wool ready for carding or grain ready for grinding. Generally speaking, the position of a cheese factory in the hamlet induced farmers to transact all their business in this locale.

In support of the cheese making industry there grew up cheese box manufacturing businesses. Boxes made for packaging cheese started being made around 1820. These were large wooden casks that could hold from four to six cheeses. They were relatively heavy and bulky to transport. However, by the 1860s individual cheese boxes of a round shape were in common use. These answered the need for both convenience and less bulk in packaging. Given the transportation system of the time and the expense of shipping produce, using containers which were less bulky could increase profit margins. As cheese factories were set up so too were cheese box making businesses. Of particular note with regard to the hamlet of Clarksville was the cheese box making business of James Pope which was located a short distance from the hamlet, relatively close to the cheese factory. Also attendant to cheese production, many local stores started selling supplies to assist this business. E. & H. Cory advertised the sale of cheese tubs and cheese hoops in their Cooperstown store.[17]

The growth of diversity in agriculture in Otsego County was a natural progression as this frontier became more settled and established in the early to mid-nineteenth century. It was viewed in a positive light by those wealthy gentlemen farmers who had founded the Otsego County Agricultural Society. Indeed, in his opening address in 1817 Jacob Morris had exhorted the farmers of the county to persevere in "the steady habits of our revered ancestors, in an honest and diligent cultivation of the earth."[18] Although the common farmers of the county were suspicious of the efforts and motivations of these men it was these wealthy gentlemen who endeavored to introduce improved animal breeds into the area as well as encourage farmers in the use of fertilizers and other soil improvements techniques. Stephen Van Rensselaer, the great landlord in the Albany region, who was also very active in local agricultural societies, even went so far as to send scientists out to lecture his tenant farmers in the most modern agricultural practices.

The advice of these wealthy individuals became difficult to ignore as these men used their position as landlords to either convince or cajole farmers and lease holders to their way of thinking. In many ways George Clarke was the most effective of these gentleman farmers and landlords in swaying his farmers and lease holders in the Middlefield and Springfield areas through example and other means as necessary to increase the output of his leased farms. Certainly by the late 1830s, this Clarke had shown himself to be quite different from his father in the way he dealt with his tenants, taking a much greater interest in his farmers' agricultural practices. It is possible that in taking a line from Jacob Morris' address of 1817, with which he must have been familiar, Clarke may have been the first person to dub Middlefield "the Land of Steady Habits" in reference to its economic base in agriculture. Almost certainly he would have viewed the town as a model of prosperity in part due to its importance to his landed inheritance and income derived as it was from his leased farms.

Clarke's endeavor to assist and educate his tenants was no doubt viewed as meddlesome. However, what bothered his tenants more was the very leasehold system that was the foundation of Clarke's wealth. Although his Middlefield tenants resented this system, it was in the neighboring counties of Delaware and Schoharie, where Clarke also had significant lands along with other large landowners such as the Van Rensselaers, that this resentment over the leasehold system boiled over. In 1839 the issue of paying back rent to the Van Rensselaers reached the breaking point and what has become known as the Anti-Rent Wars erupted. Although the disturbances of these anti-renters were minimal in Otsego County, it is illustrative of their character to see how the leaders in Otsego viewed this movement that was ultimately successful in obtaining many of its stated demands.

The leasehold system as it developed in New York had three main variants. In some cases there were provisions for the tenants to eventually purchase the land. Other leases lasted for the life of one or more (usually three) persons. In these cases, the landlord retook possession of the property with all its improvements upon the death of the last listed person in the lease, leaving heirs with the option of signing a new lease or leaving the land. Finally, there were perpetual, or durable, leases, which lasted forever. Tenant farmers had labored under this system in the Hudson Valley since the colonial period. As settlement moved along the Mohawk Valley and into central New York, this system, in many cases, followed. Although the Clarkes had allowed some tenants to purchase their land, particularly in hamlets and villages, most farmers leasing from the Clarkes had not been given the option to purchase their land. This served Clarke's interest well since he derived the vast majority of his income from this leased property.

Under this leasehold system it was not uncommon for farmers to fall behind on their rents in years of poor harvests. Usually these arrearages would be paid at a later time. However, it had also become not uncommon for landlords to go for long periods without demanding rent. The situation came to a head in 1839, after the death of Stephen Van Rensselaer, the Old Patroon, when his son, Stephen Van Rensselaer IV demanded payment of all back rents in order to settle the estate of the Old Patroon. Many farmers throughout the Van Rensselaer lands could not, or would not, settle. Indeed, they used the occasion to band together in resistance to what they viewed as an unjust system. These men believed that the leasehold system was unjust and that they had already paid for the land many times over with rents they and their ancestors had paid. Landlords countered the position of the anti-renters by pointing out that these renters had taken title to these farms subject to lease terms. Many of their deeds or instruments by which they acquired the property contained legally recognizable language of their lessor status. Many people throughout the region, especially those among the landed elite and politically well connected, who believed in the sanctity of contracts, upheld the lease system.

There were other issues at work in this struggle, though. Resentment over the leasehold system had also been brought to the fore as many farmers had seen the prices paid for their produce drop as cheaper farm produce was brought via the Erie Canal, to more urban areas. This was compounded by the fact that these farmers had to pay taxes which helped to pay New York State's Erie Canal debt.[19]   Clearly, the Anti-Rent Wars were about more than just rents. Farmers' anger was fed by frustration over the entire economic structure and malaise in New York State that seemed to be handicapping the farmers of Delaware and Schoharie counties specifically, but also Otsego County to a lesser degree.

This general dissatisfaction with the economic situation in New York State can be seen in one of the few violent incidents of anti-renter activity that occurred in Otsego County. In early 1845 a group of anti-renters from Schoharie County disguised as Indians rode into Otsego County to prevent the sheriff from serving papers on a farmer to compel payment of a store debt. As this case makes clear, the anti-renters were concerned with more than just rents, and this uproar was growing into a wider struggle pitting farmers and tenants against those perceived to have property, wealth, political influence and power.[20]

As the struggle escalated, the anti-renters were rounded up and charged accordingly. In one case in 1845, Dr. Smith A. Boughton stood trial on a charge of robbing Sheriff Henry Miller of papers. Boughton's attorney was Ambrose L. Jordan, who had studied under Jacob Van Rensselaer and later had relocated to Cooperstown in 1812. He was also a one-time mill owner, along with Peter Besancon, in Clarkesville. Jordan had offered his legal talents to the anti-renters, which clearly indicated what side he took in the dispute. This trial of Boughton ended in mistrial. At the retrial in September 1845 the situation in Delaware County had become so volatile that Jordan and the Attorney General of New York State, John Van Buren, son of President Martin Van Buren, got into a fist fight in court.[21] Indeed, so violent had the area become that on 27 August 1845 New York Governor Silas Wright had declared Delaware County to be in a state of rebellion.

One of the first leaders of Otsego County to come out in support of the landlord's titles was James Fenimore Cooper. It must be remembered that during this time, even though he was a successful author, he still rented out farms, which he had inherited when William Cooper died in 1809. At that time he had inherited twenty-three farms paying an annual rent of 650 bushels of wheat. Based on the price of wheat in Albany on 1 January 1840, this rent would have been valued at $734.50. Early in the anti-rent struggle he characterized the landlord/tenant relationship as "entirely natural and salutary." In 1841 Cooper went even further and chastised New York Governor Seward for meddling in a matter, that between landlord and tenant, in which he had no right to meddle. Cooper even accused the Governor of "recommending a pecuniary compromise that is flagrantly wrong . . ."[22] So bitter were his feelings, that he went so far as to write three novels, known collectively as *The Littlepage Manuscripts*, showing the laudatory qualities of the landlords.

During this period, George Clarke remained quiet. However, in 1848 he roared forward when an action was started to allow the state to recover any manor lands unless clear title could be proved. If there was no clear title, then those lands would devolve to the state. Viewing this as a gross violation of the rights of property and a potentially ruinous action to his landed interests and income, Clarke vowed to spend the enormous sum of $25,000 to defeat the measure. It was even rumored that he paid men $2 a day to solicit petitions against anti-rent legislation.[23]

Since Otsego County remained relatively quiet during these troubled times, there had developed only a weak tenant organization by 1845. Where it did exist, it was most notable in the area of the towns of Milford, Middlefield, and Westford. This corresponded to the area in which George Clarke held significant land holdings. However, in this county, unlike other areas, the anti-renters and tenant farmers formed an alliance of sorts with others of differing political stripes. Anti-renters allied themselves with the political causes of the Whigs and some dissident Democrats. In the case of Otsego County, the cause of this group was aimed more at challenging the landed elite's political power. Chief among the men furthering this alliance were S. S. Bowne, who defended many anti-renters in Delhi, Levi S. Chatfield, who, in 1846, represented Otsego County along with Joshua Spencer at the New York State Constitutional Convention, and Sumner Ely, who seemed always to be furthering liberal and egalitarian causes. Ely had considerable sway with this group since it was clear he had great political influence already, having served in the state senate from 1840 to 1843. The alliance of these sometimes disparate political groups proved so successful that their candidates for sheriff, state senator, and assemblyman easily out-polled their opponents.[24]

It is not necessary here to discuss the whole of the Anti-Rent Wars. It needs to only be stated that ultimately, the landlords lost this battle. New York State held a constitutional convention in 1846. Many counties that had significant amounts of land being farmed by tenant farmers sent delegates who were anti-rent sympathizers. Among these was Levi Chatfield from Otsego County. This convention made many changes to the constitution to answer several tenant concerns: income from leases would henceforth be taxable, leases could no longer exceed twelve years, and impediments to the transfer of titles were eliminated. Perhaps more troubling for landlords though, was the provision that even though leases made before the constitutional convention would stand, the legislature seemed ready to challenge manor titles in court.[25]

In 1850 Justice Ira Harris of the state supreme court ruled that the titles Van Rensselaer held to his lands were invalid. This decision was reversed on appeal when the court of appeals ruled that an 1830 statute clearly stated that land titles had to be questioned within forty years of their original sale. However, this upheaval spelled the end of the feudal-like system of land tenure that had grown in New York. Although this is highly significant to the nature of Clarke's titles, as well as those of all the other New York landlords, it must be remembered that the Clarke family had withstood such a challenge to the titles to its Middlefield lands in 1811. These court cases involving Van Rensselaer were no doubt watched closely by George Hyde Clarke. During the height of the Anti-Rent Wars he had taken very concrete steps to protect himself against the eventuality of the landlords losing the legal struggle. As a result, he continued to hold vast stretches of land and continued to derive vast sums of money in rents from his tenants. As late as the 1870s many Middlefield farmers were still leasing their farms from Clarke. Lucian Hinds, who lived at the southern end of the town near Milford, was one of the most significant tenants. He was leasing 700 acres of farm land from Clarke in 1872. Closer to the hamlet of Clarksville and much more typical in farm size were Samuel Preston and John Risendorf, both of whom were renting 160 acres each from Clarke in that year.[26]

It must have been clear to Clarke during these anti-rent disturbances that the old semi-feudal land holding system in New York was unsustainable. Accordingly, he began to change the nature of his leases to his tenants. Indeed, as astute as he was, he began altering his lease terms in the mid-1830s. As leases expired or as tenants fell behind on rents, Clarke altered the lease terms to resemble a share farming system. Under this system, his tenants would farm as before and be supplied with farming supplies. In return Clarke would receive, in some cases, up to half of the farmer's crop in lieu of a cash rent payment. This system eased the socially perceived inequality of the durable lease system because it was viewed as more democratic. It was seen as an honest contract between two parties. In the cases of hop growing, for example, Clarke would supply land, a dwelling, a garden plot, timber for fuel and fencing, hop roots, hop poles and the tenant would supply his labor to plant, pick and dry the crop.[27]

This system of land tenure appeared to many land owners to show more sustainability in the current political climate and this led many other landowners to emulate Clarke's method of share farming. One of the effects of farming on shares though was the elimination of any sense of a paternalistic bond between landowner and farmer. The farmer as renter no longer had security of tenure. Landowners, since they would receive a portion of crops produced, wanted ambitious, industrious farmers. Farmers who were lazy or indolent were among the poorest members of society; unable to get good tracts of land to farm and unable to care for their family. Henry Conklin of Blenheim Hill in Schoharie County, complained in his memoirs about his father, blaming him for the family being sometimes "half naked and sometimes hungry and cold and no place to lay our heads that we could call our own . . ."[28]

Farming on shares led farmers to compete for better tracts of farm land as they became available, even going so far as to give references of previous landlords from whom they had farmed as in the case of George Potts. In 1836 when Potts wanted to take over a farm tract in Middlefield owned by William B. Campbell, he not only referenced the previous farm he had leased, but he also spoke highly of his own abilities to work a farm well.

I have under stood that Mr. Allison and Mr. Davison were a going from your Farm next Spring if so I would like to take it or rint [sic] it as we could agree not that I wish to under mind Mr. Allison and Mr. Davison but if they do quit I would like to get it I have worked Jeremiah Reads farm where John Prince lived on Shears I took it for 2 years from last Spring and he has sold it and wants me to leave it next Spring I worked it at halvs [sic] *and he says what he has got for his part is worth over $200 and if I get yours I will try to do as well by you.*[29]

The Clarke family's efforts to convert their tenant's leases to this new share farming system did not always progress smoothly. When George Clarke had died in 1835, he had made some minor progress in this direction, but it was left to his son, George Hyde Clarke, to finish the process. This younger Clarke was much more forceful in his approach with his tenants. First, like Stephen Van Rensselaer IV, Clarke demanded payment of back rents, which had been allowed to go uncollected in many cases since his father had died. Second, he instructed his attorney, Richard Cooper, to investigate life leases to determine if all people named in the lease were still living. If they were not, then the lease was considered terminated. Many tenants, of course, would not disclose this information, as it would mean they would have to either sign a new lease or vacate the property, leaving improvements such as houses, barns, and fences without compensation. Through both of these courses, Clarke endeavored to obtain new share leases. Indeed, by the late 1840s he had successfully converted most of his lands to share leases producing hops and dairy products. It was not until over thirty years later that Clarke could feel that his conversion to share farming was complete. In 1878 his agent, T. C. Smith, informed *The Freeman's Journal* that all of Clarke's 56 farms in Otsego County were rented and that nearly all of his 170 farms outside of Otsego were rented. It was happily reported that, "All the old anti-rent troubles have ceased."[30]

There was another effect of this share lease system that the farmers would not have foreseen. In many ways it would force them to produce for market, such items as dairy products, hops, and other crops rather than produce for their family's consumption. John Chamberlain, who leased a farm from George Clarke in 1857 in Cherry Valley, had clear obligations to Clarke, which were typical. He had to deliver to Hyde Hall by the first of November 208 bushels of oats, 20 bushels of barley, and all the hops grown on the farm. The hops were to be well dried, cleaned and in good order.[31]

George Clarke became, in this way, a significantly different sort of landlord than his father had been. Whereas that first Clarke had set up his semi-feudal manor system in the manner of the Van Rensselaers, Philipses, and Livingstons, this younger Clarke was not averse to use his position as landlord to exert a more direct influence on his tenant farmers. However benign his motivations may have been, this was still viewed as meddlesome. It has already been discussed how he sought to introduce better bloodlines and breeds into the livestock of the county. He went significantly further when it came to crops. There was a growing body of literature expounding the virtues of agricultural specialization throughout the northeast. Starting in the second quarter of the nineteenth century it was thought advantageous for farmers to think more commercially and to gear their farm produce more toward market demands rather than toward self sufficiency or subsistence. This drive was led by such publications as *The Massachusetts Yeoman, The New England Farmer, The Genesee Farmer*, and, closer to Otsego, from Albany, *The Ploughboy*.

George Clarke was, no doubt, familiar with many of these publications and his actions convincingly assert that he subscribed to their espoused philosophy. He saw great financial benefits to his farmers and himself in commercially driven, specialized farms in light of the share farming system he was developing. Indeed, this system could be much more financially advantageous to him than a semi-feudal rent based system, at least in good years. With regard to specialized farms, Clarke took a great interest in hop growing. This crop, an essential ingredient in the production of beer, was incredibly lucrative for growers as well as agents who bought hops on speculation early in the season and hoped to sell at enormous profits at harvest time. Clarke grew hops on his farm in Springfield around Hyde Hall, but he also acted as an agent. This led him to pressure his tenant farmers to grow hops for him to sell on the open market.

Hops had been actively cultivated in Otsego County since the early nineteenth century. It was only one of many crops being grown during that period as agriculture was rapidly diversifying. In fact it even made sense to grow hops with another crop simultaneously in the same field since hop plants took two years before they would bear fruit for harvesting. This lag time between planting and the ability to harvest a marketable commodity meant that a farmer had to have his cash tied up for two years before he could hope to make money. This notwithstanding, the climate and soil conditions in Otsego were such that the county became known for its high yielding hop fields. By about 1835 Otsego County became the foremost producer of hops in the United States, followed quickly by Madison County just to the west, with Cooperstown as the center of this trade. Five years later the crop from this county totaled 168,605 pounds, while the crop from all of New York State totaled 447,000.[32] That is, 38% of the entire New York hop harvest came from Otsego County alone.

Growing hops could be a very expensive enterprise for a farmer to start. There was the cost for hop poles, field boxes, sacking and cording, but added to this was the expense of paying and boarding, as necessary, additional hop pickers. Of course, with Clarke's share farming system, his farmers did not bear many of these costs. This made his system seem less onerous to his tenants. The cost of additional workers, though, was borne by the farmers themselves. These extra workers were required because the harvest was so labor intensive that family members could not do all the work. Henry Hilton Wood gives a good first hand account of the labor involved in harvesting his hop crop in Middlefield in the 1860s.

[Hops] was usually a good paying industry, but like many other things there was no great excellence without much labor. This crop was gathered during the month of September. We had to have four men for box tenders and about twenty women, or girls and boys to gather

the hops. We had to drive many miles to get all the help we needed, as everybody picked hops at about the same time. We had to lodge and board them, and give them the very best bed and food that could be found or they would leave and go to some other hop field where pickers were needed. Our pickers gathered about thirty ten-bushel boxes a day. This was 300 bushels daily. The hops that were picked during the day I dried at night. We had a large kiln built for that purpose. The hops were carried to the second floor of the building and spread out in a large room, on a thin cloth. Under this cloth were narrow slats, so the heat could come through. There was a room the same size, beneath this one, containing a large furnace. It was my work to tend the furnace, and keep the fire just hot enough that the hops would be dried about 8:00 o'clock in the morning. While they were cooling I helped in the house, as there was always plenty to do there. After dinner I moved the hops out of the drying room into the storage room adjoining. I often had to be out in the field to look after things. Hop picking lasted from two to three weeks. When it was done, wife and I were about done, too, and when the hands were paid off our money was done also.[33]

Another expense alluded to in Wood's memoir was that of constructing a hop house which was built to have a drying kiln to dry the hops before baling them. All of these expenses taken together spelled a significant gamble for the average farmer. Quantifying these costs is difficult though, because of the paucity of accurate records kept by many farmers in this period. However, James H. Dunbar of Hamilton, New York, did keep such a record in 1837. Hamilton was a community about 50 miles west of Middlefield so it can be surmised that costs to a Middlefield farmer, such as Wood, would have been similar. Dunbar's balance sheet shows a cost of approximately $96 per acre to cultivate hops. It must be pointed out though that his costs do not include the expense of building a kiln nor does he show any costs associated with purchasing hop poles for the vines to grow up.[34]

The costs of these buildings and the hop kiln could be prohibitive for the average farmer. In 1853, Brewster Conklin of Springfield, where Hyde Hall was located, estimated these costs for George Clarke. According to Conklin, a barn would cost $2,600 and a hop kiln and stove would cost $780. Additionally, Clarke would usually supply his share farmers with a dwelling, a garden plot, timber for fuel and fences, hop roots, and poles. Clearly, the only way for the vast majority of farmers to enter the sometimes lucrative hop business was via share farming for Clarke or someone like him: a man who had the means and the land to set up a farmer on a workable plot.[35]

As with other sectors of the agricultural industry, whole businesses sprang up to service the needs of the hop farmer. Although some farmers no doubt were able to make some of their own supplies such as hop poles, other items needed to be purchased. Of particular interest to farmers was the portable hop press, which started replacing stationary presses in the 1820s. This novelty did not supersede the stationary press until the Civil War. However, as early as 1826 Joseph Wilson & Co. of Otsego advertised that he had "obtained the full and exclusive right and liberty of making, constructing, using, and vending to others to be used, a Machine for pressing HOPS . . ."[36] This type of portable press caught on quickly because it was easy to move and was less expensive than constructing the stationary presses with the large wooden screws that were housed permanently in barns and hop houses.

The extraordinary growth in the number of acres devoted to cultivating hops spurred many entrepreneurs to set up stores catering almost exclusively to the hop trade. By the Civil War era it was not uncommon to see numerous advertisements in *The Freeman's Journal* of Cooperstown from competing stores all catering to this industry. J. H. Story spoke of his "usually large store of GOODS" for hop growers which he promised to sell "at prices defying competition." Another merchant in the same paper referred to his ability to sell goods "at the very lowest market price, and we can assure our friends and the public that we were never better prepared to do them Justice than at the present time." Finally, directly below these two advertisements, R. Russell & Co. exhorted growers "IF YOU WANT HOP GOODS at low prices, go to the Central Cash Store . . ."[37] In fact, with three advertisements in this one issue devoted entirely to hop articles, this was the single most advertised industry in this paper.

These many stores catering to the needs of the hop grower were able to flourish because of the sheer amount of hops being grown in the county. By 1865 Otsego County was producing 3,451,761 pounds of hops. Leading the towns in the county was Middlefield, which accounted for 11% of the total for the county. In 1865 Middlefield farmers produced 391,861 pounds of hops. Even more astounding was the fact that as hop cultivation fell off in Otsego County, dropping to 1,976,623 pounds in 1874, Middlefield was still producing 323,303 pounds of hops in 1875.[38] This phenomenal growth and staying power in Middlefield was tied directly to some key hop agents and dealers situated in the town. Primary among these men were James F. Clark, whose hop fields were situated around the hamlet of Phoenix Mills at the southern end of the town, and Harrison North, who was a hop dealer in the hamlet of Clarksville. Towering above both of these men, though was George Clarke of Hyde Hall who used his position as a landlord to push his tenant farmers in Middlefield to grow hops for him. In all cases these agents and dealers hoped to make huge profits by selling these hops on the open market at harvest time.

Of these three men, Harrison North was the most minor of the hop dealers. He had numerous business interests both in his own right and in combination with his friend Moses Brown of Clarksville. However, in 1868 he was described as a dealer in hops and wool.[39] In contrast to North, James F. Clark was a hop dealer of immense proportions. However, he was also a well-respected citizen of the community. He was a one-time sheriff of Otsego County as well as an executive in the Hop Growers Association. Further, he was a commissioner of the Cooperstown & Susquehanna Railroad, which opened in 1869. It was through this means that he was able to get the rail line running from Colliersville to Cooperstown along the Susquehanna River to pass over the Middlefield town line right near his property. This area, in which his fields were located, north of the area of Middlefield known as Phoenix Mills, was commonly referred to as "Hop City." During the height of hop picking season, Clark would have up to 1,000 persons working for him, up to 700 of whom may have stayed on the farm in the four buildings he had erected for pickers. These pickers were feeding seven hop houses and two hop kilns on this farm. However, it was not only work that Clark provided. He also had a hall for entertainment, dances and such, built as a place for his pickers to find amusement. Ultimately, Clark's fortune was lost and he went bankrupt on a scheme to ship hops to England to get a better price than the American market could provide.[40]

George Clarke's hop interests took a slightly different angle from those of James Clark and Harrison North. His share farming arrangements meant that he did not actually grow hops, although he did have some hop fields around Hyde Hall. He acted more as a factor or agent to his tenants and some other hop growers. After he had enticed or cajoled his tenant farmers into growing hops at the expense of growing other crops, he could hope to reap huge profits. Indeed Clarke's share farming system was designed solely to move a large portion of these hop profits to his accounts. As the hop market matured, Clarke's efforts altered in a much riskier direction. No longer was he happy to use his tenants to grow hops for him. He, like many others, contracted with farmers at the time of planting to purchase their hops at a set price, regardless of the market price. It was hoped, by people like Clarke, that the contracted price would be significantly less than the market price at harvest time, thereby ensuring him a sizeable profit. Non tenant farmers were tempted by this arrangement because it spared them the risk of losing money, although some thought that by holding out longer they might possibly get a higher price. Whatever the rationale, many farmers bowed to his pressure and grew hops under contract to him.

It was after the Civil War that all hop related activities, other than actually growing the plants, was removed from the growers due to the large number of agents, factors and brewers who were contracting to buy hops. In many cases these men would even advance to the farmer sufficient dollars for the farmer to buy his hop roots and other items as well as enough money to pay his pickers, thereby freeing the farmer of even the risk of borrowing money from his bank. Although this arrangement was completely in place after the Civil War, it had started developing long before that time. As early as 1845 *The Freeman's Journal* was devoting space to the speculations that were causing havoc in the hop market. It was reported that in 1844 the market price of hops had been nine and a half to ten and a half cents per pound, but that price had escalated to fourteen cents per pound due to speculation. In 1845 the price had started at the same level in the market. However, speculation had driven the price up to twenty-five cents per pound in Boston and thirty to thirty-five cents per pound in New York.[41]

By the 1860s the hop market and Clarke's speculative activities had started getting the better of his judgment. He began purchasing more farm land throughout Otsego County, in many cases paying a premium for that land. The only rationale for his behavior was the anticipated profits from his speculative hop activities. However, by the late 1870s hop production began shifting to the western states. As with the wheat market, fresher land produced higher yields. The Otsego lands could not match these yields and Clarke saw his profits begin to evaporate. Furthermore, in his efforts to procure ever more land for growing hops he had used his existing land holdings as collateral. As the hop harvests became smaller and of lower quality, it became increasingly difficult for Clarke to meet his credit obligations. With land serving as collateral to purchase additional lands on credit and with crops declining, Clarke found himself in grave financial straights. Unable to meet his credit obligations, he risked not only the lands purchased on credit, but also lands that were serving as additional collateral, and indeed even Hyde Hall, the house his father had built. Two years before his death in 1889, George Clarke was forced to declare bankruptcy in what became the largest bankruptcy filing in the nation's history to that point.[42] It is not necessary here to relate the details of this bankruptcy case. George Clarke, at this point, serves as the most spectacular of the hops speculators of the era.

Harrison North of Clarksville serves as a more conservative and dramatically smaller scale hops dealer and agent than either George Clarke or James Clark. His hop activities remained one of several businesses with which he occupied himself. He was born in 1817, the youngest son of Daniel North and a brother of Benjamin North who had purchased the tavern in town from Joshua Pinney. Like so many other children in Clarkevsille in the 1820's, he attended the school taught by George Washington Johnson. For the second term in 1827, his father paid $1.37 for his two youngest children, Aaron and Harrison, to attend school for 90.5 days. It is not clear if either of these children attended the select school organized by Sumner Ely and taught by Johnson as well. Once out of school and set on his path in the world he married Helen Parshall, who was eleven years younger than he.[43]

Early in his business career, North entered the hop business. In 1846 he purchased his first parcel of land. This was a 160-acre tract from James Cornwall of Rensselaerville for $25. This piece of land was situated outside the boundaries of Clarksville. It was located west of the hamlet near lands owned by Peleg Coffin and William Shipman. He later had a hop kiln situated in this area. The following year he purchased another tract, this time thirty acres from George L. Briggs near Newtown-Martin, or Middlefield Centre as it came to be known. This parcel came at the much higher price of $700 and, no doubt, had considerably more improvements by way of buildings and fences than his first parcel.[44] Indeed, it may have even had hops growing on it already, which would help explain the greater cost. It is unclear how North managed to make these significant purchases, but it is probable that his father, Daniel, who had made a considerable fortune through his businesses, was able to extend him credit, ready cash, or assist him in getting credit from other sources.

North's acquisitive impulses were not sated at this point, though. Just months after making his first land purchase, he purchased the stone school house which had served as George Washington Johnson's select school, from Aaron Van Allen for $200. It is unclear what this building was to be used for, but North purchased it subject to an existing lease, which Van Allen had made with Harrison Griffin. It is unclear what use Harrison Griffin was making of this building. However, this purchase serves to illustrate that North was not averse to becoming a landlord, since Griffin was now under obligation to pay North rent. As time went on, he showed himself ever more willing to rent lands to farmers. He was also not against the idea of building business partnerships. In line with his endeavors, he purchased half of his uncle's store in 1847 for $300. This was the store building Benjamin D. North had bought from Joshua Pinney. Harrison eventually bought out the remainder of his uncle's share in this business for $600 in 1851.[45] This approach was in keeping with the path several other Clarksville entrepreneurs had taken before; using business partnerships to help build their fortunes. In this way, men were able to pool both resources and talent. So, too, could they spread their money and time over several business ventures.

It was at this point that Harrison North purchased his first house. This was in the hamlet, near the distillery and was the former residence of Stephen Wickham, who had sold it to John Seymour of Utica. North paid $525 for this house.[46] The proximity of this house to North's store and other village lot, the stone school house, was surely a motivating force in his choice of this house. His marriage to Helen Parshall may also have prompted his need to buy a house.

Two years after the purchase of his house, Harrison North formed one of his most enduring partnerships: that of North and Brown. Moses R. Brown was three years older than Harrison and came from a well-established Middlefield family. Indeed, the brothers Thomas and Amos Brown, and the family of Benjamin North, Harrison North's grandfather, had all come from Chatham, Columbia County in New York, where they had been neighbors, to Middlefield together after the Revolutionary War. Both families settled in close proximity to each other on plots of land north of the hamlet. Thomas and Amos Brown had lived north of Clarksville near the Indians' *niskayuna* rock; Benjamin North's family settled a little east of this spot. By 1800, Amos had moved to the Westville area near Moses Rich. His son, also named Amos, born in 1791, later married Moses' daughter, Alsey Rich. To them was born Moses R. Brown in 1814.[47]

When Moses Brown and Harrison North formed their partnership, Brown had been living in the hamlet in a house he purchased from Azel Metcalf for $400. When Metcalf sold this house he moved to the tavern which Benjamin D. North had taken over from Joshua Pinney. Metcalf chose not to operate a tavern.[48] In addition to his business partnership with North, Brown was very involved with the political life of the town and served as the town supervisor for two years, starting in 1851. He also served one year as town clerk under William Compton in 1855.

Harrison North was the senior partner in this arrangement and his name appears first on all their joint properties. North also went on to make significant additional land purchases on his own and with other partners. However, the partnership of North & Brown always remained North's strongest business relationship. This partnership acquired two parcels totaling nearly 131 acres in 1849 and 1850. The first parcel was nearly 20 acres stretching back from the hamlet along the Long Patent Road near the Methodist church. This was purchased from Orra Knapp for $400.00. The other parcel was a large farm that was owned by Eugene and Clarissa North and rented to George Potts. They paid $850.00 for this 111-acre tract. In addition to these two purchases, they also bought a village lot in Clarksville from Luke Swan for $1,300.00 and a much larger parcel in the hamlet from George Clarke for $536.50. The lot acquired from Swan was an improved lot near the corner of the Long Patent and Whiteman Hill Roads. Finally, they acquired a village lot from Nathan Watson containing a little more than thirteen perches of land for $468.53. This lot was along the road leading out of the hamlet toward Cooperstown.[49]

North built another, much more limited, partnership with Erastus Belknap in 1858. In that year these two men purchased a one-half interest in a 130-acre tract in Middlefield from Hiram Palmer for $900.00. This purchase gave North the most trouble of any of his land acquisitions. The year after this purchase North and Belknap had to bring suit against the heirs of Zimri Palmer to take possession of this parcel. Eventually, North and Belknap prevailed and the land had to be seized and sold at auction. At auction the land and improvements sold for $3,150.00.[50] The exact nature of this suit is unknown, but it seems probable that the heirs of Zimri Palmer disputed the legality of Hiram Palmer's right to sell this land.

In his quest for ever more hop lands, North ventured into the neighboring town of Westford as well. There he purchased a 21-acre lot from Joseph Chiles for $800.00. He also partnered with Daniel Aldrich to buy a 75-acre lot in Westford from Levi Cummings for $500.00. These purchases in Westford were logical as Westford farmers in the 1860's were having a fair amount of success growing hops. In fact, in 1869 the *Schenevus Valley News* reported that the crop was quite heavy that year. Further, Westford was quite close to Clarksville and land prices seem to have been cheaper there than in Middlefield. Finally, in 1872, just three years before his death, North made his final land purchase. Here he purchased the two parcels which made up the estate of Peleg Coffin. These lands were very near the first lands he had purchased in 1846. He paid $5,810.00 for Coffin's 100 acres.[51] This is a striking increase over the $25.00 he had paid for the 160-acre tract a little more than a quarter century earlier and illustrates the increase in land values in the area, especially for those lands suited for growing hops. This also corresponds to the period when George Clarke, among others, was feverishly buying land thereby pushing lands values artificially high. This price would also support the assumption that there were many improvements on this land, thus raising its value.

It is obvious from this rash of land purchases that North was not working this land himself. In fact, he was clearly engaging in land speculation, the simple practice of buying and selling land to make quick profits. This was not his main impetus, though. His real intent was to find tenants for this land. He wanted these farms rented and the tenants to grow hops for North to sell on the market, much as George Clarke was doing. This explains his land acquisition activities and his repeated references to himself as a hop agent. Much of this land was still wooded when he and Brown purchased it too. This, of course, led to other avenues to make money. Certainly North & Brown engaged in selling pot and pearl ash produced from the burning of tree stumps. Additionally, they operated a lumberyard in the hamlet to dispose of the timber from their lands as they were being cleared.

Harrison North's involvement in agriculture extended further than just his ownership of land and leased farms. By the early 1860's he was also an active member of the Otsego County Agricultural Society, along with his older brothers Thomas and Aaron. These North brothers were joined in this society by other men from Middlefield; namely William Compton, who served as the society's vice president in 1863, Benjamin Pierce, and O. N. Shipman. The fact that the roster of members from Middlefield is so short is testimony to what the Society itself recognized when it reported that in many districts and remote areas of Otsego County "there is not a single member of the Society . . ." Like so many other landlords in central New York, Harrison North sought to bring innovation to agriculture. However, rather than foster better cattle bloodlines, as George Clarke was doing, North sought innovation through machinery. To this end, he exhibited a new double acting force pump in the 1862 Otsego County Fair for which the society awarded him a prize of $1.00.[52] This sum brought more prestige in the community than the nominal cash amount would imply.

Among one of Harrison North's most enduring achievements, though, had nothing to do with his land or mechanical innovations. Early in his career, North purchased a fifteen-acre parcel from George Clarke in the hamlet of Clarksville across the street from the house to which Azel Metcalf had moved in 1842, the former Pinney tavern. He purchased this lot for $1,000 subject to two leases: one to Caldwell Clarke and one to Moses Rich. Further, it excepted certain other lots which had been previously conveyed to others. The lot was surveyed in 1850 by Barnabus Gilbert and was found to contain a little over ten acres after previous conveyances were subtracted. It is probable that this large parcel in the hamlet was used for storing the products of his rented lands. Among these would obviously have been his hops, but also the wool, a product in which he had started dealing. However, the bulk of this property was devoted to the North and Brown lumberyard. It is probable that the purchase of this lot was prompted by the desire of North and Brown to start a lumber business. Again, it is clear that Harrison North was the senior partner in this arrangement since Moses Brown's name does not appear on the property deed.[53] The bulk of the lumber inventory was a by-product of clearing the jointly owned land preparatory to growing hops Since this hamlet parcel was not owned jointly, it was, no doubt, recognized that the jointly owned lumber business would only last as long as there was jointly owned land to be cleared.

It was on this land that Harrison North erected one of the last houses to be built in Clarksville. By the late 1850's he was a man of considerable wealth and importance in the hamlet. Through his hop dealings with farmers and others in Westford he met William O. Ashley, a stonemason. Ashley had moved to Westford shortly after 1850. Over the next twenty years, his handiwork was seen throughout the town. The stonework of the foundation for his house, which was built in 1869, shows exemplary skill. His skill is also seen in the stonework of the Westford cemetery crypt. This structure was built in 1871 when Ashley was president of that association.[54] In addition to working as a stone mason, he was a noted builder. It was in this capacity that North hired Ashley to build his house in Clarksville in 1859.

The house North had built stood out as one of the most stylish homes in the hamlet at the time. It was built following many of the standards of the Italianate fashion. Typical features of this architectural style were low-pitched roofs with overhanging eaves supported by prominent, decorative brackets. Windows were tall and narrow. The main section of the house was usually square and blocky, capped with a cupola or square tower. Harrison North's house encompassed all of these features. On the five bay front façade was a well-proportioned Doric styled Greek Revival portico. The house was capped with a square cupola, which helped accentuate the verticality of the overall appearance, making the structure seem very tall and stately. This house, though, combined details that were new and fashionable with a basic house design that was familiar. The overall symmetry was indicative of the Federal style. The portico and heavy frieze were Greek Revival embellishments. In many ways it was a house of Italianate details grafted onto Greek Revival modifications of a Federal structure. It was a vernacular interpretation of the Italianate ideal.

The interior of the North house was as striking as the exterior. The front foyer boasted a sweeping circular staircase designed and built by Daniel Green. In 1859, Green was already 55 years old and had built two other circular staircases in Clarksville. The first was in the Briggs house, which was on the Whiteman Hill Road leading out of Clarksville toward Westford. This house stood on the opposite side of the street from the academic school and had been constructed by George L. Briggs sometime after he purchased this parcel from Alfred G. Cross in 1844 for $75. It stood as a fine, fully developed Greek Revival structure with an asymmetrical central block flanked by two matching wings. Heavy exterior moldings coupled with newer style six over six, large pane windows gave the house a modern look when it was built. The other staircase was in a house on the Cooperstown Road leading out of the hamlet toward Cooperstown.[55] However, the staircase Green built for the North house stood out as his masterpiece. Its graceful lines and sweeping banister made this foyer a sight of almost unparalleled beauty in Clarksville architecture. In many ways, the construction of this house was Harrison North's crowning achievement. It stood out as a magnificent piece of architecture in the hamlet.

The large amounts of money men like Harrison North and Moses Brown were making through agriculture only bolstered the rural economy which fed the other professions and businesses in Clarksville. The prosperity of the hamlet, after all, was built largely on the prosperity of the surrounding farmers. It was only through the needs of these farmers for myriad products and services that businesses were able to form a solid foundation and flourish in Clarksville. George Clarke had known this would be the case in the 1790's when he noted that this crossroads would make a good spot for a tavern or store. Joshua Pinney brought form to that vision when he started renting Clarke's house to use as a tavern. Opportunity then led Pinney to open his store and found many of his other enterprises. By the mid-nineteenth century, the surrounding agricultural output had become a solid base for a nearly self-sufficient network of businesses and services to flourish in Clarksville.

One of the more crucial services in the hamlet was medical care. This need had been filled largely by Dr. Ely since the early part of the century. In 1840, when Dr. Metcalf returned from Owego with his wife, Anna Maria, and their two young children, Charlotte born in 1836 and George Washington born in 1837, he too launched a medical practice. At this time the population of Clarksville and the surrounding area was sufficient to support both doctors. Shortly after his return to the hamlet from living in Owego, Metcalf purchased Benjamin North's tavern on the Long Patent Road for $2,500.[56] Unlike this house's two previous occupants, the Metcalfs did not operate a tavern, instead this magnificent building returned to the use George Clarke had initially envisioned in the 1790's; a fine country home. Metcalf operated his medical practice from a small office he had built on the front lawn of his home. This building was a miniature of the fine Greek Revival buildings then prevalent in much of the county.

Azel Metcalf's son, George Washington, chose to follow in his father's footsteps and become a doctor as well. Accordingly, he embarked on his course of study. In 1855, he entered New York University Medical College in New York City where he spent two years, graduating in 1857. The next year father and son formed a partnership to practice medicine in Middlefield out of Azel's office in Clarksville. Three years after launching their partnership, on 9 January 1861, in a service conducted by the Reverend Ingraham Powers, George Washington Metcalf married Nancy Wickham. She was the daughter of Stephen and

Irene Wickham, who had purchased Daniel Cummings' house on the Long Patent Road in 1841 for $200. Stephen served as a justice of the peace in Middlefield in the 1840's and as postmaster for Clarksville for one year in 1861. As a girl, Irene had attended the academic school taught by George Washington Johnson. She was also the sister of William Shipman, who was running a tannery in the hamlet.[57]

The same year that George Washington Metcalf formed his partnership with his father, another young man embarked on a medical career in Clarksville. Jeremiah B. North was born in the same year as Metcalf, and, like Metcalf, he had to wait until his twenty-first birthday before New York State would allow him to practice medicine. He was well educated and studied medicine under Dr. Minzo White of Cherry Valley for five years. During this time he also attended lectures in the medical college at Castleton, Vermont, receiving his degree in 1856. Unfortunately, North was denied the opportunity to build a career that was afforded to Metcalf. He died at his father's house in Clarksville on 30 October 1858 after contracting black diphtheria from a family in the nearby hamlet of South Valley who were afflicted with the disease.[58]

Jeremiah's father, Harry, was the son of Benjamin and Waity North. This Benjamin North was the cousin of the Benjamin North who owned and operated the tavern in town. Harry North had been born in 1811 and was the cousin of Harrison North.[59] Harry lived in a small house across from the Ely residence. This house stands out for the strikingly delicate Federal style front door surround, which is noteworthy for its little fans carved in the corners of the entablature. Given the location of this house it is possible that, as with Metcalf, Jeremiah studied under Ely.

As the 1850's began it is probable that Dr. Sumner Ely was looking forward to retiring from his medical practice and no doubt looked on fondly as Azel Metcalf began to care for more and more people in and around Clarksville. Certainly his other business interests were also taking their toll on him. Most notably, his partnership with Alexander Murray in the distillery became a large millstone around his neck. By 1851 the partnership of Ely & Murray had become indebted to Sumner Ely for $2,400 through various notes and advances of cash. Further, Alexander Murray was personally indebted to Ely for another $1,000. It became obvious to Ely that the partnership was completely incapable of discharging this debt when these notes would start becoming due in July of 1851. Therefore, Ely sought to dissolve the partnership and force a sale of its assets to cover these debts. Accordingly, on 14 July 1851 the partnership of Ely & Murray gave over to Anson C. Parshall, as assignee, all the land and assets of the firm to be sold.[60]

The bulk of the assets of this partnership was tied up in a thirty-six-acre parcel of land that was located behind the Baptist burying ground, on the road leading out of the hamlet toward Pleasant Brook, and behind the houses which had been built along Whiteman Hill Road leading out of the hamlet toward

Westford. After these house lots were subtracted from the parcel, the land was approximately thirty acres. This plot of land sold to Harrison North and Moses Brown who, no doubt, leased it out for the growing of hops like so many other of their parcels. They paid $450 for this land, hardly enough to cover the debts of Ely & Murray. By the terms of the insolvency filing, Alexander Murray would be liable to take a note "for seven hundred and fifty dollars or thereabouts payable to the order of Sumner Ely . . ."[61] This was a most unfortunate conclusion to their partnership and friendship.

Although Ely may have been eager for retirement, he remained practicing for several more years. As a leading physician in the area he necessarily invested in new equipment for his practice. One such piece of equipment was a "turn-key." This was used for the extraction of teeth since doctors also served as dentists in small communities. A first hand account of this device as used by Ely describes the procedure. This device had a hook which would be hitched to the tooth to pull it in one direction, by disconnecting the key and removing a pin the hook would then pull in the other direction until the tooth came free.[62] Although this was excruciatingly painful, people had relatively few other choices.

It was only six years after these events, just before Jeremiah North obtained his medical license, that Sumner Ely departed this world. In January of 1857 he suffered a fall, which led to an inflammation of his brain. During his last days his family was in attendance, three of his four sons having traveled from distant parts of the state to be in Clarksville. He died on 3 February, thus ended a long and fruitful life in the history of Middlefield and, indeed, Otsego County. His funeral in the Baptist church was largely attended even though a heavy snow followed by a drenching rain had fallen making roads nearly impassable. The Reverend Battin delivered what has been described as "an eloquent and impressive address." So deeply was Ely's passing felt that all businesses in the hamlet were closed. Dr. Jenks S. Sprague summed up the feelings of the community when he wrote:

> *His death, even at this advanced period of life, caused a deep and painful sensation in the entire community. All felt that they had met with a loss that could not soon be supplied. A father and friend and benefactor had been removed from among them. And although he had lived out man's allotted period in their midst, yet so gently had the hand of time fallen upon him that he had neither lost the genial smile, nor scarcely the elastic step of his early days of manhood.*[63]

Dr. Sumner Ely had made a solid and lasting contribution to the development of Clarksville during the first half of the nineteenth century. At the time of his passing he was no doubt proud that two of his sons had become doctors and that he had successfully nurtured the early career of Dr. Metcalf, who would be able to tend to the people of Middlefield. He could rest easy knowing that two newly licensed doctors, George Washington Metcalf and Jeremiah North, would soon be tending his patients as well. He could not have foreseen events that led to the relocation of Metcalf or the tragic, premature death of North.

As these doctors had been building careers in Clarksville, so too were other professionals. It should not be surprising that with the large number of land transactions and the occasional lawsuit, a lawyer would find his way to the hamlet. Leroy E. Bow[64] had been born in Hartwick, the town just west of Middlefield, on 25 July 1819. His father, Edward, had moved to Hartwick from Connecticut after the Revolutionary War. The elder Bow had been taken prisoner by Indians, but had been released through the influence of Benedict Arnold, to whom Edward always referred to as having been poorly treated. Leroy attended the Delaware Literary Institute in Franklin, Delaware County, a county just south of Otsego County. From thence he attended Hartwick Seminary. During the course of his career he was admitted to the bar of New York State, the bar of the supreme court in New York City, and the bar of the chancery court in Saratoga.[65]

Bow studied law with E. E. Brown, who was practicing law in the village of Milford, located at the southern tip of the town of Middlefield. In the 1830's, after Benjamin and Elizabeth North had moved from their house across from Daniel Cummings to the tavern formerly owned by Joshua Pinney, Bow took up residence in their house. He rented this house for several years before finally buying it in the spring of 1848 for $630.[66] He made several alterations to the exterior of the house around 1840, even though he did not own the house at this point. This seems to not have been an uncommon occurrence throughout central New York in the pre-Civil War period. His first change was to add a two-room wing extending from the northern side of the original square, symmetrical Federal style house. This wing, with its separate entrance, served as his law office in the village. He, then, had a stately Greek Revival portico added to the front of the house. This portico boasted a heavy frieze supported by six square columns topped with tasteful, but unpretentious capitals. These two additions testified to the growing prosperity and more cosmopolitan tastes of the hamlet. Bow was making his house both more commodious and fashionable. The Greek Revival style was at its peak and the Federal style in architecture was looked upon as old-fashioned.

Bow took a keen interest in the affairs of the town of Middlefield. He was very actively assisting in the numerous land transactions of the residents. Certainly, his services were sought out by Sumner Ely, when Ely was seeking to dissolve his distillery partnership with Alexander Murray by a forced bankruptcy. Ely and Bow lived next door to each other and it seems only natural that Ely would turn to Bow when it was clear that his distillery was insolvent. This area of the law was of particular interest to Bow, who in 1873 was appointed by the Chief Justice of the United States as register in bankruptcy. Beyond legal issues, Bow was also active in the politics of the town and county. Starting in 1858 he served two years as town supervisor. Later, in 1862, the residents of Otsego sent him to the New York State Assembly.[67]

With his practice becoming more secure, Bow married Caroline Eddy of Milford. As both his family and his legal practice grew, it became necessary for him to erect a separate building to serve as his law office. This building was a simple, vernacular Greek Revival structure next to his house to the north. It had a story and a half, three-bay façade with a front facing gable. The entrance was placed between the front ground floor windows. It was an ambitiously large building for an office, significantly larger than the office Dr. Metcalf built for his medical practice. However, Bow felt a need for space for a legal library as well as private areas within this building for documents. Unlike a doctor who often went to his patients, Bow's clients came to him and he would have to have a more commodious area for this purpose.

In this growing, self-sufficient community, professional men such as doctors and lawyers filled very specific needs for the residents. However, along side these professions were other businesses which served the more immediate needs of both the surrounding farmers and those people living in the hamlet. These included such businesses as tanneries and blacksmiths. Tanning was a smelly and messy operation, and to some degree dangerous. The tanning process also required large amounts of water and tree bark. For these reasons, tanneries were usually set up away from hamlets, or at least on their outskirts, and near creeks and other sources of water. It was a common practice for poorer farmers to peel bark from trees (not always on their property) to sell to tanneries as a way of making extra, much needed money. There were two tanneries in Clarksville operating by the 1850's. The first of these had been started by John Hayden, who sold it to the partnership formed by George Pratt and John Eckerson. As has already been discussed, this was along the Cherry Valley Creek near the Gilbert & Ely mill; a location which provided ample water both from the creek itself and from the millpond used to power the Gilbert & Ely mill. Neither Hayden nor Pratt and Eckerson owned the property on which their business stood.

The other tannery in the hamlet was one being operated by William Shipman and Harrison Bailey. Shipman's father, Samuel, had brought his family from Connecticut to Otsego County in the early years of the nineteenth century. They settled north of Cooperstown in the vicinity of Oaks Creek. In 1819 William and his brother, Robert, purchased forty-four acres from their father for $500. However, in 1841, William moved to a seventy acre parcel of land north of Clarksville referred to as Metcalf Hill, which he purchased for $1,200 from Jonah and Clarissa Griffin. Finally, in 1851, probably after the tannery had already started operating, he bought a village house and lot near the Gilbert & Ely mill from Daniel and Marcia Green for $110.[68] Harrison Bailey's father was Nathan, who has been mentioned as living at the top of Whiteman Hill heading toward Westford and had been a school trustee when George Washington Johnson had been hired to teach the academic school. He was also one of the early leaders in the Baptist church. Harrison attended this school along with three of his siblings, Nathan, Margaret, and German.

The information about this tannery is scant. It is probable that it, like the Pratt and Eckerson tannery, was located along the Cherry Valley Creek. This makes more sense in light of the fact that Shipman's house was located in this vicinity as well. In testament to the dangerous nature of the tanning business, in just the three years between 1853 and 1856 the Shipman and Bailey tannery caught fire three times. On all three occasions the fire was put out with the assistance of residents. However, in about 1859, this tannery caught fire again and was completely burned out. Shipman moved to McDonough, a town in Chenango County to the west, where he returned to farming until he died in 1883.[69] It is not clear what became of Bailey.

Blacksmithing was also a gruelingly hard and dangerous business. Within the hamlet during much of the early nineteenth century Carlton Briggs was one of several blacksmiths. He was born in New England in 1776 and came to Middlefield when quite young along with his wife. He operated a farm for only a few years before moving into the hamlet to open his smithy. Whether or not he gave up farming because he felt he could make a better living at smithing or because he did not like leasing land is unclear. What is clear is that he never bought land on which to farm in Otsego County. It is also unclear when he began operating his blacksmith shop. However, Briggs did buy a village lot from Gilbert & Ely in 1835, although it seems likely that he was living here and operating his blacksmith shop from this location prior to that date. This lot was located on the westerly side of the Cherry Valley Creek, on the north side of the road leading out of Clarksville near the Gilbert & Ely Mill. The idea that he may have given up farming because he disliked renting land is implausible in light of the rental clause in his deed with Gilbert and Ely. In this deed, Briggs was obligated to pay one dollar each year for the natural life of the longest survivor of Daniel Gilbert, Sumner Ely, Elijah Wickham, or Reuben Rich.[70] These last two names appear on this deed because Gilbert and Ely were under a similar lease obligation to them. This deed was merely the continuation of that prior agreement.

Briggs taught at least one of his sons to be a blacksmith. Elihu C. Briggs was born in Clarksville on 10 May 1824 and lived out his days in the hamlet. Indeed, he lived at his parent's house until they died. Carlton died in May 1842 and his wife, Louisa, died in February 1845. Elihu married S. Amanda Cook on 11 July 1847. At some point early in his career, he also learned the wagon-making trade. Until the Civil War, Elihu lived in the house where his parents had lived. In 1849, though, he bought a little over six acres across the street from his house. This parcel came from Sumner Murphy for which Briggs paid $76. It was here that he operated his shop. George Washington Parshall came to Clarksville in April 1853 to learn the wagon-making trade and may have worked with Briggs, although, much later in his life he noted that there were actually three wagon shops in the hamlet at this time, together with four or five black-smith shops.[71]

Elihu Briggs' decision to change from being a blacksmith to a wagon maker was probably prompted, like so many other changes in a person's career, by better opportunities to make more money. Even though an apprentice wagon maker could only expect to make around $50 per year, a fully trained craftsman could make substantially more depending on the amount of work in the area. Briggs must have gauged that there was plenty of work in and around Clarksville to make a better living as a wagon maker than a blacksmith. From accounts in the nearby town of Laurens it is possible to see costs for various types of wagons in the 1850's. For a simple two-wheeled carriage, called a sulky, one could expect to pay about $65. However, an open buggy could sell for about $90 and a two-horse buggy could be as much as $165. Custom-made wagons of various types could be $100 or more.[72] In addition to the construction of wagons, there would necessarily be repair work, which could add substantial income to the business. Further, Briggs' early training as a blacksmith, no doubt, meant that he did not leave that craft in his past. Surely he would have used those skills to fashion the iron work needed for wagons. Briggs probably had available for purchase at his shop paint and varnish for wagons as well. Taken together, a former blacksmith could use those skills while operating a wagon shop to augment income in a business that already had several ways to make money in addition to wagon construction.

It seems highly unlikely that Briggs operated the only blacksmith shop in the vicinity of Clarksville. Certainly the amount of such work available to service both the hamlet population and the surrounding farm population would have necessitated more blacksmiths. By the late 1840's Jordan Follett was operating a blacksmith shop. Initially he sited this shop on the same side of the Long Patent Road as the Methodist church, only a few buildings away and closer to the center of the hamlet. Later, he seems to have moved his shop across the street, perhaps as the business was growing, since by this time he had constructed his Gothic Revival house near where the shop had originally been. As with most people, Follett became a very constructive, respectable member of the community as he matured and his smithy business prospered. By 1854 he was elected as a clerk for the Trustees of the Baptist Society. He had certainly come a long way from the mischievous boy who had carved *J C Follett* in the railing of the balcony of the Baptist church. In addition to Follett, James and Samuel Allen operated another blacksmith shop on the other side of the hamlet. This shop was past the four corners in the hamlet leading toward the Baptist church, but on the other side of the street. It was still operating in the 1880s under the name J. J. Allen & Son.[73]

As these small hamlets and communities throughout central New York were becoming ever more self-sufficient during the first half of the nineteenth century it became apparent that one of the surest ways to building a prosperous career was through the ownership of a store. Joshua Pinney had been keenly aware of these prospects very soon after establishing his tavern in Clarkesville. Benjamin North, no doubt, saw how lucrative this store was and this is what induced him to buy it. The same held true for Benjamin's nephew Harrison in 1847 when he bought half of his uncle's store business. These stores necessarily dealt in the entire gamut of household staples, from foodstuffs and hardware to fabric and tinware. However, the cost of transporting goods across rough roads, often in bad weather, from the place of manufacture to the store could add substantially to their final cost. Well maintained turnpikes and waterways assisted greatly in easing this transportation hurdle for goods, but, as has been shown, these improvements largely bypassed Clarksville. Store merchants, therefore, found their best profits in items that had a high value in relation to their weight, such as butter, maple sugar, potash, livestock that could be herded along by drovers, salted meats, and whiskey. Not surprisingly, these were items which could be produced in close proximity to these stores as well.[74]

Some of the items the store merchant could make easily available to residents were not viewed in a universally good light. The ready availability and ease of transport associated with whiskey led to a host of perceived ills in these communities. Pinney erected his distillery for the profits he could make by controlling the whiskey supply for his tavern and his store. Surely he sold it to other stores as well. It was the reality of these profits that led Sumner Ely and Alexander Murray to purchase this distillery when Pinney chose to divest himself of all things associated with alcohol. Both the ease of transport of whiskey and its ready local supply led it to be a high profit item for store keepers while keeping it a relatively inexpensive product at the retail level as well. The concerns which had surfaced in Clarksville regarding drunkenness in the 1820s and 1830s continued to plague the area. *The Freeman's Journal* of Cooperstown noted two upcoming temperance meetings in the edition of 21 February 1846; one was set for Oneonta, the other for Milford Center. Both meetings invited people from all neighboring towns to attend. The Oneonta meeting even referred to itself as a "Temperance Convention."[75]

The Baptist church in Clarksville had a large contingent of members opposed to alcohol as well. The Pinneys only represented members of that first frontier generation of temperance advocates. In November of 1854 a resolution was debated against drinking alcohol. Within this motion, alcohol used for medicinal purposes was excluded, but even then it was to be in keeping with Biblical teaching, specifically in accordance with "Proverbs 31st chapter and 6th." This same motion contained strictures against dancing and gambling. Although the motion was hotly debated, it does not seem to have been carried. Drunkenness was a problem with very few easy solutions in light of the cheapness of liquor. It became a nearly perpetual problem. Over twenty years later, James Holmes, a carpenter in Westford, noted attending a temperance lecture that brought out a large crowd.[76]

The case of whiskey, though, was certainly the exception to the rule. Store-keepers were viewed in a very positive light for their ability to bring the necessary staples and a few luxury goods to these communities. Many owners of stores would take out advertisements in local papers to let residents know when new shipments, particularly of more exotic goods, came in. It is important to note that central New York was still largely an area with little cash circulating. Out of necessity stores would thrive on the barter system. The ledger from the Manning and Mortimer Gilbert store in Clarksville is riddled with the constant barter transactions between the Gilbert brothers and both farm and hamlet residents.[77] In some cases, store owners would alleviate the lack of specie in these areas through the issuance of script. Note has already been made to the script Joshua Pinney issued as early as 1816. This issuance of script, however, was most useful to merchants who had multiple businesses where this script would be honored. It also served to keep customers locked into doing business at specific stores.

This barter system could mean a double profit for the storekeeper, though. By taking in an item on barter at less than the item's perceived retail value in exchange for another item at its full retail value, the storekeeper made money on the initial transaction. However, he would then sell the original item for its full retail value, thus gaining a double profit. It was through this barter system that the bulk of merchandise made it's way to stores, and an enterprising storekeeper could send much of this merchandise to more urban areas for sale. This was his primary source of cash. However, here, too, he often found that he was bartering these goods in trade for finished goods unavailable in small inland communities like Clarksville.[78] Alternatively, the store keeper could find himself using these goods to pay his credit account with urban suppliers.

Mid-way through the second quarter of the nineteenth century Clarksville had grown to a point that it could support several stores. Competition does not seem to have been fierce even with multiple stores operating in the crossroads at one time. Several of these enterprises have already been discussed, but by the 1840s and 1850's many had begun changing ownership. It has already been noted that in the 1840s Harrison North was in the process of buying out his uncle's interest in his store. Harrison completed this process of buying his uncle's store, which had operated out of the stone building Joshua Pinney had built, in 1851. The North & Brown partnership also ran a store located on the parcel that Harrison purchased in the hamlet from George Clarke. This centrally located building was well-suited for the post office when Harrison North became postmaster in 1853, a position he held until 1861. It was on this parcel that he later built his fine Italianate house.[79]

Directly on the crossroads of Clarksville, on the northwest corner, was the Parshall store. James Parshall Jr. had purchased this parcel of nine perches very early in the nineteenth century and sold it to his son Clark D. Parshall in 1826 for $300. Clark retained ownership of this store until his death in 1889 at the age of 85. However, his son, Anson, took an ever-growing level of management in the business as the nineteenth century wore on. This store was painted the ubiquitous red that was used on more utilitarian building during this time. The process to make red paint was inexpensive and, therefore, became prevalent on stores, barns, and various buildings where it was not deemed necessary to be ostentatious in any way, including the backs of even the most elegant of houses. At some point, Anson's control of the business was such that he was able to bring a partner into the enterprise in the person of Egbert Marks. Marks was a descendent of Benoni Marks, who came to Middlefield with the first influx of settlers after the Revolutionary War. Benoni was a farmer of limited means. He purchased a slip in 1826 when the Baptist church was auctioning slips. However, the price he paid was in the lower tier of slips based on price paid. With Marks as his partner, this store focused on selling dry goods and groceries.[80] Egbert's introduction into the merchant business with Anson would have represented a significant advance in prospects.

In addition to Parshall's store, there were two others located at the crossroads, filling three of the four corners with stores. Diagonally across from Parshall's store, on the southeast corner, was a store operated by John Seymour. This he sold to Luke Swan in 1853 for $650. For some reason, Swan did not stay long in Clarksville and sold his store to Chauncey Yager in 1856 for $900. Even though other opportunities beckoned Swan, he certainly was able to make a healthy profit on his real estate in three years. This certainly indicates that real estate values were being driven up in the hamlet at a rapid rate, which could only mean that Clarksville was becoming quite a bustling community where people saw the chance to accumulate wealth. Yager had as his partner in this enterprise Harry North, Harrison's cousin and the father of the future Dr. Jeremiah B. North. The Yager and North store was noted for tinware, stoves and general hardware. This effort aimed at specialization which was a way for stores to avoid competition and, thereby, allowed all merchants to make a decent living.[81]

The third store to operate on this crossroads was that established by the brothers Barnabus M. and Mortimer Gilbert. Barnabus was likely the junior partner in this business combination, known as Manning and Mortimer, in the sense that he was probably not actively involved in the day-to-day operations of the store. Instead, he was more actively involved with his surveying business. It is through his work in this area for George Clarke that so many fine maps of the hamlet and surrounding area were made. These brothers purchased the lot, one rood and twenty perches, from Stephen and Irene Wickham, in April of 1841 for $775. It is unclear if this lot was developed with any buildings at this point. The seemingly high price of the parcel may not indicate a building present. The price could have had as much to do with the location of the parcel at the crossroads of a busy community and the rising value of land. In the early 1860's Manning was required to take a much more active role in the store business with the death of his brother in 1861 at the age of 47. Seven years later, he purchased his late brother's half of the business from Amanda, Mortimer's daughter, then living in Orange County, New York, for $120. However, Barnabus never seems to have given up his surveying business and as late as 1872 he was still calling himself a surveyor.[82]

The Gilbert brothers built their house next to the store, along the road leading out of the hamlet toward Cooperstown. In keeping with the current architectural style in central New York, they employed classical elements typical of the Greek Revival fashion. The front façade was symmetrical with five bays. There were two balanced wings each fronted with a portico, supported by heavy square columns. The house and the porticoes had a hipped roof.[83] This is notable in that it was much more difficult to construct than a more common gabled roof. The frieze along the eaves of the roof of the house and the porticoes was heavy and bold, again in keeping with the Greek Revival style. One of the most pleasing, almost cosmopolitan, features of the house was the front door surround. As expected, it was heavy and bold, but in keeping with the Gilberts' level of education, they employed a design of the architect Asher Benjamin, whose design had been used in the 1820's for the Baptist church. In this case they took plate 28 from his plan book, *The Architect, or Practical House Carpenter*, first published in 1830. As was so often the case in Clarksville, the Gilberts were showing off wealth and education in the tasteful design for their house, with particular emphasis to the front door and its surround.

Coupled with these outward displays of wealth and good fortune, the Gilberts continued a long family tradition of active involvement in the life of Clarksville. Barnabus seems to have been more inspired in this direction. Throughout his life he was an active participant in the Baptist church as his family had been since its very beginnings. Starting in 1859, Barnabus served as a trustee for the church, a position not conferred lightly on any individual. His devotion to the Baptist Society must have been well known and outwardly obvious.[84]

All three store buildings on the crossroads were strikingly similar in appearance to each other. All were built in the prevalent Greek Revival style, mimicking the look of a Greek temple. They each were of two stories with the second story having a three bay façade, and each was capped with a front-facing gable ornamented with a heavy frieze. The second floor overhung the front portico, which was supported by four heavy, square, austere columns. These columns were almost identical to those used on the Gilbert house and the Leroy Bow house. With broad steps leading up to the portico, the buildings were inviting for people to enter, stay, and converse about topics of local interest. These stores served as local gathering places for both the people who lived in the hamlet, but more for farmers in the surrounding areas where they could catch up on local news. Most of all, though, these places were inviting so people would come in to shop.

In addition to stores there were other merchants in these communities.

Peddlers served the same function as storekeepers. Peddlers, though, as their name implies, brought their goods from either a store or warehouse of some sort and criss-crossed the countryside visiting farms and communities that could not easily get to a store. By 1841, New York State had licensed 302 peddlers. Of these, 227 traveled on foot rather than using a wagon. It must have been a lucrative business since men were prepared to pay the $20 annual fee to maintain their license. The penalties for not having a license were stiff. Peddling goods without a license would get the merchant a $25 fine. Further, he could be charged a $10 fine for simply refusing to produce a license. The overseer of the poor was given the duty of enforcing these regulations. Clarksville had such a peddler in 1853 in the person of Alfred Hayden, who is noted to have had a well-stocked warehouse. By the time of the Civil War, Hayden was joined by fellow peddlers Leopold Rice and Hiram Pitts, all of whom plied the hills and valleys of Middlefield bringing much needed supplies, implements, and, perhaps, some luxuries to isolated farmers who would not be able to get to the hamlet often or conveniently.[85]

Joining these numerous businesses in Clarksville were several hotels. The term hotel was coming more into fashion and served to replace the older term, tavern. Perhaps it was felt that the word hotel denoted a more genteel environment, or maybe tavern was being used for more rural establishments as opposed to those being run in more settled hamlets and villages. It has been noted that by 1842 the tavern established by Joshua Pinney, then sold to Benjamin North, ceased operating as a tavern when the Metcalf family purchased it. It is unclear what motivated North to sell his tavern. It could have been as simple as a desire to retire from business, which makes sense since he was selling his store at about this time to his nephew, Harrison. Of course, it could have been his recognition that competition in the tavern business was becoming too fierce. For whatever reason, once the Metcalfs purchased the tavern from North, there is no indication that it ever served that purpose again.

Hannah Howard continued to operate her tavern under the name Pinney & Howard. Whether or not she referred to this as a tavern or hotel is unclear, although an 1856 map notes the business as a hotel under a subsequent owner.[86] Three years after the Metcalfs purchased the North tavern, Howard sold her tavern business. Nathan Watson bought the business for $220.00 on 7 May 1845. There is scant information about Watson, whose career seemed relatively short-lived in Clarksville. Interestingly, he sold this tavern to Harrison North and Moses Brown in 1854 for $468.53, and the next year Brown bought out North's interest in the building for $500.00. It seems probable that the business partners North and Brown had a pre-existing buy out arrangement.[87]

It seems that North had multiple and varied business interests and was an astute enough businessman to know how to take advantage of opportunities as they presented themselves. However, North kept his primary interests in agricultural produce while his partner, Brown, moved in different directions.

Brown's interests seem to have been grounded more in the North and Brown store and this tavern. It is most probable that Brown started referring to this as a hotel, though, rather than a tavern. He was of a younger generation than the businesses previous owners and would have been more in tune with the updated phrase. Perhaps he was also trying to make a break with the past to build a new image for his business. This business became known as the Central Hotel.

Directly across the street from Brown's hotel was another hotel, which by 1856 was called the American Hotel, and in that year was being run by A. Loyd.[88] James Jones, however, was running a hotel business on this spot starting at least nine years earlier, and, probably even earlier than that. Jones had moved to Clarksville from the village of Milford. He owned a one-acre lot in that village which he sold to John Newell for $325.00 in 1841. He then took this money to Clarksville to establish himself in business as a hotelkeeper. George Clarke sold him the parcel on which the hotel stood for $50.60 in 1847. Previously, Clarke had been leasing this parcel to Caldwell Clarke, who, when he died, was the last named person on the life lease for this parcel. When Caldwell Clarke died is unclear, but Jones' deed to this parcel states that "the estate hereby conveyed being the reversion in fee of the said party of the first part [George Clarke] on and after the termination of the said Lease to the said Caldwell Clarke."[89]

For George Clarke to have sold this parcel for the insignificant amount of $50.60 it seems unlikely that there had been many improvements to the parcel. It would appear probable that when Jones sold his Milford property in 1841, he, then, moved to Clarksville to assume a lease on the property he later purchased. Many of Clarke's leases at this time were verbal. In all likelihood he had the American Hotel built in the early 1840s, which corresponds to the time when Benjamin North was seeking to retire from the tavern business. Jones probably saw this as his opportunity, and one that he used well. Not only did he derive a living from this hotel business, he was able to sell the property to Charles Warner in 1849 for $700.00.[90] It does not seem likely that Warner operated a hotel. It seems more likely that Warner was the owner and A. Loyd was the manager or lessor or some other such arrangement.

Moses Brown and James Jones, like so many men previous to them, had found keeping a tavern very financially rewarding, like keeping a store was. With affluence and social standing came responsibility. Accordingly, in 1845 Jones started serving as clerk for the trustees of the Baptist church. Of course taverns came in a myriad of sizes. The common denominator was that they were established on busy thoroughfares. Clarksville could support multiple taverns and hotels because it had been a destination and a large center of business for the surrounding countryside. However, major traffic patterns were bypassing Clarksville. Therefore, as the nineteenth century wore on, if Clarksville was not actually a person's destination, it was easy to bypass it. Most notable among these new routes, was the road on the west side of the Cherry Valley Creek which led from the village of Cherry Valley to the village of Milford via Rose-boom. This was quickly becoming a highway of choice because it was direct and allowed a traveler to avoid crossing the Cherry Valley Creek. There were also several taverns along this route where travelers could stop. Peter Brockham was one such man who saw his opportunity along this route. By the late 1840's he was leasing a building a short distance from Clarksville on the west side of the Cherry Valley Creek to serve this traffic route.[91]

As the people of Clarksville were building these businesses throughout the 1840's and 1850's, they remained preoccupied with the education of their children. The academic school has been discussed in some detail, but this seems to have ceased operation by the 1830's. Certainly by 1834, when the building was purchased by Erastus Sterling for his residence, the need for a new school building was brought to the fore of people's minds. They established their new school on the south side of the road leading from Clarksville toward Cooperstown. This was a short distance from where the American Hotel was erected. This was a small building, having one room and an attached wood shed, situated a considerable distance from the road. This schoolhouse had a remarkable suspended ceiling, which allowed the classroom area to be one open space, without interior supports. It served as the local school until 1875 when a much larger school building was constructed behind the mill complex along the Cherry Valley Creek.[92]

Taken together, these businesses, along with the school and the two churches in the hamlet, paint a picture of a bustling, prosperous community in Clarksville. George Washington Parshall noted that in 1853, in addition to the businesses discussed above there were also two tailoring establishments, one run by Orra Knapp and one run by James Parshall, and two harness shops, one run by Edwin Macumber and one run by George Herdman.[93] All of these businesses were supported largely by the agricultural prosperity of the surrounding area and the rising level of wealth building upon itself within the hamlet by the local businessmen and their families. As is natural, these newly prosperous people sought outlets to show their wealth.

Harrison North's construction of his fine house with its newly fashionable Italianate embellishments was one example of the prevalent avenue to show wealth. Using one's money to build fine houses was nothing new in Clarksville. When a person was not in a position to actually build a new house, though, they could add to an existing house. Indeed, all over central New York, newly prosperous people embellished existing houses by enlarging them and employing builders who could add details in the latest architectural styles. Quite often, as in the case of Leroy Bow, that could be accomplished simply by adding a stylish new Greek Revival portico to the front of an "old-fashioned looking" Federal style house. However, for others, like North, embellishing an existing house was not deemed sufficient to show their new station in society.

Harrison North was not doing anything that had not been done before when he used his newly found wealth to build his new house. More than twenty years prior, other men had taken this route. In three cases, men had used their wherewithal to build stylish new houses along the Long Patent Road and in each of these cases they chose to employ the fanciful Gothic Revival style. This was a style which gained prevalence in America shortly before 1840 and extended through the 1850's. As the name of this new style implies, the models were the great stone cathedrals of Europe erected during the thirteenth to sixteenth centuries. As the Greek Revival style had answered the needs of the new American republic to emulate the ancient Greeks through architecture, taking on that ancient mantle of democratic ideals, so did the Gothic Revival answer the needs of the American people during the mid-century religious revival, known as the Second Great Awakening, thereby emulating the religious fervor that animated the Europeans of the Middle Ages. The Gothic Revival style, as executed in wood through the use of the new scroll saw, was distinguished by gingerbread trim, bargeboard ornamentation, steeply pitched gables, and an emphasis on verticality.

First among the men in Clarksville to employ this style was Orra Knapp, who had a tailoring business. In 1835 he purchased a small village lot from Clark Parshall for an unrecorded amount of money.[94] On this lot he built a one and a half story house with very steeply pitched gables and tall relatively narrow windows complete with drip hood moldings. There was even an asymmetrically placed umbrage, or entry porch, leading to the front door. Along the eaves of the gable there was a wide, pierced trefoil decorative bargeboard. These elements were all characteristics of the Gothic Revival style of architecture as executed in wood. Following Knapp's example in this new style were houses built by Jesse Brown and Jordan Follett.

When Jesse Brown came to Clarksville in the 1840's he started leasing land from Erastus and Hannah Belknap. His lease agreement stipulated the lease term would be for twenty-six years starting on 22 February 1841. Brown would pay $6.65 yearly for the village lot plus all taxes. During the course of the next ten years, he built the second Gothic Revival house in Clarksville. This house was similar to that built by Knapp except that the bargeboards running along the eaves, instead of having a complex and pleasing pierced trefoil design, had a more coarse, sawtooth design. In 1851, Brown sold this house and its accompanying lease to Robert W. Taylor for $1,100.00. Taylor had been living on the edge of the hamlet across from the Gilbert and Ely Mill on a lot he was probably leasing from George Clarke since there is no record of him purchasing other property in the hamlet. He sold his Gothic house to Henry Guy four years later at a loss of $375.00.[95] There is no record to explain what prompted Taylor's sale at a loss.

Guy had been an active member of the community for quite some time. In 1849 he was elected to the first of several three-year terms he served as a trustee for the Baptist Society. The terms he served ran in conjunction with terms being served by Daniel North.[96] This property that Guy purchased continued to be subject to the original lease terms. It was not uncommon for even quite prosperous people during this period to buy a house that was built on a leased parcel of land. As this lease shows, ownership of the house was held separately from ownership of the actual land. This was not an uncommon occurrence during this period.

The third house in this style was built by Jordan Follett on forty perches of land he bought from North and Brown near the Methodist church. He purchased his lot in 1852 for $285 and built perhaps the most simple of the three Gothic Revival houses.[97] The exterior had a very similar façade as the other two. However, the windows were less narrow and the bargeboard along the eaves was even simpler and less delicate than that of the Brown house. The result was to make a house that should have appeared light and tall, to instead appear more heavy and squat. Clearly the two houses built after Knapp's fine example represented attempts by Brown and Follett to emulate Knapp and his architectural choice. Knapp was the most successful financially of the three, and was able to afford to execute this style in its best rendering in Clarksville.

Outlets for displays of wealth were not limited to such ostentatious and flamboyant items as new houses and house alterations. The mid-century saw a proliferation of newspaper advertisements devoted to new products aimed at filling hitherto unknown needs. Numerous examples from *The Freeman's Journal* serve to demonstrate where this affluence was being channeled. J. Russell advertised in 1839 that he had just received an extensive array of goods from New York City. Among this shipment were such things as gloves, hosiery, parasols, lace, satin, scarves and ladies cravats, French crape, and taffeta. Beyond items suited for personal adornment were such things as table linens, *piano forte* covers, looking glasses, china, and glassware. Items catering to people's vanity increased with growing prosperity. In 1846 P. E. Johnson was advertising that at his store in Cooperstown there was an assortment of perfumes for sale. By the 1850's there were advertisements for products which restored hair, freshened breath, and enhanced one's complexion. The local population was certainly past being entirely concerned with the basics of life.[98]

The people of Clarksville were not so self absorbed that they neglected to improve their hamlet. In fact, they used their prosperity in concert to make Clarksville as stylish as other neighboring communities. The most obvious and long-lasting contribution these people made was the addition of a new clock to the Baptist church tower which overlooked the hamlet. In 1852 the Van Riper clock factory in Cazenovia, New York delivered a new clock to the Baptist church. Austin Van Riper was born in Cazenovia in 1825 and lived out his days there. He entered the tower clock-making business under Jehiel Clark Jr. sometime before 1850 and he went on to become one of the most prolific tower clock designers in nineteenth century America. His firm hired Jonah Moor to travel throughout New York State selling tower clocks. Cooperstown acquired a

Van Riper clock in 1850 and this may have prompted the people of Clarksville to contract with Van Riper for a clock of their own shortly thereafter.[99]

Van Riper clocks quite often had design changes every year so it became easy to date these devices. The clock that was brought to Clarksville was of a design distinct to 1852. It had a cast iron frame with a "straight line architectural and Gothic design." Once installed in the Baptist church, the multiple clock faces were seen from the front and two sides of the church. Along with the new clock came a bell. The bell was fashioned by the Meneely Bell Foundry in West Troy, New York. The Van Riper and Meneely firms worked together on many such clocks, quite often one firm would refer business to the other firm.[100]

By the middle of the nineteenth century the people of Clarksville could be very proud of the state of their community and the level of self-sufficiency it had gained. Outward displays of prosperity were not only evident in the adornments both personal and architectural, that people used, but also in the ability to meet all of a person's basic needs. Indeed, by this time, the people in and around Clarksville could purchase anything they needed in the hamlet. The necessity to travel to neighboring communities for finished goods had nearly completely disappeared. Further, the rising level of wealth being created in Clarksville by these businessmen and their families was leading to a desire for ever more luxurious products. This need too was being served by the local businesses. By the mid-nineteenth century, for the first time, Clarksville represented a self-sufficient central New York community. This level of self-sufficiency becomes even more obvious in hindsight. Clarksville saw no significant new construction within its boundaries after the Civil War with only the notable exception of a new schoolhouse which was built in 1875. Simply stated, by the time the Civil War erupted, the hamlet had all the businesses and services needed or desired by its inhabitants.

Chapter Six

AN ABSTRACTION CALLED WAR

The attack on Fort Sumter in 1861 was met with universal indignation and an outpouring of patriotic fervor throughout central New York. With war imminent it was confidently predicted that this would be a conflict of short duration. The Union army would be able to subdue the southern states quickly and life would remain only indirectly affected in much of the North. As the war entered its second year, though, it became clear that victory, if it came, would not be swift. It was not until President Lincoln instituted a draft that a very real and direct impact was felt on the inhabitants of many Northern states. For the first time in its history the United States would force families to give up members to take up arms. This impact became rather more profound in New York since it was perhaps the most populous state and would be called upon to give the most men. When the draft was implemented, authorities in Washington, D. C. would find it to be only a qualified success. Conscription represented to many central New Yorkers of independent Yankee stock a deprivation of freedom of choice and an interference with the normal course of life.

It must be remembered that war, until quite recently, was not an event that had a direct impact on people unless they lived close to the military campaigns. Men left their families to serve and while many came back horribly wounded and disfigured, many more did not come back at all. However, unless families had a member serving, the war was little more than an abstract idea, a distant conflict. For the vast majority of people in central New York, even though New York gave the most men to the Union Army, the Civil War was not an event with which they had direct contact. Unlike parts of the south where armies battled, fields and houses were burned, towns and villages were pillaged for supplies, and civilians were caught in the cross currents of struggling and desperate armies, the people of the North remained immune to the direct horrors of the war. Their awareness of the conflict was in-depth and unavoidable through newspaper reports and letters from soldiers to family members and friends. This notwithstanding, there were no pictures of carnage on the field and to many people casualties were only numbers printed with other news in the papers. The only depictions of battles were sanitized drawings and sketches.

On the home front life went on as before. People voiced their support or opposition to the war and the president's policies, women knitted socks, gloves, and other items for soldiers, and merchants shipped vast supplies to the Union Army, but these actions were taken at a distance from the gruesome carnage. People in central New York did not see the ravages of war. In most ways it was an abstract idea. It was a conflict in a distant region that the vast majority of people in Otsego County had never visited. There was little first-hand knowledge of the southern states or its antebellum lifestyle. What there was in Otsego County was a growing repugnance toward the institution of slavery, an institution long abolished in New York. This led to the feeling, after the war erupted, of a sense that justice was on the side of the North. These were only ideas. They were ideas discussed in the warmth and comfort of homes that were in no danger of destruction by virtue of being in the path of a military campaign.

Opposition to slavery in Otsego County in general and Middlefield specifically was not new. Sumner Ely's vocal opposition to the spread of slavery in the 1830's has already been discussed. As the slavery debate became ever more divisive, many people in the North sought to actively assist runaway slaves as best they could. The legal impediment to such assistance was a constitutional provision adopted by the nation's founders which allowed slave owners to recover runaway slaves in non-slave states. This provision was aided by the Fugitive Slave Law that Congress passed in 1793. Under these legal provisions, a person from a slave state could claim ownership of a Negro who had "fled" to a non-slave state with very little obligation to prove ownership. Tempers were further inflamed in the North when the Supreme Court, under Chief Justice Taney, voided all state laws that attempted to make slave owners prove ownership of a Negro as a slave before they could be removed from a non-slave state. The 1842 decision in *Prigg v. Pennsylvania* was viewed as a frontal assault on Northern abolitionist efforts to place limits on the seizure of Negroes, both legally free and runaway slaves, in non-slave states.[1]

The laws notwithstanding, abolitionists in the North disregarded these legal strictures. Many otherwise law-abiding citizens actively assisted runaway slaves by use, most notably, of the Underground Railroad. However, many more people quietly assisted Negroes to escape north to Canada. So rapid was this flight, that during the 1850's the Negro population of Ontario, Canada had doubled to eleven thousand. One case in Westford, just east of the hamlet of Clarksville, is illustrative. In May of 1854 a Negro "who represented himself as a fugitive slave who had made his escape from his master in Virginia" had made his way to that small community. When officers arrived in the community to apprehend the fugitive, the local population rescued him and gave him money to make his way to Canada. In the words of *The Freeman's Journal*, these people in Westford were "determined to cheat the Fugitive Slave Law out of a victim."[2]

With passions raging over this issue, it is not surprising that people from the North greeted the onset of the Civil War with patriotic fervor. This despite that fact that many, less informed farmers who had little access to news reports, had little inkling that war between the states was imminent. Many men, though, enlisted during the first year of hostilities, both in support of the Union, but also because military pay compared well with local farm wages. In 1860 a laborer on a farm in Otsego County could hope to make about $200 per year. Five years later that same farm worker could hope to make about $300 annually, perhaps a little more during the busy summer season. This inflationary increase in farm wages was due to the huge need for foodstuffs to feed the Union forces. The Union Army was offering a $200 bonus in 1862 to simply sign up for service for three years. Additionally, a soldier would receive $13 each month. Even though this seemed a small monthly pay, Colonel Silas Burt, the Assistant Inspector General of the New York State National Guard, pointed out that this was in addition to, "food, clothing, quarters and medical attendance."[3]

Coupled with a soldier's pay, many small communities offered financial assistance to a soldier's family. Cooperstown stood out as an example when, in May of 1861, a subscription fund was started for this purpose. In advertising this fund, *The Freeman's Journal* stated that, "If we have those among us who desire to enlist under the Stars and Stripes at this time, the Citizens of Cooperstown will not be backward in subscribing aid toward the support of their families during their absence."[4] Clearly people understood how financially ruinous it could be to many farmers and poorer laborers to have the male bread winner enlist.

Although it cannot be doubted that men flocked to the aid of the Union out of a deep-seated sense of loyalty to the nation, it cannot be ignored that financial inducements and the widely held belief that this would be a short conflict played a role as well. Certainly the signing bonus, military pay, and civic-sponsored aid all sounded enticing when newspapers like the *Oneonta Herald* were predicting that the war would be "concluded within a year" with the rebellious south "crushed out."[5] This is not to impugn the sentiments of those who served. However, it does point out that there were more considerations to serving than simply patriotism. Why else would the Union need to offer such a generous signing bonus? Further, men must have weighed the likelihood of being mortally wounded during a short war against the quick financial rewards. Obviously, the shorter the war, the less likely would be the chance of grave suffering. Finally, by early 1862 the extreme carnage of the war was unknown and men with horrific disfigurements had not returned home yet.

Many communities hosted patriotic gatherings where speeches were made to stir men to enlist. Westford hosted one such gathering in the summer of 1861 which was attended by many men from the surrounding area, including Clarksville. Quite often men forgot all other considerations as they signed up for service, and, in many cases, later regretted their decision as sombre reality dawned over them. On the walk home after one such gathering where he had enlisted, Henry Conklin considered what he had done and "almost repented signing the paper." Upon telling his wife of his actions, all she could do was cry as she looked at their children.[6] One can only wonder at her grief thinking of possibly losing her husband and caring for their three young sons alone.

During the early months of the war, Dr. George Metcalf of Clarksville decided to join the Union efforts as a surgeon. It had only been a few months previous to this that he had married Nancy Wickham. After passing a qualifying examination, Metcalf received his regimental commission. Accordingly, he reported for service in Cherry Valley where a volunteer regiment was being formed around the 39th New York Militia. Metcalf was given the position of "Surgeon of the Regiment and Examining Surgeon of the post." In January of 1862, with only a partially formed regiment in existence, orders came to leave Cherry Valley for Albany. Upon arrival this militia unit was divided between the 76th New York Volunteer Infantry and the 3rd New York Artillery. Metcalfe, who had added the final "e" to his name in Cherry Valley, accepted the position of Assistant Surgeon with the 76th Regiment.[7]

Metcalfe's unit made its way to Fredericksburg, Virginia by July of 1862. It was here that the surgeon of the unit, Dr. J. D. Nelson was required to resign his commission due to poor health and Metcalfe was promoted to Surgeon of the 76th Regiment. Civil War camp life was not always pleasant and conditions were at times unsanitary. Metcalfe contracted malarial intermittent fever and chronic diarrhea which resulted in health problems that afflicted him for years. In the late summer and early autumn, this unit underwent a series of forced marches and skirmishes as the advancing armies positioned themselves for battle.[8]

The summer of 1862 made it clear that this was not going to be a short war. The Union defeat at First Bull Run in 1861 was followed by ghastly casualties at Shiloh and George McClellan's failure to capture the Confederate capital at Richmond. Faced with dwindling ranks, President Lincoln, in July 1862, called on governors in loyal states to raise 300,000 men. Families made difficult choices during this time. The Wood family near Middlefield Centre decided it would be best for all three sons, James, John, and Henry, to enlist together at this time. The hope being that the three men could help keep each other safe. Many years later Henry Hilton Wood remembered that time in his life clearly.

> *Father and my brothers James and John came to see me and wanted me to enlist, as Lincoln's second call for 300,000 more volunteers had been issued. They thought it would be better for the three of us to go together. I went home with them and on the 12th day of August, 1862, we three brothers enlisted in Co. E. 121st Regiment Volunteer Infantry of New York.[9]*

In support of Lincoln's call for these additional men, many towns sought ways to raise additional funds to entice these men. The usual amount in central New York seemed to have been $25 for each man who enlisted. On 9 August 1862, one day after the town of Otsego, the town of Middlefield had a meeting to consider such an idea. The committee which had been charged with getting volunteers to fill Middlefield's quota, led by C. F. Allen, met at the Presbyterian chapel in Bowerstown, a small hamlet of Middlefield very near the village of Cooperstown. At this meeting Benjamin Pierce moved that the town borrow up to $900 to pay thirty-six men $25 each to enlist. The town of Otsego's resolution called for the same bounty to be paid for at least fifty men who answered the call to serve from that town. This bounty was to be paid in two parts; "one half when the volunteer is mustered into the Regiment and the other half when mustered into the service of the United States . . ." Leroy Bow served as secretary on this committee.[10]

Along with these financial inducements, women throughout the community banded together to knit and sew items for volunteers. As early as June 1861, Mrs. Lyman Foote reported that she had received a "thank you" letter from Colonel J. Lafayette Rider for the supply of havelocks that the "women of Cooperstown" had sent. He expressed his gratitude for "their patriotic efforts in a common cause." These caps, which extended over the back of the neck for protection against the harsh southern sun, were a welcome gift to men unaccustomed to the much hotter weather of the southern states. By the winter of 1862 care packages were being sent frequently by local inhabitants to soldiers in the field. Donated yarn for knitting was being distributed for women to use to make garments as well. *The Freeman's Journal* was frequently reminding readers that the needs of soldiers was great.[11]

All this time, the central issue of the war, slavery, remained divisive in Clarksville. The question seems not to have been whether or not slavery was justified or an abomination, but whether slavery should be contained within a handful of states in the south or allowed to spread into the new United States territories in the west. This was a nuance of the debate over what stance Christians should take on slavery generally. As late as 1862 Clarksville was still wrestling with this debate. In November of that year, Robert Crandall's efforts to inflame passions over the abolition cause had become too impassioned for many in the community. At their meeting on 15 November the congregation of the Baptist church debated a resolution "that the Church appoint a committee to visit R. Crandall to request him to leave off his abolition doctrine or else leave the Meetings of the Church." Clearly, his efforts had become too unsettling to the serenity of the church congregation and may have been driving a wedge between too many members. Voting on this resolution was deferred until the next meeting, although at that subsequent meeting it was not mentioned.[12] It seems likely that a group of people spoke to Crandall and came to some understanding. However, this incident is illustrative of the point that even during the war, the disposition of slavery was not a settled issue.

There had long been a strained relationship between abolitionists and the Protestant sects in America. Many ministers had been reluctant to take a firmly anti-slavery stance for fear of alienating members of their congregations. Meanwhile, many staunch abolitionists were refusing to even commune with people

who were not openly anti-slavery. This nascent schism had led the great abolitionist William Goodell to declare in 1853 that in light of its unwillingness to
take a firm stand against slavery, American religion had become one of the chief
obstacles to abolition.[13] It seems very likely that Crandall agreed with this more
militant stand that abolitionists nationally were taking, while the Baptist congregation in Clarksville was desperately trying to maintain harmony.

As the war dragged on, the early and enthusiastic response to the call to service waned. War weariness set in with the grief and anguish that accompanied
the first large casualty reports to appear in newspapers. This was coupled with
the return of men from the front who had been wounded and maimed. By
1863, war weariness had turned to near opposition to the war effort in some
areas as a result of the 1863 Conscription Act. This act had been passed by
Congress after the Militia Act, passed in July of 1862, proved insufficient in raising enough Union troops. The Militia Act allowed Lincoln to call up local mili-
tias for up to nine months of service to the Union Army. However, it also required all men between eighteen and forty-five to register for the draft. For
these reasons, the Militia Act became known as a "disguised conscription law."[14]

So serious was the opposition to the draft from all quarters that President
Lincoln perceived a danger that it might be ruled unconstitutional. Accordingly,
he instructed his New York born secretary of state, Seward, to visit Supreme
Court Justice Samuel Nelson, then at his residence in Cooperstown. There was
at this time a case in Pennsylvania being presided over by an associate of Nelson's in which the constitutionality of the draft was at issue. The judge in this
case was a Democrat, like Nelson, whose party stood in opposition to Lincoln.
It was felt by Lincoln and Seward that Justice Nelson could be persuaded to use
his influence over this justice from Pennsylvania to rule in favor of the Administration on the draft issue.[15]

Seward was successful in his mission and the constitutionality of the draft
was upheld. However, that did not end opposition to conscription. In Burlington, a town only a few miles west of Middlefield, five men were arrested in August of 1862 for trying to evade the Militia Act and flee north into Canada.
After the passage of the Conscription Act in 1863 opposition increased because
it was felt that the draft unfairly targeted poorer people who could not pay others to do their service for them.[16] It had become a frequent occurrence that
more affluent families would pay poorer men to serve in their stead if they were
called upon to serve via the Conscription Act. Indeed, a song of the time high-
lighted this distaste for the seeming social inequity of the draft.

> *We're coming, ancient Abraham, several hundred strong*
> *We hadn't no 300 dollars and so we come along*
> *We hadn't no rich parents to pony up the tin*
> *So we went unto the provost and there we mustered in.*[17]

A year later, many towns in upstate New York were forced to use bounty money to pay blacks from Tennessee and Kentucky to fill the draft quotas because local men would not. This was prompted as much by opposition to the war and the draft as it was to the lack of men left in many communities. In 1863 Otsego County alone had been called upon to furnish nearly one thousand men.[18] This was certainly a large number for the small, tight-knit communities of the county.

The war took an even heavier toll on the poor in society because military bonuses and pay were slow in coming. Henry Conklin was saddened to hear of his family reduced to begging and becoming county paupers because he had not received his military pay. In fact, he reported that he went for over eight months without receiving any pay.[19] As stories of hardships like this circulated on the home front, it was no wonder that draft dodging became rampant.

Attempted flight to Canada was not the only means of evading the draft. Many men were much more creative. When Middlefield compiled its *Enrollment of Persons Liable to Military Duty* in 1864 there were a surprising number of men who were presumed to be living in Middlefield, but gave their place of residence as another town. Among these were John Camp, Horace Pratt, Philo Thayer, and Charles Wager, who all claimed residence in Westford. However, several men noted other towns of residence such as Thomas Page and Nelson Thayer, who stated they lived in Otsego. What is curious about these instances is the verbiage in the enrollment book which often used the word "claimed" and the curious fact, certainly not lost on John Marsh and Daniel Temple, the enrolling commissioners, that they assumed these men all lived in Middlefield.[20] It is possible that if a man lived on the town line, there might be confusion about which town he actually considered his. It is also possible that men were simply evading by telling the commissioners in each town that they lived in the other town. It is unlikely that commissioners from various towns compared notes.

Many more men simply claimed to be aliens, rather than give a town of residence. These claims, too, were no doubt met with skepticism. Indeed, in two such cases, those of William Fenly and Patrick Kiley, it was noted that, although they claimed to be aliens, they had voted in Middlefield. Of the 575 men who were listed as liable for military duty, 23 of them, or 4%, claimed residence in other towns or alien status. In many instances the commissioners probably had serious doubts about these claims. After all, as members of the same community, these commissioners knew where people lived. For this reason, they found the claim of Henry Brown acceptable. He claimed his occupation as "daguerrean" and his residence to be Norwich in Chenango County.[21] As new as the field of photography was in 1864, a man who claimed this as his occupation would have aroused significant interest and people would have known without a doubt if he lived in Middlefield. Brown, no doubt, made his way across the countryside as an itinerant photographer. Whether or not he reported back to Norwich to register is unknown.

There were other ways of evading the draft. Usually men stated that they had some physical handicap. The most commonly claimed handicap was eye trouble, although surprisingly this is usually noted as "poor eyes" rather than actual blindness. It was much easier to claim something as vague as "poor eyes." There were cases of men in central New York putting pepper in their eyes to simulate eye trouble. Eight men claimed eye trouble, another eleven claimed some other health problem. Very few claimed health ailments which were easily proven or disproved. Exceptions to this include the cases of Jonah Campbell and Chancellor Snyder, both of whom were missing two fingers on their right hand. This was certainly a legitimate disqualification for military service that the commissioners could easily see. Perhaps the most curious draft dodging attempt was the case of Louis Ismond who the commissioners noted next to his name in big letters "Claims to be a priest." In a town with very few Catholics, this claim would most certainly have raised eyebrows, particularly since most of the members of the Ismond family seem to have been members of the Methodist church in Clarksville. Taken together, slightly over 7% of men in Middlefield found reasons to not be liable for military service.[22]

As widespread as draft dodging may have been during the Civil War, it was not considered honorable, nor was it as common as enlisting. Of all the men who avoided service by either legitimate or non-legitimate means, there were more who enlisted. The vast majority of those enlisting, though, were farmers. This is perhaps because they were the most unlikely to be able to pay someone else to serve their commissions. Nearly 10% of the 575 men who were liable for service in 1864 actually enlisted. This is in addition to all those men who had enlisted prior to this 1864 report and some, who are known to have served, but are not noted as enlisting in this report. Among these men was Timothy Dodge, who was a mulatto and enlisted on 5 September 1864. The percentage of men listed in this report and who enlisted represented a respectable percentage when compared to comparable communities throughout central New York. In fact, for this same period among the Northern states, the percentage of draft dodgers grew to 24%. In many cases, when these men were called up for service, they simply did not show up for their examinations.[23]

There are many reasons why men chose to evade service in the war and do what was viewed as dishonorable by their contemporaries. In most instances, though, it came down to economic self-interest, which was inextricably tied to a man's need to care for his family. To understand more fully the logic in many people's minds it must be remembered that in 1857 a severe economic depression hit the United States. This depression was so harsh that its effects were still being felt in Otsego County as late as 1860. During this time crops prices, that backbone of the local economy, plummeted, wiping out people's savings and sense of financial security. Many farmers, followed by many merchants, had to contract debts to meet obligations. With the Civil War came a period of inflation. Debts contracted during the depression could now be repaid with artificially inflated dollars. This was coupled with the Union's extreme need for foodstuffs to feed the massive army. Farmers throughout the Northern states saw an opportunity to make tidy sums of money if they could remain home and work their farms. Merchants, too, saw an opportunity to profit by staying in their communities with these newly prosperous farmers.

Economic self-interest was coupled with the lack of a perceived military threat by the southern states to the northern states. New Yorkers did not feel threatened by the Confederacy's military prowess and indignation over slavery was insufficient to sustain the home front's fervor for the war in the face of casualty figures and first hand accounts of death. The casualties at Shiloh, over 20,000, and Fredericksburg, over 13,000, seemed an undue price to pay by Northerners safe from the secessionist states. Henry Hilton Wood noted this colossal loss of life when he wrote that, "In a battle near Salem Church our regiment was almost annihilated, especially my company. Out of seventy-seven men only seven answered roll call next morning; the others were killed, wounded or missing. Nine of these young men went from Middlefield Centre; only one answered roll call. My brother, John, was among the wounded."[24] Given this carnage, it can not be surprising that men would chose evasion to service.

Clarksville, like so many hamlets throughout central New York, was touched by the loss of men during the Civil War, but also took part in the prosperity visited upon farmers by the increase in the prices for grain and dairy products to feed the Union army. These notwithstanding, people in the region could only view the war distantly. Direct contact was only felt intermittently through letters and news reports, and, even these, were hard to comprehend in more than an abstract way. The disastrous aphid attacks which reduced the hop harvest by three quarters in 1863 and 1864 were more immediate concerns than attacks on the war front. When the war did end, soldiers very quickly re-assimilated themselves into the life of the community as if the war had only been a brief interruption. Upon his return to Middlefield, Henry Hilton Wood, like many returning soldiers, re-enrolled in school to finish his education. He was shepherded through his studies by his teacher, Emma Marsh. He also joined a debating society, which had been in existence since the 1840's, becoming one of the most talented of its members.[25]

Life for the Metcalfe family went on during the war as it had before the war, even with one of its members serving on the front. About the time George was receiving his commission, his sister Charlotte married Eli William Stone of Owego, a place the Metcalfes knew well. In September of 1862, George learned of the birth of Charlotte's first child. He also was informed of the tragic death of his much younger brother Willis, which was due to a fall. This death had more immediate bearing on the people of Clarksville than did the news reports of thousands of deaths on the front. People knew Willis and the Metcalfe family directly. When the Metcalfes decided to move back to Owego in 1862 to be closer to Charlotte, the people of Clarksville would have noted the loss of their doctor as more tragic than the loss of a battle in a distant war. Luckily for Clarksville, the void created by the loss of Dr. Azel Metcalf was filled by Dr. Erastus Warren, who practiced well into the 1870's and traveled extensively to tend to his patients.[26]

The alternating joy and tragedy that visited the Metcalfe family in quick succession, came to other families as well. In October of 1864, Egbert Marks, Anson Parshall's business partner, married Emma Griffin. This is a noteworthy marriage in that Marks left the Baptist church to become a member of his wife's church, becoming a communicant of the Methodist church. Two months later, Elder Ingraham Powers, the Baptist minister who had married George and Nancy Metcalfe, gave the funeral sermon for Benoni Marks, Egbert's father. Egbert remained a member of the Methodist church until his death in 1868. His widow, Emma, remained active until she was "removed without letter" in 1873 from the Methodist membership rolls.[27]   It is probable that she remarried and left Clarksville as her body was not laid to rest in the local cemetery.

Two months before the passing of Benoni Marks, the Baptist congregation noted the passing of Susan Boyce. Although little is known of this woman beyond the fact that she had married into one of the families that had formed the earliest core of Baptists in Middlefield, the fact that her death was recorded in the Baptist congregational minutes indicates she was a woman held in very high esteem by the congregation. Certainly her passing due to "Cancer of the breast" at the age of 32 would not have gone without notice by many of the women of Clarksville.[28] The monument marking her grave speaks both of her devotion to a good Christian life and her battle with cancer.

Her acts are past her work is done
And she is fully blest
She fought the fight her victory won
And onward into rest[29]

When the Metcalfes returned to Owego, they sold their house to Elihu C. Briggs. This ushered in a period of nearly one hundred years of Briggs family ownership of this house. Alanson Briggs moved in with Elihu and his wife Amanda in 1863, when the two brothers decided to share the house. Alanson paid Elihu $500 for half of the house, which was divided down the middle.[30] During this time, it is presumed, a grand room, subsequently known as the "South Parlor," was added to the house. With a Victorian bay window overlooking the south lawn and a high, stately ceiling, this was the largest room in the house. Access to this room was through the closet that George Clarke had had built in the room where the Norths later commissioned murals to be painted in the 1830's. This closet was a uniquely English domestic feature that had become a general feature of manor houses by the end of the seventeenth century. It was a small space attached to both bedrooms and parlors, and, being very small and enclosed by a door, afforded privacy and warmth for reading and writing. In the case of this house it had been positioned between the chimney-breast and the front wall of the house with a door separating it from the parlor and a window overlooking the south lawn.[31] Apparently, as large as this house was, when it became a shared residence between Elihu's family and Alanson, more space was needed and sacrificing this wonderful closet was deemed advisable in order to access the addition of the South Parlor.

Shortly after the Metcalfes left Clarksville, so too did the last of the Ely family. With the death of Dr. Sumner Ely in 1857, his widow, Hannah, continued living in their house on the Long Patent Road with one of her sons who remained in Clarksville. Adriel, the oldest, and Benjamin both moved to Girard, Pennsylvania where they became physicians like their father. Sumner Stow Ely became an attorney and moved to New York City. Theodore died unmarried in 1869. However, William Horace Ely remained in Clarksville through the 1860's. In 1855 he married Ellen Caryl, who was the daughter of Leonard Caryl, a wealthy merchant in East Worcester, a hamlet in the town of Worcester, southeast of Middlefield. William may have gotten to know Ellen through his brother, Benjamin, who was married to Ellen's sister, Elizabeth.[32]

William was a merchant in Clarksville and probably this provided another tie to his father-in-law, although very little is known about William's business. He was actively involved in politics, as his father, Sumner, had been. In 1863 he was elected town supervisor of Middlefield, a position he held through 1866. William had avoided military service because he had "deformed shoulders." After his mother died in 1868, he moved to East Worcester to reside with his wife's family. Ellen's father had erected an impressive three-story brick house on Main Street in East Worcester in 1841. That was the same year that Leonard was elected to the state legislature. It seems very likely that Sumner and Leonard may have been responsible for introducing their children since Sumner served in the state senate from 1840-1843, which corresponds to the time Leonard was serving in the legislature.[33] Perhaps there is a certain poetic justice in the fact that as much as Sumner Ely abhorred slavery, it fell to his son William to be at the helm of the town's government during much of the war that eradicated this institution from the Nation.

From the conclusion of the Civil War until the end of that tumultuous decade, Clarksville went through another period of change and the departure of familiar faces, similar to that experienced in the late 1820's and early 1830's. Some of these changes were very pleasant in nature. It is surmised that shortly after the war, the Baptists first acquired an organ for their church. In May of 1866 the first mention of singing is recorded in the congregational minutes.[34] The acquisition of the organ at this time is bolstered by a long oral history of the organ coming to Clarksville over snow-covered roads from Springfield. Specifically, Carlton Hinman, who was born in 1898, related stories to this effect, which had been told to him by his grandfather, Julius, who would have been age 23 at the time. By the 1860's this would already have been an ancient instrument. It had been constructed before the Revolutionary War and came from England.

Among those who left during this period, the Metcalfe family was perhaps most notable. The loss of the Ely family through death and emigration has also been related. However, March 1868 saw the Bow family leave Clarksville, an event marked by their names being removed from the membership rolls of the Methodist church. Leroy and Caroline took their young daughter, Addie, to live in Otego, a town in the southwest corner of Otsego County. There Addie later married and the family lived out its days, becoming active members of that community and joining the local Methodist church.[34]

The Civil War was perhaps the most pivotal event in the course of American history after the Revolutionary War. It may seem to be contrary to logic to characterize it as an abstraction to people throughout central New York. That is indeed the reality, though. As wrenching as this war was to the fabric of the union of states, it was neither fought within the bounds of the northern states, nor was its central issue, slavery, directly relevant to central New York. Middlefield residents had shown abhorrence over human bondage for much of the nineteenth century, and Sumner Ely along with other men stood out against slavery, or at least its expansion into new United States territories, which many in the southern states viewed as nearly identical. However, that moral indignation was only an idea and slavery's direct reality had long ago been erased from New York. During the war, the home front functioned much as it had before the outbreak of the rebellion. Life went on. War was a distant conflict reported in the newspapers, not dissimilar to the conflicts which had been reported as raging in Europe and viewed in the same abstract manner. Further, when the war ended and after the celebrations of victory were over, men returned to what they had done before. Re-assimilation into Otsego society was quick and complete.

It would be wrong to slight the sacrifices and service of those men who enlisted. Certainly they rendered a true service to freedom and the preservation of the union in a way that was more relevant to the United States than most other conflicts in which Americans have fought. The large number of families who lost fathers, sons, and brothers in the war were deeply affected by the war and their profound loss. These people would be deeply scarred by their loss. However, the relevance to the safety and way of life of people in Otsego County in general and Clarksville specifically, was not as profound. People in Clarksville knew that Confederate victory would not dramatically change their lives even though it would have meant the ripping apart of the Union. Both the causes of the war and Union victory or defeat were thoroughly understood, but it is hard to believe either was dreaded with the same immediacy in Clarksville as they were in the nation's capital.

A close examination of any hamlet in central New York through the late eighteenth to the mid-nineteenth century necessarily delves into all the component parts of society. One sees great fluidity in society as social *mores* change, based not only on the level of education in a given community, but as economic stratification and diversification occurs. That is, as people are freed from the strait jacket of exerting all their energies to survive in an untamed wilderness, they can focus their efforts on other pursuits. Throughout this region of New York, these vastly divergent levels of economic success led to centers of prosperity and wealth. Usually centered in hamlets and other close communities, people vied with each other to show outwardly their level of prosperity, usually through the architectural sophistication of their homes. Further, whole communities would band together to accomplish the same ends by the beauty of their public buildings, which normally meant their churches in these smaller enclaves.

Clarksville follows this model, and, thereby, serves as an excellent case study of central New York antebellum development. Before the first foundation was laid at the four corners of the hamlet, when George Clarke stood at that point and noted that this would be a good place for a tavern or store, it was recognized that this was a spot that could serve as a magnet for people. This led him to have his excellent house built on that spot. When it was noted that the alluvial lands of the Cherry Valley Creek valley were fertile for growing the vast stores of grain needed to feed a hungry America and a hungry Europe, settlers came racing to the valley to farm. Concurrent with them came trades people and craftsmen. Much was needed. Saw mills, grist mills, and smithy's were all erected in quick succession, but so too were churches, schools, taverns, and stores. These first settlers were in no respects prepared to be self-sufficient, even though they knew they would have to work hard to subsist in a wilderness with few of the comforts of the communities of the Hudson River valley or the eastern states which had produced most of these early settlers.

Before town borders were marked, hamlets began to coalesce. These hamlets formed at locations that usually combined two prime features: a crossroads and a water source. Although it is without doubt that roads were cut to suit the needs of migrants on an *ad hoc* basis, it is equally true that many roads were cut in an almost random fashion to serve as routes from one point to another. In this way, quite often, unintentional crossroads were formed before there was any real settlement at that given location. Where these crossroads formed near a water source, a perfect site for a settlement cluster was formed. Besides the obvious fact that water provided a basic building block for the preservation for life, it also provided a power source for those myriad necessary services that were essential to settlement, *i.e.*, those mills which would churn out lumber for erecting buildings and those mills which would grind grain. This water was needed for the tanning of hides which were vital for clothing as well.

A crossroads provided additional incentives for enterprising businessmen. These would quite often become more traveled routes than single lanes would be, therefore, it became logical to site taverns and stores at a crossroads. In this way, travelers would conveniently stop and lighten their purses. This led to the next step in development, social gathering places. Once this cluster had built itself into a social gathering place as well as a center of business, regardless of how big or how many businesses were set up in those early stages, a certain inertia took over. Business and social activity built upon itself. All this occurred in Clarksville, as it did in so many other places. Even though there were many different permutations and orders in the specific businesses, the basic pattern was the same, and was repeated *ad infinitum*.

The pattern of initial development was quite often similar throughout the region because it was internally based. That is, the needs of the community were met by the community as those needs became relevant to the individual members in that community. Churches were erected as the community grew and either the home of the minister, or some other church member, or perhaps a communal meeting house, was outgrown by the congregation. In this way Clarkesville required a Baptist church in 1825 when the meeting house, used as a church, a town meeting building, and a school became insufficient for their needs. So too was there a multiplication of service businesses. As society grew more than one store, or tavern, or blacksmith was needed to fill the needs of the hamlet and the surrounding farm populace.

This pattern of development began to be divergent throughout the region as external forces came to bear on the hamlet. As a communication network grew and matured through better roads and then canals and finally railroads, certain hamlets grew to villages and cities and, in time infinitely interconnected communities, while others became isolated. Clarksville fell into this latter category. Even though this is a phenomenon which is best seen through the prism of hind sight, it was noted in specific ways at the time. Clarksville became ever more isolated as more major thoroughfares developed on the opposite side of the Cherry Valley Creek, and as rail lines skirted the town. In response, many people left the hamlet in search of seemingly greater opportunities in the path of these transportation lines. Others, either through talents or because existing ties were too strong to leave, chose to stay.

The people of Clarksville found their own unique solutions to dealing with isolation from major transportation lines. Stores began to specialize in certain product lines. This led to a more indirect competition among merchants, many of whom were related by blood and/or strong social ties. Growing populations within and surrounding the hamlet, though, allowed similar businesses and services, which could not specialize to avoid competition, to flourish as well. In this way, multiple taverns, blacksmiths, tanners, and doctors were able all make good and fruitful livings. There was a proliferation of seemingly unlikely business partnerships. Dr. Ely's partnership with Daniel Gilbert to own a mill is only one of many examples. In this way, men from vastly different backgrounds could participate in the overall prosperity of the hamlet in many ways. It allowed people with limited means but necessary skills to band together with men of greater financial wherewithal to found economically rewarding businesses.

Crucial to the financial foundation of Clarksville as a prosperous community was the prosperity of the surrounding farm families. Although it is true that a certain internal momentum could sustain the hamlet's component businesses, this was insufficient without the influx of money and bartered goods brought into the community by the local farmers. Even with only limited amounts of specie during the frontier period, and, indeed, well into the mid-nineteenth century, economic activity based on barter provided a vital link in the financial cycle. Fortunes were made by merchants and professionals in the hamlet often based on the value of farm produce from the countryside. What the residents of Clarksville did with these business profits tells its own story about these people. They displayed this wealth, in its varying degrees, both in outward, ostentatious ways, but also in internal, intellectual ways.

Outwardly these people constructed a fine collection of architectural monuments. George Clarke's house and the Baptist church based on designs by Asher Benjamin certainly rank in the first tier of these buildings. Both of these structures display what was finest about the Federal style as it was transplanted inland to central New York. In an area covered in vernacular interpretations of fine architectural styles, there were some surprises in Clarksville. Notably, the fine tripartite Federal style house of Dr. Sumner Ely, which seems loosely based on a house he certainly knew in Lyme, Connecticut. Finally, of note for its overall beauty, was the Harrison North house, a tribute to the budding fanciful architectural edifices of the Victorian period. This one, being adorned with so many fine Italianate features, make it an overall exceptionally pleasing composition. Lastly, was the appearance of the Gothic Revival, which came to Clarksville in three interpretations, with varying degrees of architectural merit.

Outward signs of prosperity were not only evident in entire houses that were built, but also in parts of those house in terms of adornment. The beautifully pleasing front door surround of the Manning and Mortimer Gilbert house, based on drawings of Asher Benjamin, is worthy of note. So too is the circular staircase in the Harrison North house built by Daniel Green as his finest effort. Men made alterations to these houses as well which served to enhance their appeal. Benjamin and Elizabeth North's addition of the fine mural in the tavern is an exceptionally beautiful example of decorative art. Equally impressive is their construction of a monumental portico stretching the full forty-two feet across the front of the tavern with a vaulted ceiling over two stories high supported by massive wooden pillars.

Inwardly, prosperity allowed the residents of Clarksville to focus attention on pressing social issues of the day. Intemperance and slavery were banes of society in many people's minds. Toward the end of the first quarter of the nineteenth century intemperance was recognized as a problem in society. It led such people as Joshua and Polly Pinney to abhor alcohol completely. It led others, like a group of Baptist communicants to offer resolutions against it. The ease of production of spirits and their inexpensive means of distribution made this a problem with few easy answers. Slavery fell into a similar category. Abolition in New York was accomplished in the 1820's, this was after the institution had *de facto* ceased to exist in Middlefield. The issue for the residents of Clarksville centered around the debate of absolute abolition and the eradication of this horror from the United States entirely or stopping the spread of slavery to new states of the union. This was only an academic question after New York abolished slavery, and remained so even while the Union was fighting a war for its own preservation over this issue. In less grandiose terms, inward displays of prosperity took the form largely of providing educational opportunities for the community's children. A school was erected very early in the settlement stage of the hamlet. When it became practical and sustainable, a select school was set up for more advanced education.

It must always be borne in mind, though, that these early residents of the hamlet were merely people. They acted on the same plane that people in the modern era do. Therefore, even while they were tending to their children's education by establishing schools, or their everlasting souls by constructing churches for the furtherance of the Christian faith, and while their minds were wrestling with the grand social questions of the day, so too were they engaged in business dealings that were at times focused on making the hamlet a better place in which to live, and at other times focused on their individual interests. These individual interests sometimes seemed overly harshly detrimental to other people. When Joshua Pinney sued Reuben Rich over an unpaid store account and had his property auctioned, Pinney, founder of the Baptist church, was behind Pinney the businessman. Likewise the case of Dr. Sumner Ely pushing the Ely & Murray partnership in the distillery to insolvency was Ely the good doctor coming behind Ely the creditor. In other ways, business was business and businessmen sought any way to make money. A perfect example is the seemingly ironic position of Joshua Pinney owning a distillery and marketing a cure for intemperance. These people were just people, and to portray them as more selfless than they truly were is to heap undue nobility on them. They were founders and builders, and they did great things, but they were not perfect and they were not saints.

Viewing the hamlet of Clarksville in the immediate post Civil War era displays the picture of a self-sufficient community. By this point, every business or service a person could need or, in most cases want, was available within the crossroads. Blacksmithing, tanning, and milling were available services in Clarksville, as was tailoring, medical care and legal advice. Multiple retail outlets provided the staples of life and numerous luxury goods for purchase, but these store owners also engaged in bartering to provide an outlet for agricultural and hand crafted items from the surrounding inhabitants. Added to this were churches and taverns which allowed opportunities for social interaction which was so vital to the health of a community. It allowed very strong bonds to form between friends, which became the bonds of blood as people intermarried in ever tightening circles of neighbors.

As a land of steady habits people knew that the steadiness of a good work ethic would lead to a prosperous and happy life. Contentment was to be found in good work and loving bonds of family and friends. This closeness of relation-ships was vital during the period of early settlement when people relied on each other to survive, but it was equally important when the question of mere surviv-al ceased to be the overarching concern. As transportation routes circumvented the hamlet and all one's needs were met internally by the community, people fo-cused inwardly as a group among themselves. This was best exposed when the Civil War erupted, but was only viewed as an abstract, external interruption in Clarksville's existence. It was so in a place that people were happy to call home. A familiar place. A place separate from, but part of, a larger world.

Notes About Map Orientation and Text

The hamlet of Middlefield was laid out on a quarter compass, meaning that the roads of the four corners ran northeast to southwest and northwest to southeast. For ease of discussion in the text, the orientation is rotated approximately forty-five degrees counter-clockwise so that northwest becomes north.

The map key lists that appear with the maps have been taken from the keys included on the original maps shown in detail and in full. Though some editing has been done to make the information uniform, there are gaps and discrepancies in the original numbering and notation of the lists, which has been retained.

Key to *Map of Subdivisions No's 17 & 18 in Great Lot No 12*
The map detail appears on the following page., the full map two pages hence.

House Lots, etc.
1. North & Brown
2. Jordan C. Follett Shop Lot
3. William D. Clark
4. School District No. 1
5. Joel Rowland
6. Leroy E. Bow
7. Henry Guy
8. Edgar Macomber
9. Sumner Ely
10. James N. Parshall
11. Orra Knapp
12. _____ Seymour
13. Benj. D. North
14. Alexander Murray
15. Elizabeth Campbell heirs
16. Ely & Murray Still Lot
17. Charles Soules
18. & 42. Stephen F. Wickham 2 Lots
19. George L. Briggs
20. James Bishop
21. Joseph W. Reynolds
22. Baptist Parsonage
23. Orra Knapp
24. Grave Yard
25. Baptist Meeting House Lot
26. Nathan Watson
27. [Not listed]
28. William Shipman House Lot
29. [Not listed]
30. School District No. 2
31. Mary S. Gilbert
32. James S. Louis
33. L. M. & B. M. Gilbert
34. North & Brown Store Lot
35. C. D. Parshall

36. James Johnson
37. Moses R. Brown
38. Polly Antisdel
39. Charles Warner
40. Nelson A. Green
41. Jordan Follett
42. Harry Van Huzen
43. Robert W. Tay Lot
44. Henry P. Thompson
45. Methodist Parsonage
46. A. Murray Shop Lot
47. Geo. L. Briggs Shop Lot
48. E. C. Briggs Shop Lot
49. S. E. Murphy
50. Anamar Knapp
51. Elihu C. Briggs House Lot
52. Geo. L. Briggs vacant
53. William Shipman Tannery

Lands Conveyed
A. Methodist Church
B. W. J. Campbell
C. Joshua L. Pinney
D. Baptist Church
E. Hosea Cummings
F. Henry Howard
G. Henry Howard
H. William Shipman
I. John Hayden
J. Ebenezer Pratt
K. Henry Guy
L. Henry Guy
M. Martin Reynolds
N. James S. Jones
O. Harry North
P. Daniel Cummings

Barnabus M. Gilbert, "Map of Subdivisions No's 17 & 18 in Great Lot No 12, and a part of Subdivision No 21 in Great Lot No 13, Oothout Patent" (1851). The map key appears on the previous page, the full map on the following page. George Hyde Clarke Family Papers, #2800, Cornell University Library, Division of Rare and Manuscript Collections, Ithaca.

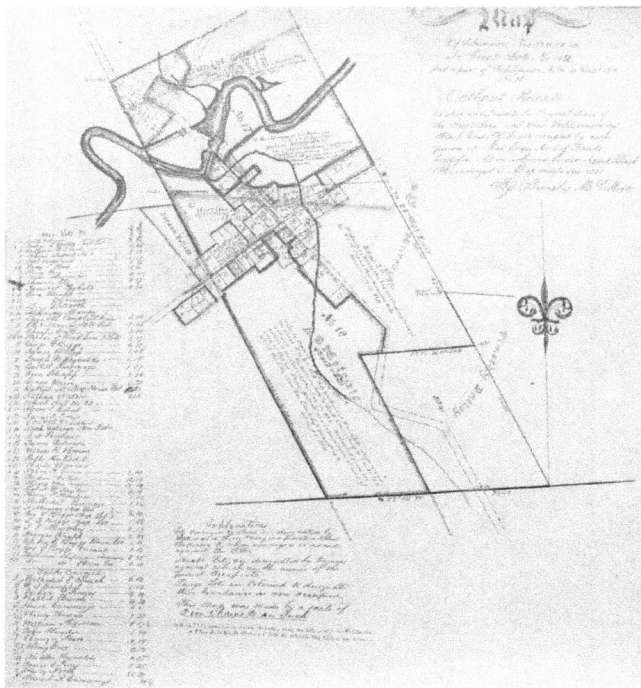

Barnabus M Gilbert, "Map of Subdivisions No's 17 & 18 in Great Lot No 12, and a part of Subdivision No 21 in Great Lot No 13, Oothout Patent" (1851). Map detail appears on the previous page, the map detail key two pages previous. George Hyde Clarke Family Papers, #2800, Cornell University Library, Division of Rare and Manuscript Collections, Ithaca.

Barnabus M. Gilbert, "A Part of Farm No 17 in the Outhout Patent, formerly owned by Gilbert Ely" (1861). Map detail and key appears on the next page. George Hyde Clarke Family Papers, #2800, Cornell University Library, Division of Rare and Manuscript Collections, Ithaca.

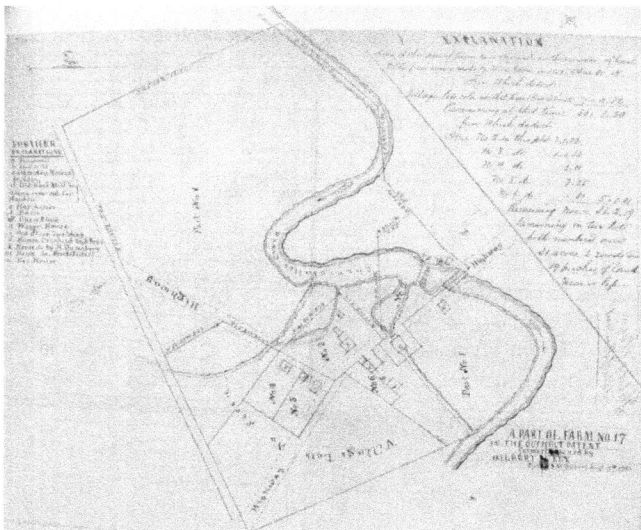

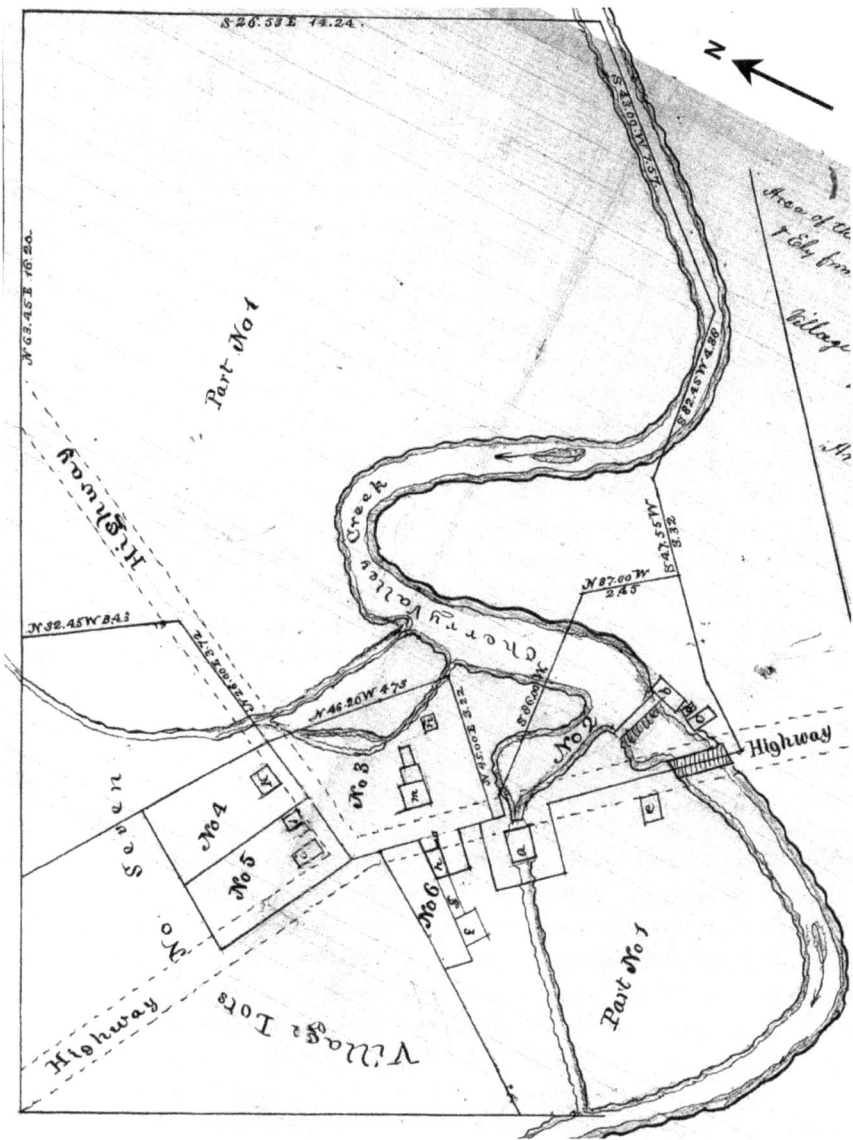

Barnabus M. Gilbert, "A Part of Farm No 17 in the Outhout Patent, formerly owned by Gilbert Ely" (1861). The table below was included on the full map (previous page). George Hyde Clarke Family Papers, #2800, Cornell University Library, Division of Rare and Manuscript Collections, Ithaca.

Further Explanations

a. Flour mill
b. Saw mill
c. Old carding machine building
d. Old bark mill building reserved for Hayden
e. Hop house
f. Barn

g. Open shed
h. Wagon house
i. Old store building
j. House occupied by B. Bray
k. House occupied by H. Dusenbury
l. [Not listed]
m. House occupied by Mrs. A. Gilbert
n. Hen house

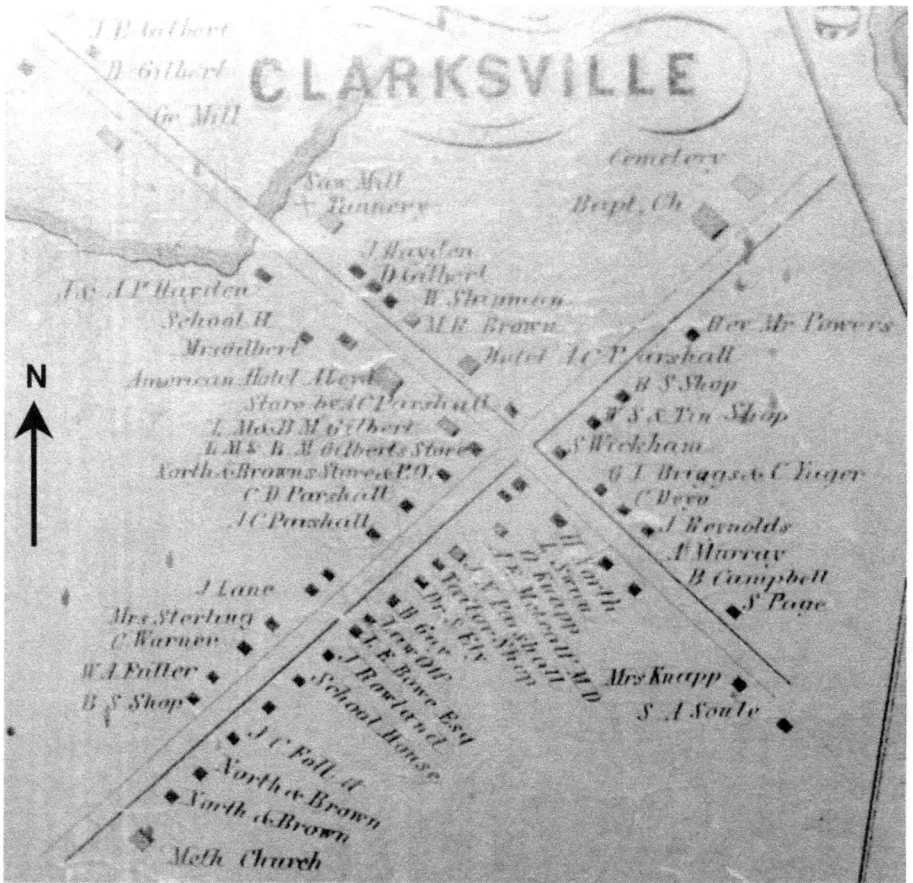

Detail from *Map of Otsego Co. New York from Actual Surveys by C. and R. C. Gates*, (Philadelphia, 1856).

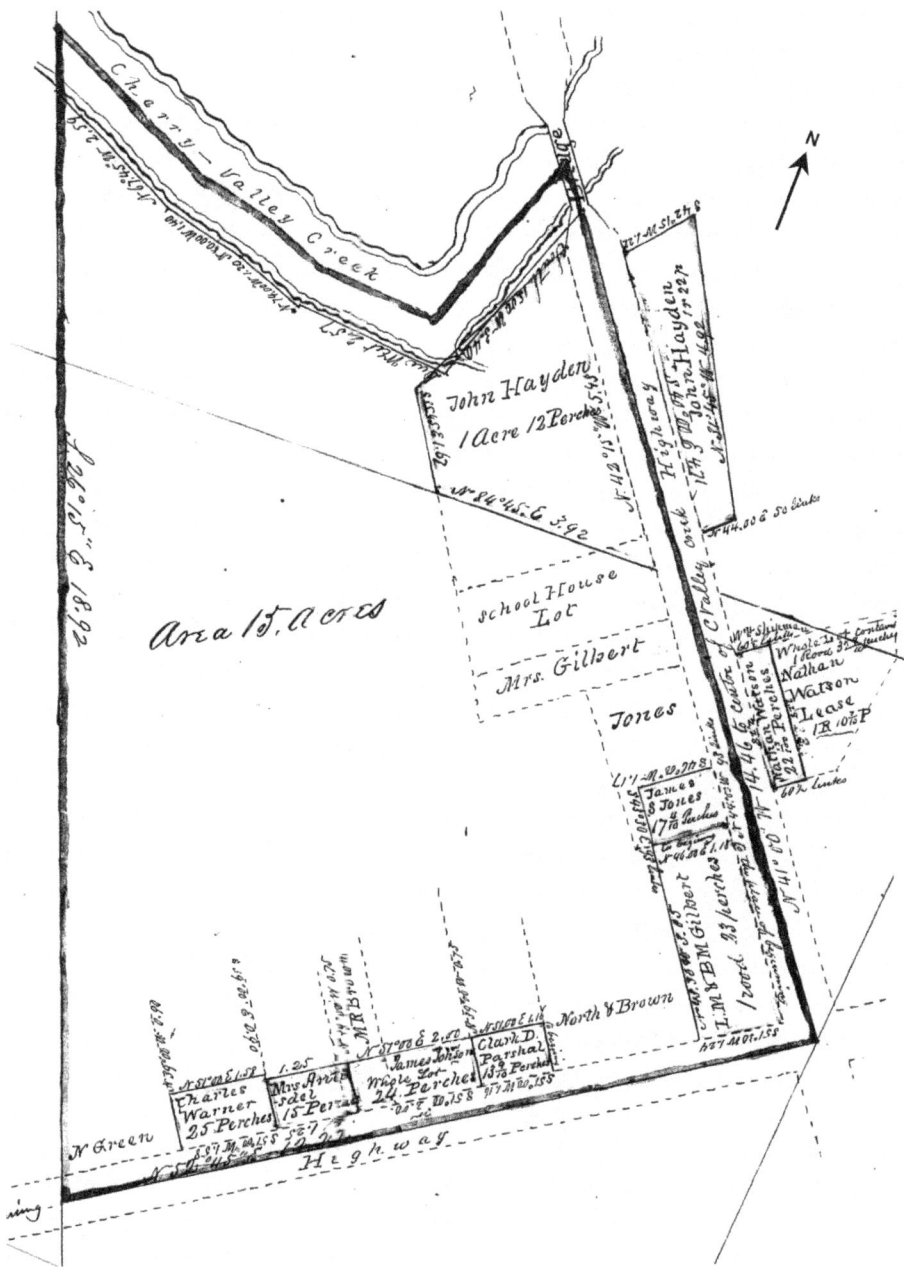

"A Map of a Lot of Land sold by George Clarke to Harrison North," George Hyde Clarke Family Papers, #2800, Cornell University Library, Division of Rare and Manuscript Collections, Ithaca.

Inset of Clarksville, from F. W. Beers, "Town of Middlefield, Otsego Co. N.Y.", *Atlas of Otsego Co. New York*, 1868.

THE KIDNAPPING OF DANIEL MCCOLLUM (1878)

The following is taken from Duane Hamilton Hurd, *History of Otsego County, New York, with Illustrations and Biographical Sketches*, (Ovid, 1978), 184-185.

During this period, and many years later, it was unsafe for women or children to venture out unprotected, as marauding bands of savages were roaming the forests in every direction. On the White farm is standing the barn near which Daniel McCollum, son of Alexander Mc-Collum, was captured by Indians in 1778. The narrative of his capture is as follows:

In the spring of 1778, then but two years of age, he went with his father and eldest brother to a "sugar-bush" located a short distance from the house, for the purpose of eating warm sugar. He soon became weary, and wanted to go home. The others, not being ready to go, showed him the foot-path, and saw him start for the house. He proceeded safely until within hearing distance of the house and near a millpond. His mother and sister in the house, hearing a scream, recognized it as that of the little boy. The mother said, "Run, Kitty; for I fear something has happened to Daniel." She immediately ran to the place from whence the sound had proceeded, but could find no traces of him save a few small footprints near the pond. She went to the sugar-camp, and there learned that they had but a little while before sent him to the house. The pond was drained, and during three days search was continued for the little one, but without success. Mr. McCollum, being a man of influence and property, left no means untried by which information might be obtained. But all in vain. The heart-broken parents were obliged to give up in despair. Daniel in the mean time was being carried on the back of a squaw towards Buffalo, by way of the Mohawk valley. This squaw had been in the habit of frequenting the McCollum neighborhood, several times visiting the house, and was often seen to take the children in her arms in a playful manner. As she was missing about this time, and was never after seen in the vicinity, it is supposed that she had taken him. He was about nine years among the Indians, when he was taken to Fort Stanwix (Rome). From here he went to Albany, and finally to Poughkeepsie, where he was taken by the poormaster and apprenticed to a man named Colonel Hay, who soon after removed to Lake George, taking Daniel with him, and naming him Clinton Hay. While at the lake he was seen and recognized by an aunt, who at once sent the information to his parents. They, however, failed to receive it, but subsequently learned from a lady residing at Cherry Valley that he was alive. Mr. McCollum immediately set out to reclaim the wanderer, and after furnishing Colonel Hay sufficient proof that the child was "Daniel McCollum," he was restored to his father and taken to his mountain home. But oh, how changed! The little prattling boy had grown up in Indian degradation and wretchedness, knowing nothing of civilized life except the little he had learned while among the whites. He spoke three Indian tongues, and upon his return he attended school, but it was with the greatest difficulty that he learned English. He grew to manhood, married, and settled on a farm given him by his father. His long captivity with the savages in a measure incapacitated him from business, and he subsequently lost his property, and to gain livelihood published a narrative of his captivity and life among the Indians.

Middlefield Town Supervisors and Clerks (1797-1877)

Year	Supervisor	Clerk
1797-1802	Samuel Griffin	Thomas Jones
1803-1805	Benjamin Gilbert	Thomas Jones
1806	Benjamin Gilbert	Samuel Griffin
1807	Benjamin Gilbert	Thomas Jones
1808-1809	Benjamin Gilbert	Samuel Griffin
1810-1811	John M. Bowers	Samuel Griffin
1812	Benjamin Gilbert	Samuel Griffin
1813-1816	Benjamin Gilbert	Sumner Ely
1817-1820	Sumner Ely	Daniel Gilbert
1821-1822	Sumner Ely	Ashael Todd
1823	Sumner Ely	Samuel Griffin
1824-1825	Sumner Ely	James J. Rice
1826-1827	Sumner Ely	Lewis Barnum
1828	Sumner Ely	Benjamin Gilbert
1829	John Denton	David Lent
1830	John Denton	Samuel Huntington
1831	Daniel Gilbert	Levi Wood
1832	Samuel M. Ingals	Levi Wood
1833	Samuel M. Ingals	Barnabus M. Gilbert
1834	Erastus Sterling	Barnabus M. Gilbert
1835	Eben B. Morehouse	Barnabus M. Gilbert
1836	Levi Wood	Barnabus M. Gilbert
1837	William Temple	Barnabus M. Gilbert
1838-1839	William Temple	Milton U. Chase
1840-1842	Eben B. Morehouse	John Hayden
1843-1844	Milton U. Chase	John Hayden
1845	Sumner Ely	Everett Henman
1846	Sumner Ely	William Brooks
1847	Barnabus Gilbert	William Brooks
1848-1849	Sumner Ely	George Henman
1850	Richard H. Denton	George Henman
1851-1852	Moses R. Brown	George Henman
1853	George R. Fowler	George Henman
1854	George R. Fowler	Orsemus Reynolds
1855	William I. Compton	Moses R. Brown
1856	Samuel H. Hunter	John Hinds
1857	Samuel H. Hunter	Elihu C. Briggs
1858	Leroy E. Bowe	Fayette L. Gilbert
1859	Leroy E. Bowe	William Brooks
1860	Levi H. Bower	William H. Ely
1861	Elihu C. Briggs	William H. Ely
1862	William Brooks	William H. Ely
1863	William H. Ely	Farrand C. Parshall
1864-1866	William H. Ely	Samuel H. Hunter
1867	William Jones	Jordan C. Follett
1868	William I. Compton	Jordan C. Follett
1869	Anson C. Parshall	Egbert Marks
1870	Anson C. Parshall	Lucien B. Bowen
1871	Egbert Marks	Martin E. Gates
1872	Egbert Marks	Lucien B. Bowen
1873	William Jones	Lucien B. Bowen
1874	Horace M. Purce	Lucien B. Bowen
1875	John G. Fowler	Delos Follett
1876	Fayette L. Gilbert	Lucien B. Bowen
1877	Adriel G. Murphy	John Peake

POSTMASTERS FOR MIDDLEFIELD (1815-1967)

NAME	ACTING PM	APPOINTED PM
Samuel Griffin		01 July 1815
Post Office discontinued		24 October 1816
Joshua L. Pinney		12 December 1819
Sumner Ely		11 March 1835
Mortimer Gilbert		22 January 1842
Harrison North		20 May 1853
Stephen F. Wickham		10 July 1861
Fayette L. Gilbert		26 December 1862
Frederick L. Gilbert		07 April 1879
Henry S. Westlake		12 April 1880
Elihu C. Briggs		16 December 1880
Charles A. North		09 March 1886
L. A. Cossart		18 March 1991
Charles A. North		01 March 1895
Charles E. Hearn		26 November 1898
Rose North	30 January 1945	05 April 1946
Eva E. Morton	31 March 1967	
Post Office discontinued		02 June 1967

After it was discontinued, the Middlefield post office became Rural Cooperstown Branch until 19 June 1976.

Petition For Middlefield Masonic Lodge (1823)

The text that follows is taken from a letter to the Grand Lodge of Free and Accepted Masons of the State of New York from a group of Freemasons in Clarkesville requesting a warrant to start a Lodge. *Source:* Freemasons in Middlefield to Grand Lodge of New York, 23 December 1823, vol. 123 of the Grand Lodge of Free and Accepted Masons of the State of New York Archives, The Chancellor Robert R Livingston Masonic Library and Museum, New York.

To the Right Worshipful Master, Wardens and Brethren of the Right Worshipful Grand Lodge of the State of New York. Greeting

The Petition of the Undersigned, Members of Otsego Lodge and others within the County of Otsego, respectfully showeth, That they are free and accepted Master Masons, that they are at present, or have been, members of regular Lodges; that having the prosperity of the fraternity at heart, they are willing to exert their best endeavors to promote and diffuse the genuine principles of Masonry, that for the convenience of their respective dwellings, and for other good reasons, they are desirous of forming a new Lodge, in the Town of Middlefield to be named "The Widow's Son"; That in consequence of this desire, they pray for letters of dispensation of a warrant of Constitution, to empower them to assemble, as a legal lodge, to discharge the duties of Masonry, in a regular and constitutional manner, according to the original forms of the Order, and the Regulations of the Grand Lodge. That they have nominated and do recommend John J. Crandall to be first Master, Bela Kaple to be first senior Warden and Benjamin Gilbert Jun. to be first Junior Warden of the said Lodge; that if the prayer of the petition should be granted, they promise a strict conformity to all the constitutional laws and regulations of the Grand Lodge - Dated at Middlefield December the 23rd A. L. 5823

Joshua L. Pinney	*Sumner Ely*
Dunham Spaulding	*Ebenezer Rice*
name crossed out	*Charles Soule*
John Hayden	*Elihu Cone*
Smith Murphy	*S. D. Jones*
Whitney Jewell	*Nelson Abraham*
Rice Pratt	*Benjamin Gilbert Jun*
James Murphy	*James Van Valkenburgh*
	Alonzo Bridges
	Daniel Starr
	Prosper Stewart
	J. J. Rice

Baptist Church Pew Auction Results (1826)

Results of the auction of slips (pews) in 1826 for the Baptist church in Clarkesville. From the record of sales as kept by D. W. Bice, clerk. *Source:* Trustee Minutes of the First Baptist Society in Middlefield, Book 1 (1825-1833).

Nos		Dolls. Cts.
Deed 1	To Amos Brown for	33.30
Deed 2	To Allen Brown for	36.50
Deed 3	To James H. Thomas for	39.00
Deed 4	To John B. North &	42.00
	Amos Butler	
Deed 5	To Paul Coffin for	38.00
Deed 6	To Ebenezar Bice	36.00
	Lewis Barnum	
Deed 7	To Joshua L. Pinney for	46.00
	_____ Graham 1/4 part	
Deed 8	To Alexander Cummings	35.50
Deed 9	To J. L. Pinney for	35.00
Deed 10	To Silas Devol for	45.50
Deed 11	To Moses Rich Junr for	39.50
Deed 12	To John F. Marks for	25.50
Deed 13	To John Manzer 1 half	25.00
	James Cummings half	
Deed 14	To Ebenezar Pratt for	27.00
Deed 15	Deeded half to Jewol Valentine	12.00
Deed 16	1/4 to Chester Wetmore	6.25
	1/2 to David Blair	13.00
Deed 17	To Harvey Henry & J. G. Bice	22.00
Deed 18	To Angus Griffin for	31.00
Deed 19	To Benonia Marks for	16.50
Deed 20	To German North for	42.00
Deed 21	To Aaron North for	51.00
Deed 22	To Benjamin D. North for	51.00
Deed 23	To John D. Griffin for	53.00
Deed 24	To Sumner Ely for	77.00
Deed 25	To Ebenezar Tucker for	90.00
Deed 26	To Joshua L. Pinney for	103.00
Deed 27	To Daniel North for	100.00
Deed 28	To Daniel Gilbert for	92.00
Deed 29	To Nathan Bailey &	51.00
	_____ Blair half ea	
Deed 30	To Elijah Rich for	38.00
Deed 31	To John Darling (one half)	39.00
Deed 32	To Erastus Belknap (crossed out)	38.00
	Henry Guy	
Deed 33	To James Murphy for	70.50
Deed 34	To James Pitts for	75.00
Deed 35	To Benjamin North Junr	74.00
Deed 36	To John J. Crandall for	87.00
Deed 37	To Elias Ismond for	62.50
Deed 38	one fourth part to James Van Valkenburgh	57.00
	one fourth part to Isaac Hubbard	
	and the other half to John Hayden	
Deed 39	To Benjamin Evins for	45.50
Deed 40	To William Bailey &	42.00
	Jeremiah Bailey	
Deed 41	To William Shipman for	33.50

Deed 42	To Aaron Brown for	26.00
Deed 43	To Ebenezar Jones for	30.00
Deed 44	To Ezra Allen for	22.00
Deed 45	To Salmon Coats 1/2	
Deed 46	Daniel Clark 1/2 & Sally Hall for	5.00
Deed 47	To John Cheles & Lydia Eglestone	25.00
Deed 48	To John Manzer & Amos ____ half	25.00
Deed 49	To Elihu Cone for	26.50
Deed 50	To Martin Gailor for	33.00
Deed 51	To Jacob Van Husen for	34.00
Deed 52	To Nicholas Hubbell for	34.00
Deed 53	To John Bice for	34.00
Deed 54	To James Parshall Junr for	41.00
Deed 55	To Jonathan Davis for	37.50
Deed 56	To Daniel A. Cumings for	34.50
Deed 57	To James Chace &	40.00
	Smith Murphy	
Deed 58	To Benjamin Lawson for	62.00
Deed 59	To Peleg Coffin one half	40.00
	Henry Bice	
Deed 60	To Daniel W. Bice for	24.00
		2471.25

I certify the foregoing to be a true copy of the records kept by D. W. Bice
Joshua L. Pinney Clerk

LIST OF STUDENTS, ACADEMIC SCHOOL (1827-28)

List of students for the academic school George Washington Johnson taught in Clarkesville. This is for the second term, 12 November 1827 to 15 February 1828. *Source:* Diary of George Washington Johnson, Town of Middlefield Historical Association.

Horace M. Crandall
Elias J. Crandall
Caroline Crandall
Rufus Crandall
Charlotte Crandall
Hammon Pinney
Mary Ann Pinney
Wm. Aug. Pinney
Edward Pinney
Emily Pinney
Silas Pinney
Hartwell Shelly
Wealthy M. Shelly
Daniel Shelly
Abigail Sherry
Henry Webster
Alonzo Webster
Elvira Webster
Manning Gilbert
Benjamin Gilbert
Mortimer Gilbert
Lucy Gilbert
Augustine Gilbert
Joseph Gilbert
Daniel Gilbert
Harrison Bailey

Nathan Bailey
Margaret Bailey
German Bailey
Albert Sawin
Marilla Sawin
Judson Sawin
Julia Sawin
Ely Cook
Seymour Cook
Alfred Cook
Pamelia Ismond
Polly Ismond
Levi Ismond
Gilbert Coffin
Farrand Coffin
Gardner Spencer
Adriel Ely
Theodore Ely
Almira Shipman
Luthera Shipman
Burnum Soules
Delia Soules
Harrison North
Aaron North
William Tabor
Sarah Tabor

Sally M. Devol
Caroline Devol
Cyrus Loveland
Reynolds Ferris
Aaron Ferris
Calvin Randall
David Randall
Harriet M. Reynolds
Lavancha Guy
Lucy Howard
George Briggs
Birdsell Rice
Clarissa Tanzer
Rensellaer Knapp
Mary A. Cummings
Isaac D. Lamatter
Betsey Thompson
Darius _____selle
George Bick (or Beck)
name crossed out
Marilla Thomas
Irene Shipman
Jemima Thompson
Joel Bailey
Clarissa Rice

NUMBER OF STUDENTS PER CLASS, ACADEMIC SCHOOL (1827-28)

Number of Students in each class for the second term of the academic school in Clarkesville as recorded by George Washington Johnson in his diary. *Source:* Diary of George Washington Johnson, Town of Middlefield Historical Association.

WHOLE NUMBER OF SCHOLARS	78
Studying the Greek Language	1
Studying the Latin Language	5
Studying Rhetoric	5
Studying History	1
Studying Composition	12
Studying the Art of Speaking	15
Studying Arithmetick	23
Studying English Grammar	10
Studying Penmanship	48
Studying Spelling	78
Studying Reading	78
Studying Pronunciation	20

School Bill, Academic School (1827-28)

School bill for the second term of the academic school taught in Clarkesville by George Washington Johnson. *Source:* Diary of George Washington Johnson, Town of Middlefield Historical Association.

Name of Proprietor	No. Days	Tax ($)	
John J. Crandall	261.5	3.97	paid to Johnson
Joshua L. Pinney	285.5	4.31	paid S. Devol
Hartwell Shelly	209.5	3.16	paid to G. W. Johnson by order of ___ Pinney
Theron Webster	182.5	2.8	Rec'd by G. W. Johnson
Daniel Gilbert	307	4.63	Rec'd by Johnson
Silas Devol	149.5	2.25	Rec'd by Johnson
Joseph W. Reynolds	65	0.98	Rec'd by Johnson
Sumner Ely	109.5	1.65	paid to Johnson
___ T. Bailey	207	3.13	paid to G. W. Johnson
Benjamin Sawin	197.5	2.98	paid to Johnson
Charles Cooke	87	1.32	p'd by Bailey to Johnson
John Cook	52.5	0.79	p'd by Bailey to Johnson
Elias Ismond	145	2.19	pd by Bailey to Johnson
Paul Coffin	46	0.69	pd by Gilbert as Trustee
William Shipman	78	1.18	Rec'd by G. W. Johnson
Newell Shipman	50.5	0.76	Rec'd by G. W. Johnson
Wm. & Newell Shipman	40.5	0.61	Rec'd half of W. N. Shipman and the other half of Wm. Shipman
Charles Soules	120.5	1.82	_____
Daniel North	90.5	1.37	Rec'd by Johnson
Thomas Taber	88	1.33	Rec'd by Johnson
Allen Brown	23	0.35	Rec'd by Johnson
Zadac Ferris	24	0.36	pd by Gilbert
Benjamin North	12.5	0.18	Rec'd by Johnson
Jacob Randall	29.5	0.45	pd by Gilbert as trustee
Henry Guy	68	1.02	paid N. Bailey
Jane Howard	57.5	0.86	paid N. Bailey (rec'd by Johnson)
Carlton Briggs	59	0.89	_____
Daniel W. Rice	75	1.14	paid N. Bailey
John Manzer Inn(?)	60.5	0.91	Rec'd by G. W. Johnson
Matthias Knapp	53	0.8	Rec'd by G. W. Johnson
Henry P. Thompson	62.5	0.93	Rec'd by Johnson
David Belknap	10	0.15	Pd by Bailey to G. W. Johnson
Jacob Valentine	12.5	0.19	pd. to Johnson
Daniel A. Cummings	82	1.24	pd. to Johnson
Mary Ann Cornwall	9	0.14	pd by Gilbert as Trustee
Whole no. of days	3412	51.5	
3412 days are 51.69 quarter at		$58.15	
For ____ part of last term, Add		5.33	for wood
		63.48	
	Deduct	11.98	public money
		$51.50	to be raised by tax

CIVIL WAR ENLISTEES FROM MIDDLEFIELD (1860-65)

The following list is taken from Duane Hamilton Hurd, *History of Otsego County, New York, with Illustrations and Biographical Sketches*, (Ovid, 1978), 191.

The following enlisted from this town (Middlefield) during the War of the Rebellion. For this list our thanks are due to Horace M. Pierce, S. W. Barnum, and Fernando Hubbell.

Fernando Hubbell, enl. in the 121st Regt.; was in the battles of South Mountain and Fredericksburg; lost right arm at Fredericksburg.

Libanus Lettuce, enl. in the 121st Regt.; in battles of South Mountain, Fredericksburg, and Wilderness.

Bennett Bray, enl. in the 121st Regt.

L. Cornish, enl. in the 121st Regt.

Harry Deusenbury, enl. in the 121st Regt.

Nathan Manzer, enl, in the 121st Regt.; in battles of Antietam, Fredericksburg, and Wilderness.

William Hoyt, enl. in the 76th Regt.; in battles of Bull Run, Antietam, and Fredericksburg, and Wilderness.

Cyrus Powers, enl. in the 76th Regt. in 1862; killed.

John Risendorf, enl. in the 76th Regt. in 1862; served during the war.

Esick Roberts, enl. in the 43rd Regt.; discharged; re-enlisted. Vet.

Daniel Reynolds.

Clark Farr, enl. in the 121st Regt.

Andrew Davidson, enl. in the 121st Regt.; prom. to sergt-major of the 121st; subsequently appointed adj. of the 30th U. S. Cav. Reg.; was capt. on staff of Gen. Bates; wounded at Salem Heights.

H. B. Walker, enl. in the 121st Regt.; prom. to lieut.

John Gates, enl. in the 121st Regt.; prom. to sergt.; killed at Salem Church.

Homer Graham, enl. in the 121 Regt.; killed.

Albert Waffle, enl. in the 121st Regt.; prom. to sergt.

James Wood, enl. in the 121st Regt.

Simeon Smith, enl. in the 121st Regt.

Darius Woodruff, enl. in the 121st Regt.

William Olive, enl. in the 121st Regt.

Henry Ludlam, enl. in the 121st Regt.; died.

Eugene Smith, enl. in the 121st Regt.

Dewitt Wells, enl. in the 121st Regt.; lost leg.

Thos. H. Bentley, enl. in the 121st Regt.

Lorenzo Smith, enl. in the 121st Regt. wounded.

Gilbert A. Parshall, capt. of Co. B, 42nd Regt. Illinois Vols; killed at Spring Hill, Tenn., Dec. 1, 1864.

Wm. H. Jones, enl. in 1ˢᵗ N. Y. Eng., Nov. 11, 1861; dis. in 1864.

The following also enlisted from this town, regiments unknown: Parshall Dutcher, M. Winnie, Norman Moyer, Henry Suits, William Neal, Josiah Bush, John Hudson, John Walker, Dewitt Andrews, Henry Daniels.

Robert Wood, enl. in the 14ᵗʰ Regt. U. S. Inf., March 19, 1862; came home sick, Nov. 26, 1864; died soon after, age 22 years 9 months.

Henry Wood, enl. in Co. E, 121ˢᵗ Regt., Aug. 12, 1862; dis. June 12, 1865.

John T. Wood, enl. in Co. E, 121ˢᵗ Regt., Aug. 12, 1862; dis. June 12, 1865.

Silas E. Pierce, enl. in Co. E, 121ˢᵗ Regt., Aug. 11, 1862; trans. t Co. F; prom. to 2ⁿᵈ lieut. and then to 1ˢᵗ lieut.; mortally wounded in the battle of the Wilderness, May 12; died May 13, 1864.

Charles Compton, enl. in Co. E, 121ˢᵗ Regt., Aug. 11, 1862; supposed to have been killed in the battle at Salem Church; never was heard from after the battle.

Albert Bailey, enl. in Co. E. 121ˢᵗ Regt., Aug. 11, 1862; dis. June 12, 1865.

Reuben H. Bates, enl. in Co. G, 121ˢᵗ Regt., Aug. 11, 1862; dis. June 25, 1865.

John Bristol, enl. in Co. E, 121ˢᵗ Regt., Aug. 12, 1862; dis. 1865.

William H. Lynes, enl. Sept. 2, 1864, in Capt. William E. Marcus' Light Battery (C), 3ʳᵈ Regt. Art. N. Y. State Vols.; dis. July 14, 1865.

Isaac Pier, enl. Sept. 2, 1864, in Light Battery C, 3ʳᵈ Regt. Art., N. Y. State Vols.; dis. June 9, 1865.

Oscar Pier, enl. Sept. 8, 1863; died in hospital at Washington in March, 1865.

Orrin Waterhouse, enl. in spring of 1862; died in hospital at Washington.

John Wheeler, enl. in spring of 1862; died in hospital at Washington.

Ervin Holcomb, enl. in 96ᵗʰ Regt. N. Y. Vols., Feb. ___, 1865, Capt. Wm. B. Brock-em, commanding; died in spring of 1865.

Timothy Dodge, enl. in Co. B, 1ˢᵗ Regt. U. S. Col. Cav., Sept. 5, 1864; dis. May 26, 1865.

William Dodge, enl. in Co. B, 1ˢᵗ Regt. U. S. Col. Cav., Sept. 5, 1864; dis. May 26, 1865.

Samuel Chase, enl. in Co. L, 2ⁿᵈ Regt. N. Y. Vol. Cav., Sept. 17, 1861; dis. Dec. 28, 1863, by reason of re-enlisting; taken prisoner in the battle of the Wilderness; died in Florence stockade, S. C., in winter of 1865.

Chapter One: THE MANORIAL VISION

1. William W. Campbell, *The Border Warfare of New York During the Revolution or The Annals of Tryon County* (Bowie, 1992), Ch. 5; T. Wood Clarke, *The Bloody Mohawk*, (New York, 1940), 252-258. These books give detailed accounts of the massacre. Peter C. Mancall, *Valley of Opportunity: Economic Culture Along the Upper Susquehanna, 1700-1800*, (Ithaca, 1991), 137-138.
2. Charles Worthen Spencer, "The Land System of Colonial New York," *New York State History: Quarterly Journal of the New York State Historical Association* XVI (1917): 154-162.
3. Barry L. Wold, *The George Hyde Clarke Family Papers, A Guide to the Collection at Cornell University* (Ithaca, 1977), 16.
4. Colin D. Campbell, "They Beckoned and We Came: The Settlement of Cherry Valley," *New York State History: Quarterly Journal of the New York State Historical Association* LXXIX/3 (1998): 221; Campbell, *Border Warfare*, 30; Mancall, *Valley of Opportunity*, 112; John Sawyer, *History of Cherry Valley From 1740 to 1898* (Cherry Valley, 1898), 3-4; Hamilton Child, *Gazetteer and Business Directory of Otsego County, N. Y. for 1872-3* (Syracuse, 1872), 66; Mancall, *Valley of Opportunity*, 112.
5. Goldsbrow Banyar to Samuel Dunlop, 28 August 1761, Banyar Papers, Box 6, New-York Historical Society, New York.
6. Sung Bok Kim, *Landlord and Tenant in Colonial New York: Manorial Society 1664-1775* (Chapel Hill, 1978), 129-142; Mancall, *Valley of Opportunity*, 106.
7. Richard Smith, *A Tour of the Hudson, The Mohawk, The Susquehanna, and The Delaware in 1769* (Fleischmanns, 1989), 97.
8. Peter Martin to Banyar, 22 September 1762, Banyar Papers, Box 6.
9. Smith, *Tour of the Hudson*, 98; Mancall, *Valley of Opportunity*, 107.
10. Kim, *Landlord and Tenant*, 24.
11. Ibid., 158, 167.
12. Smith, *Tour of the Hudson*, 107; James Arthur Frost, *Life on the Upper Susquehanna, 1783-1860*, (New York, 1951), 21.
13. Campbell, "They Beckoned", 223. George Clarke had died in 1760, unbeknownst to Dunlop.
14. Mancall, *Valley of Opportunity*, 112.
15. Duane Hamilton Hurd, *History of Otsego County, New York, with Illustrations and Biographical Sketches*, (Ovid, 1978), 184-185. A complete reprint of the Daniel McCollum incident, as presented by Hurd, appears in the appendix. Catherine Snell Crary, "Forfeited Loyalist Lands in the Western District of New York - Albany and Tryon

Counties," *New York State History: Quarterly Journal of the New York State Historical Association* XXXV/3 (1954): 241.

16. Campbell, *Border Warfare*, 122.

17. Child, *Gazetteer and Business Directory*, 69-70.

18. Otsego County was broken from Tryon County in 1791. It was in 1784 that Tryon County was renamed Montgomery County. It was thought inappropriate to have a county named for a British governor after the Revolution.

19. Campbell, *Border Warfare*, 40-42; Alexander Clarence Flick, *Loyalism in New York During the American Revolution*, (New York, 1969), 93, 110.

20. Mancall, *Valley of Opportunity*, 122; Flick, *Loyalism in New York*, 86; Alan Taylor, *William Cooper's Town: Power and Persuasion on the Frontier of the Early American Republic*, (New York, 1996), 58-60.

21. Colin G. Calloway, *The American Revolution in Indian Country: Crisis and Diversity in Native American Communities*, (New York, 1995), 122; Mancall, *Valley of Opportunity*, 131, 140-142 which discusses in detail the reasons for the Indians adherence to the Crown's cause.

22. Clarke, *The Bloody Mohawk*, 259-272; Edward Countryman, *A People in Revolution: the American Revolution and Political Society in New York, 1760-1790*, (Baltimore, 1981), 150.

23. E. Pomeroy Staats, *Town of Middlefield, Otsego County, New York*, (Middlefield, 1991), 27.

24. Levi Beardsley, *Reminiscences; Personal and Other Incidents; Early Settlement of Otsego County; Notices and Anecdotes of Public Men; Judicial, Legal and Legislative Matters; Field Sports; Dissertations and Discussions*, (New York, 1852), 36; David Maldwyn Ellis, *Landlords and Farmers in the Hudson-Mohawk Region, 1790-1850*, (New York, 1967), 74. Ellis cites three sources: Ulysses P. Hedrick, *A History of Agriculture in the State of New York*, (Albany, 1933), 109-110; John Wilgram, *John Wilgram's Proceedings on Goldsbrow Banyar, 1812*; and O. Turner, *Holland Purchase*, 565. However, he clearly views this claim with skepticism.

25. George Hyde Clarke to James Duane, 4 January 1789, Duane Papers, Vol. 8 #70, New-York Historical Society, New York; George Clarke Junior to James Duane, 1 January 1789, Duane Papers, Vol. 8 # 69.

26. Wold, *Clarke Papers*, 16-17; E. B. O'Callaghan, *Voyage of George Clarke, Esqu., to America with Introduction and Notes*, (Albany, 1867), lxxvi-lxxviii.

27. George Clarke to James Duane, 26 December 1791, Duane Papers, Vol 9 #22.

28. George Hyde Clarke Family Papers, #2800, Division of Rare and Manuscript Collections, Cornell University Library, Ithaca.

29. Ibid., box 137, folder 3.

30. Staats, *Middlefield*, 38.

31. John Shy, *Winding Down: The Revolutionary War Letters of Lieutenant Benjamin Gilbert of Massachusetts, 1780-1783*, (Michigan, 1989), 69, 81, 95, 100.

32. Rebecca D. Symmes, *A Citizen-Soldier in the American Revolution, The Diary of Benjamin Gilbert in Massachusetts and New York*, (Cooperstown, 1980), 82.

33. Benjamin Gilbert to Daniel Gilbert, 16 July 1785, Gilbert Folder, New York State Historical Association, Cooperstown.

34. Diary of Benjamin Gilbert. 1782-1786. New York State Historical Association, Cooperstown.

35. Symmes, *Diary of Benjamin Gilbert*, 15.

36. Taylor, *William Cooper's Town*, 192.

37. Ibid., 269.

38. Beardsley, *Reminiscences*, 65; Frost, *The Susquehanna*, 38, 137; *Otsego Herald* (Cooperstown), 25 September 1800.

39. Elihu Phinney, *Reminiscences of the Village of Cooperstown*, (Cooperstown, 1891), 11; Henry Hardy Heins, *Throughout All The Years: The Bicentennial Story of Hartwick in America 1746-1946*, (Oneonta, 1946), 162; Frost, *The Susquehanna*, 40; Subscription List for the Otsego Academy, 5 April 1795, William Cooper Papers, New York State Historical Association, Cooperstown.

40. James Fenimore Cooper, *Reminiscences of Mid-Victorian Cooperstown and a Sketch of William Cooper*, (Cooperstown, 1936), 19; Dixon Ryan Fox, *The Decline of Aristocracy in the Politics of New York*, (New York, 1919), 134, 182n; Edward P. Alexander, "Judge Kent's 'Jaunt' To Cooperstown, 1792," *New York State History: Quarterly Journal of the New York State Historical Association* XXII/4 (1941): 453-4.

41. Minute Books of Otsego Lodge No. 138, Free and Accepted Masons, Cooperstown.

42. Albert T. Van Horne, *History of Otsego Lodge No. 138, F. & A. M. and Mark Lodge, Chapter, and Council*, (Cooperstown, 1896), 11.

43. *Otsego Herald*, 29 June 1797.

44. When this first lodge building was sold by the Freemasons in 1886 the cornerstone was removed and placed in their new lodge room. It remains in the possession of Otsego Lodge No. 138 F. & A. M. The translation of the cornerstone is given by Albert T. Van Horne as follows:

> *On the 24th day of June, in the year of Light 5797, this*
> *Hall was erected by the Otsego Society of Latimorus, E. P. M.,*
> *and was dedicated to the use of the Brethren of Light.*
>
> *We're born and live not to ourselves alone;*
> *But equally for country and friends of every home.*

45. Elihu Phinney to William Cooper, 4 January 1796, William Cooper Papers, Hartwick College Archives, Oneonta.

46. These daughters were: Hannah, who married Dr. Sumner Ely in 1816, Elizabeth, who married Benjamin D. North Jr. in 1823, and Esther, who married Dunham Spaulding in 1823. The son was Daniel.

47. Mancall, *Valley of Opportunity*, 203.

48. Smith, *The Susquehanna*, 128n. It must be concluded that Banyar's efforts on behalf

of the Wallaces must have also been employed to save Clarke's lands. In both cases these efforts were remarkably successful as both the Wallace and Clarke lands remained intact. Flick, *Loyalism in New York*, 159.

49. Ellis, *Landlords and Farmers*, 38, 42.

50. William North to Benjamin Walker 16 May 18__, William North Papers, New York State Library, Albany.

51. William Cooper, *A Guide in the Wilderness*, (Cooperstown, 1936), 12.

52. Clarke Family Papers, #2800.

Chapter Two: THE DEVELOPMENT OF THE HAMLET

1. The text will use the spelling of Clarkesville that George Clarke used in his papers until common parlance in the community dropped the "e". The original spelling of Middlefield Centre employed the British style. It was changed to the American style Middlefield Center on 12 December 1893. This was in keeping with a recommendation of the U.S. Board on Geographic Names as set forth in their report of 5 January 1892. Dorothy Scott Fielder, *Otsego County Postal History*, (Walton, 1994), 18.

2. Richard Smith, *A Tour of the Hudson, The Mohawk, The Susquehanna, and The Delaware in 1769* (Fleischmanns, 1989), p. 101. Colin D. Campbell, "They Beckoned and We Came: The Settlement of Cherry Valley," *New York State History: Quarterly Journal of the New York State Historical Association* LXXIX/3 (1998): 228-229.

3. Jeptha R. Simms, *The Frontiersmen of New York*, (Albany, 1882), vol. 2, 240.

4. Duane Hamilton Hurd, *History of Otsego County, New York, with Illustrations and Biographical Sketches*, (Ovid, 1978). In each quotation of the Town of Middlefield board minutes the whole town is referred to as Middlefield rather than Newtown-Martin. Unfortunately, it is impossible to consult the actual minutes as all town board minutes prior to 1918 were destroyed in the Parshall house fire when he was town clerk. See also William W. Campbell, *The Border Warfare of New York During the Revolution or the Annals of Tryon County*, (Bowie, 1992), 38, who states that Middlefield was known as Newtown-Martin prior to the Revolution.

5. J. H. French, *Gazetteer of the State of New York*, (Syracuse, 1860), 534. Hamilton Child, *Gazetteer and Business Directory of Otsego County, N. Y. for 1872-3* (Syracuse, 1872), 105; Joel Perlmann and Robert A. Margo, *Women's Work?: American Schoolteachers 1650-1920*, (Chicago, 2001), 15.

6. Hurd, *History*, 186-7.

7. Louis C. Jones, *Growing Up in Cooper County: Boyhood Recollections of the New York Frontier*, (Binghamton, 1965), 116.

8. John Sawyer, *History of Cherry Valley From 1740 to 1898*, (Cherry Valley, 1898), 58. Levi Beardsley, *Reminiscences; Personal and Other Incidents; Early Settlement of Otsego County; Notices and Anecdotes of Public Men; Judicial, Legal and Legislative Matters; Field Sports; Dissertations and Discussions*, (New York, 1852), 63.

9. Peter C. Mancall, *Valley of Opportunity: Economic Culture Along the Upper Susquehanna, 1700-1800*, (Ithaca, 1991), 174.

10. David Maldwyn Ellis, *Landlords and Farmers in the Hudson-Mohawk Region, 1790-1850*, (New York, 1967), 123. The price in Albany is reported in shillings, but Ellis states that 8 shillings were equal to 1 dollar.

11. James C. Parshall, *James Parshall and His Descendants*, (Syracuse, 1900); E. Pomeroy Staats, *Town of Middlefield, Otsego County, New York*, (Middlefield, 1991), 36; Congregational Minutes of the First Baptist Society in Middlefield, Book 1, 1810-1829, 14 & 15 October 1815.

12. Mancall, *Valley of Opportunity*, 177. Ellis, *Landlords and Farmers*, 113.

13. Alan Taylor, *William Cooper's Town, Power and Persuasion on the Frontier of the Early American Republic*, (New York, 1996), 107.

14. Child, *Gazetteer and Business Directory*, 105. Staats, *Middlefield*, 61.

15. Hurd, *History*, 187.

16. Rent Roll, George Hyde Clarke Papers, New York State Historical Association, Cooperstown.

17. Hurd, *History*, 187.

18. George Hyde Clarke Family Papers, #2800, Division of Rare and Manuscript Collections, Cornell University Library, Ithaca; Colin D. Campbell, "Rural New York in a Woman's Hand: The 1833 Diary of Sabrina Campbell," *New York State History: Quarterly Journal of the New York State Historical Association* LXXXII/4 (2001): 342.

19. Mancall, *Valley of Opportunity*, 205; Overseer of Highways contract between David Hilts and the Town of Cobleskill, 18 March 1858, Collection of Dominick J. Reisen. These contracts were both of a standard form from community to community and remained largely unchanged until after the Civil War.

20. French, *Gazetteer*, 534.

21. "Map of the Oothout Patent with lists of lots, acreage and lessees" (c.1820), George Hyde Clarke Family Papers, #2800, Division of Rare and Manuscript Collections, Cornell University Library, Ithaca.

22. United States Department of Commerce, Bureau of the Census.

23. Harry Bradshaw Matthews *The Abolitionist Movement and Reconstruction: Family Legacies in Cooperstown Village and Towns in Otsego County, New York*, (Oneonta, 1994), 5.

24. *Otsego Herald* (Cooperstown), 19 September 1799.

25. Sawyer, *Cherry Valley*, 70.

26. Clarke Family Papers, #2800. There is also a handbill in the NYSHA collection (hung on the wall of Bump Tavern at The Farmers' Museum) dated 1817 which references Joshua L. Pinney operating a tavern in Clarksville for 14 years. This establishes the fact that Pinney began operating his tavern not later than 1803.

27. George Clarke to William Cockburn, 9 July 1797, George Clarke Papers, New-York Historical Society, New York; Barnabus M Gilbert, "Map of Subdivisions No's 17 & 18 in Great Lot No 12, and a part of Subdivision No 21 in Great Lot No 13, Oothout Patent" (1851), Clarke Family Papers, #2800.

28. John Harriott, *Struggles through Life, Exemplified in the Various Travels and Adventures in Europe, Asia, Africa and America*, (London, 1808), vol. 2, 116.

29. Cummings Deed recorded 12 July 1822, liber DD, 524; Howard Deed dated 8 April 1822, liber FF, page 144; North and Brown Deed recorded 30 March 1855, liber 102, 565, Otsego County Clerk, Cooperstown.

30. Clarke Deed recorded 30 June 1810, liber M, 69, Otsego County Clerk.

31. Cynthia A. Kierner, *Traders and Gentlefolk: The Livingstons of New York, 1675-1790*, (Ithaca, 1992), 247; Beardsley, *Reminiscences*, 445; Ellis, *Landlords and Farmers*, 151.

32. Thomas Summerhill, *Harvest of Dissent: Agrarianism in Nineteenth-Century New* York, (Chicago, 2005), 26.

33. William Salzillo, *Philip Hooker and His Comtemporaries: 1796-1836*, (Clinton, 1993), 144-152, 160-174.

34. Roger G. Kennedy, *Architecture, Men, Women and Money in America 1600-1860*, (New York, 1985), 195.

35. William North to Benjamin Walker, 4 September 1801. William North Papers, New York State Library, Albany.

36. *Otsego Herald*, 23 April 1814; Staats, *Middlefield*, 24, 37.

37. *Cooperstown Federalist*, 25 July 1812, 25 May 1814.

38. Hurd, *History*, 190.

39. Taylor, *William Cooper's Town*, 227; Sawyer, *Cherry Valley*, 47; Hurd, *History*, 190.

40. Congregational Minutes, First Baptist Society in Middlefield. For baptisms, see 21 October 1810 which has the first written record of a baptism in Clarkesville, that being for Whiteford Gillett.

41. Ibid., 14 April 1811, 29 May 1813.

42. Ibid., 20 June 1812, 18 July 1812, 3 November 1821.

43. Ibid., 14 September 1816, 18 August 1821.

44. Staats, *Middlefield*, 39; Diary of George Washington Johnson, Town of Middlefield Historical Association Collection, 17 September 1828.

45. *The Freeman's Journal* (Cooperstown), 8 July 1858. Hurd, *History*, 36, 186.

46. Virginia and Lee McAlester, *A Field Guide to American Houses*, (New York, 1998), 169.

47. Minute Books of Otsego Lodge No. 138, Free and Accepted Masons, Cooperstown. The wing that was on the southwestern side of the house has been moved to the back of the American Hotel building.

48. Clarke Family Papers, #2800; Pinney Deed recorded 30 March 1814, liber S, 51, Otsego County Clerk.

49. Ely Deed recorded 1 February 1819, liber Z, 258, Otsego County Clerk.

50. Throop Wilder, "Jedediah Peck: Statesman, Soldier, Preacher," *New York State History: Quarterly Journal of the New York State Historical Association* XXXIX (1940): 292; Martha Reamy, *Early Families of Otsego County, New York*, (Westminster, 2001), vol. 1, 156.

51. Minute Books of Otsego Lodge, Cooperstown.

52. *The Freeman's Journal*, 8 July 1858.

53. Will of Benjamin Gilbert dated 28 March 1828, Otsego County Surrogate's Court, Cooperstown.

54. Alf Evers, *The Catskills: From Wilderness to Woodstock*, (New York, 1972), 335. This weather phenomenon was due to the eruption of the Tambora volcano on the island of Sunbawa in Indonesia in 1815. The eruption and its aftermath killed over 90,000 in the Pacific region, and led to widespread crop failures in Europe, the first famines in Ireland, devastating floods in China and widespread snow and frost over most of North America in June and July. Rich Deed recorded 12 April 1818, liber X, 500, Otsego County Clerk.

55. Rich Deed recorded 10 October 1816, liber QQ, 259, Otsego County Clerk.

56. McAlester, *Field Guide*, 139.

57. Sawyer, *Cherry Valley*, 103.

58. Jordan Deed recorded 23 February 1819 liber Z, 23-24, Otsego County Clerk. Both Moses Richs appear on later year censuses as being in the Westville area. This is not stated explicitly on the censuses, but is deduced from the fact that other names listed on the censuses in the proximity to the Rich names can be traced to Westville. The order of names on these early census listings tended to follow the resident's physical location as they were listed in the order in which the census taker obtained the information by means of walking from house to house.

59. Census for 1800, United States Department of Commerce, Bureau of the Census; Minute Books of Otsego Lodge, 21 July 1812, Cooperstown; Membership Return for Otsego Lodge No. 138, Free and Accepted Masons, July 1809-August 1812, Cooperstown.

60. Taylor, *William Cooper's Town*, 361; Hurd, *History*, 283; Minute Books of Otsego Lodge, 8 December 1818, Cooperstown; Albert T. Van Horne, *History of Otsego Lodge No. 138, F. & A. M. and Mark Lodge, Chapter, and Council*, (Cooperstown, 1896), 40-41; *Otsego Herald*, 22 June 1818.

Chapter Three: PROSPERITY AND SOCIAL EPIPHANY

1. Cummings Deed recorded 11 May 1821, liber CC, 88-90, Otsego County Clerk, Cooperstown.

2. Quoted in Carol McCabe, "Figured Woods," *Early American Life*, April 2003, 50.

3. Dorothy Scott Fielder, *Otsego County Postal History*, (Walton, 1994), 16.

4. Ibid., 91.

5. Ibid., 91-92. A full list of the post masters for the hamlet appears in Appendix 3. John Sawyer, *History of Cherry Valley From 1740 to 1898*, (Cherry Valley, 1898), 87.

6. Fielder, *Postal History*, 188.

7. Horatio Gates Spafford, *A Gazetteer of the State of New York: Embracing an Ample Survey and Description of its Counties, Towns, Cities, Villages, Canals, Mountains, Lakes, Rivers, Creeks, and Natural Topography*, (Interlaken, 1981), 316-317.

8. Barnabus M. Gilbert, "A Part of Farm No 17 in the Outhout Patent, formerly owned by Gilbert Ely" (1861), George Hyde Clarke Family Papers, #2800, Division of Rare and Manuscript Collections, Cornell University Library, Ithaca; Hayden Deed recorded 12 September 1820, liber BB, 259-260, Otsego County Clerk.

For reference to Hayden as a deacon see the obituary of his daughter, Stella Hayden, in *The Freeman's Journal* (Cooperstown), 10 November 1883.

9. Documentary evidence noting exactly when this distillery was set up is lacking in light of the fact that Pinney set it up privately and on his own land. His obituary does note that he was involved in distilling when he kept a tavern in Clarkesville. For this obituary, see the *Owego Gazette*, 25 October 1855. For the sale of the distillery by Pinney to Sumner Ely and Erastus Sterling, see Ely/Sterling Deed recorded 1 October 1831, liber ZZ, 368-369, Otsego County Clerk.

10. Gilbert Deed recorded 23 February 1819, liber Z, 24-25, Otsego County Clerk; Will of Benjamin Gilbert, 28 March 1828, Otsego County Surrogate's Court, Cooperstown.

11. Diary of George Washington Johnson, Town of Middlefield Historical Association. In the entry for 22 December 1827, Johnson states that he settled his bill for goods for $2 from Gilbert and North. Gilbert, "Map of Farm No 17," Clarke Family Papers, #2800.

12. North Family Folder, Town of Middlefield Historical Association; *Otsego Herald* (Cooperstown), 23 April 1814; Johnson Diary, 17 December 1827. This entry has the invitation to a "social dance" at the "Assembly Room of Benjamin D. North . . ." E. Pomeroy Staats, *Town of Middlefield, Otsego County, New York*, (Middlefield, 1991), 43.

13. Gordon S. Wood, *The Radicalism of the American Revolution: How a Revolution Transformed a Monarchical Society into a Democratic One Unlike Any That Had Ever Existed*, (New York, 1992), 223.

14. Freemasons in Middlefield to Grand Lodge of New York, 23 December 1823, vol. 123 of the Grand Lodge of Free and Accepted Masons of the State of New York Archives, The Chancellor Robert R Livingston Masonic Library and Museum, New York; Johnson Diary, 13 June 1828. This entry refers to "Mrs John Hayden and her sister Charlotte (Pinney)". Although Charlotte's surname is not noted, the entry mentions their trip to Westerloo and other references in the diary mention Charlotte Pinney as going to Westerloo shortly before this entry. Gilbert, "Map of Farm No 17," Clarke Family Papers, #2800.

15. Albert T. Van Horne, *History of Otsego Lodge No. 138, F. & A. M. and Mark Lodge, Chapter, and Council*, (Cooperstown, 1896), 16.

16. Membership Return of Widow's Son Lodge No. 391, 18 July 1824 through first Wednesday of June 1825, and Daniel Gilbert to Grand Lodge, undated, vol. 123 of Grand Lodge of New York Archives, Livingston Masonic Library; Nancy Grey Osterud, *Bonds of Community: The Lives of Farm Women in Nineteenth-Century New York*, (Ithaca, 1991), 37-38.

17. Thurlow Weed, "The Fate of William Morgan," in *Morgan's Freemasonry exposed and Explained showing the Origin, History and Nature of Masonry; Its Effect on the Government and the Christian Religion and containing a Key to All the Degrees of Freemasonry*, William Morgan, (New York, 1882). For a more detailed history of the Morgan Affair and the various theories of what exactly happened to William Morgan, see Herbert T.

Singer and Ossian Lang, *New York Freemasonry: A Bicentennial History 1781-1981*, (New York, 1981), 76-89.

18. Van Horne, *History of Otsego Lodge*, 18-20. It was in June 1819 that, due to a reordering of lodge numbers by Grand Lodge, the number designation for Otsego Lodge was changed from 40 to 41.

19. The author learned from Rodney Johnson who, with his wife Jeanne, took ownership of the former Joshua Pinney tavern, that when the house was inventoried in 1957 for the estate of Mable Folmsbee, it was noted that on the third floor the furniture and working tools of a Masonic lodge were still in place. The piece of furniture that had served as the Master's Station was given to the New York State Historical Association in Cooperstown (there is a shadow of this piece on the floor of the third story of the tavern building), and the remainder of the working tools (ritual paraphernalia) were sent to the Grand Lodge in New York. These were later returned to the Town of Middlefield Historical Association. In light of the fact that the lodge room had remained set up from the 1820s to 1957, it is not beyond the realm of speculation that men in Clarkesville had been meeting as a clandestine Masonic Lodge long after their charter was declared forfeit in 1834.

20. Edmund W. Sinnot, *Meetinghouse and Church in Early New England*, (New York, 1963), 72.

21. Trustee Minutes of the First Baptist Society in Middlefield, Book 1, 1825-1833, 24 January 1825.

22. Clarke Family Papers, #2800.

23. Trustee Minutes, 2 April 1825, First Baptist Society in Middlefield.

24. Asher Benjamin, *The Country Builder's Assistant: Containing a Collection of New Designs of Carpentry and Architecture*, (Bedford, 1992), plate 27; Sinnot, *Meetinghouse and Church*, 80-82.

25. Trustee Minutes, 21 May 1825, First Baptist Society in Middlefield.

26. Deed between Faithful Smith and the Trustees of the First Congregational Church and Society of New Lisbon recorded 22 October 1908, liber 270, 491, Otsego County Clerk; New Lisbon Congregational Church, Church Records No. 2, 1825, Collection of New Lisbon Town Historian.

27. New Lisbon Congregational Church Records.

28. Pinney Script issued in 1816 redeemable at his store in Clarkesville or Worcester, New York State Historical Association, Cooperstown; Sayles and Antisdel Script issued in 1862 redeemable at their store in Clarkesville, Collection of Rodney and Jeanne Johnson.

29. Trustee Minutes, 28 January 1826, 22 November 1826, 14 February 1828, 31 October 1828, First Baptist Society in Middlefield.

30. Joshua L. Pinney to J. & J. Townsend, 10 January 1825, 11 February 1828, Johnson Collection. The documents cited are photocopies, the originals were reported as being on display at the Sharon Springs Central School, in Sharon Springs, NY. They are part of a large collection of unstamped covers arranged by Harry E. Mitchell. They were franked by J. L. P. as postmaster. Mitchell was a former resi-

dent of Middlefield and ran the A. C. Parshall store. He married the daughter of Edward Buell, a later resident of the hamlet.

31. Spafford, *Gazetteer of the State of New York*, 316.

32. James Arthur Frost, *Life on the Upper Susquehanna, 1783-1860*, (New York, 1951), 109.

33. *The Freeman's Journal*, 21 April 1828; Terri L. Premo, *Winter Friends: Women Growing Old in the New Republic, 1785-1835*, (Chicago, 1990), 60, 140.

34. The parcel on which the academic school was located was not divided from the Pinney parcel until after Joshua and Polly Pinney sold the tavern to Benjamin D. and Elizabeth North in 1833. The school building was then sold to Erastus and Florrilla (Polly) Sterling for $85. Sterling Deed dated 15 July 1835, liber 52, 132, Otsego County Clerk.

35. *The Freeman's Journal*, 15 May 1826, 27 March 1826.

36. Joel Perlmann and Robert A. Margo, *Women's Work?: American Schoolteachers 1650-1920*, (Chicago, 2001), 13, 62; Geraldine Joanne Murphy, "Massachusetts Bay Colony: The Role of Government in Education" (Ph.D. Dissertation, Radcliffe College, 1960).

37. Johnson Diary, School Bill for November 12, 1827 to February 15, 1828, 17 March 1828. This school course enrollment list is reproduced in Appendix 7 and the school bill is reproduced in Appendix 8. *Owego Gazette*, 25 October 1855.

38. *The Freeman's Journal*, 15 May 1826, 27 March 1826.

39. Spafford, *Gazetteer of the State of New York*, 168. *The Freeman's Journal*, 3 March 1826.

40. Johnson Diary, School Bill and enrollment list. See Appendix 8 for the school bill and Appendix 6 for the enrollment list.

41. Ibid., undated entry.

42. Julia Hull Winner, ed., "A Journey Across New York State in 1833: As Recounted in His Manuscript Journal, by George Washington Johnson," *New York State History: Quarterly Journal of the New York State Historical Association* XLVI/1 (1965): 60.

43. *Cherry Valley Gazette*, 27 November 1821. *The Freeman's Journal*, 21 February 1846.

44. Johnson Diary, 31 October 1827.

45. Ibid., 27 January 1828.

46. Ibid., 10 August 1827.

47. Ibid., 10-12 February 1828.

48. Douglas Hamilton Hurd, *History of Otsego County, New York, with Illustrations and Biographical Sketches*, (Ovid, 1978), 190.

49. Johnson Diary, 26 May 1828.

50. Ibid., 30-31 October 1827, 10 September 1828.

51. Ibid., 17 March 1828, and the accompanying select school bill.

52. Harry Bradshaw Matthews, *The Abolitionist Movement and Reconstruction: Family Legacies in Cooperstown Village and Towns in Otsego County, New York*, (Oneonta, 1994), 1; U.S. Department of Commerce, Bureau of the Census; Spafford, *Gazetteer of the State of New York*, 393.

53. Winner, "A Journey Across New York State," 61.

54. *The Freeman's Journal*, 7 September 1835.

55. Dominick J. Reisen, *Inscriptions from the Middlefield Baptist Cemetery: With Select Genealogical Information*, (Middlefield, 2002), 58.

56. Barbara Dayer Gallati, "The English Victorian Nude in the United States," *The Magazine Antiques* (2002), 104.

57. *The Freeman's Journal*, 5 June 1826.

58. Richard Kluger, *Simple Justice: The History of Brown v. Board of Education and Black America's Struggle for Equality*, (New York, 1975), 36.

59. Congregational Minutes of The First Baptist Society in Middlefield, Book 1, 1810-1829, 17-18 September 1819.

60. *The Freeman's Journal*, 9 July 1827; Harry Bradshaw Matthews, *African American Freedom Journey in New York and Related Sites, 1823-1870: Freedom Knows No Color*, (Cherry Hill, 2008), 134-135.

61. Seth Williston, A. M., "A Sermon Upon Intemperance" (1808), Special Collection, New York State Historical Association, Cooperstown.

62. Osterud, *Bonds of Community*, 39.

63. *The Freeman's Journal*, 16 November 1835.

64. Staats, *Middlefield*, (Middlefield, 1991), 38; *The Freeman's Journal*, 21 February 1846, 14 March 1878.

65. *The Freeman's Journal*, 28 January 1828.

66. Congregational Minutes, First Baptist Society in Middlefield. See the entries for 14 April 1811 for the case of Jesse How, and 29 May 1813 for the case of Amos Jones.

67. Resolution of Widow's Son Lodge No. 391 dated May 18 A. L. 5826, Grand Lodge of New York Archives, Livingston Masonic Library.

68. Ibid., A True Copy from the Minutes of the Lodge May 28 A. L. 5827; Van Horne, *History of Otsego Lodge*, 17.

69. Deed between Joshua L. Pinney and Sumner Ely and Erastus L. Sterling recorded 30 December 1833, liber ZZ, 368-369, Otsego County Clerk.

70. Deed between Joshua L. and Polly Pinney and Benjamin D. North recorded 15 November 1833, liber ZZ, 367, Otsego County Clerk.

71. *Owego Gazette*, 25 October 1855.

72. Alf Evers, *The Catskills: From Wilderness to Woodstock*, (New York, 1972), 355.

73. Nina Fletcher Little, *American Decorative Wall Painting, 1700-1850*, (New York, 1972), 148-149; Diantha Dow Schull, *Landmarks of Otsego County*, (Syracuse, 1980), 257.

74. Cummings Deed dated 8 April 1822, liber DD, 524, and Howard Deed dated 8 April 1822, liber FF, 144, Otsego County Clerk.

75. Watson Deed dated 7 May 1845, liber 99, 181, Otsego County Clerk.

Chapter Four: THE CHANGING OF THE GUARD

1. *Otsego Herald* (Cooperstown, 22 June 1818.

2. Ibid., 23 October 1820.

3. Duane Hamilton Hurd, *History of Otsego County, New York with Illustrations and Bio-*

graphical Sketches, (Ovid, 1978), facing page 124. Joseph White was the father of the aforementioned Delos White. Paul Starr, *The Social Transformation of American Medicine: The Rise of a Sovereign Profession and the Making of a Vast Industry*, (New York, 1982), 40-46.

4. Levi Beardsley, *Reminiscences; Personal and Other Incidents; Early Settlement of Otsego County; Notices and Anecdotes of Public Men; Judicial, Legal and Legislative Matters; Field Sports; Dissertations and Discussions*, (New York, 1852), 49-50.

5. *Transactions of the Medical Society of the State of New York: From its organization in 1807, up to and including 1831*, (Albany, 1868), 378; Vol. I 1832-1833, (Albany, 1833); Vol. II 1834-1835, (Albany, 1835).

6. For information on the history of poor relief in England see: Linda Colley, *Britons: Forging the Nation 1707-1837*, (New Haven, 1992); M. Dorothy George, *London Life in the Eighteenth Century*, (Chicago, 1984); Paul L. Hughes and Robert F. Fries, *Crown and Parliament in Tudor-Stuart England: A Documentary Constitutional History 1485-1714*, (New York, 1959); A. P. Thornton, *The Habit of Authority: Paternalism in British History*, (Toronto, 1966).

7. *Biographical Sketches of the Leading Citizens of Otsego County, New York*, (Boston, 1893), 401-402; Albert T. Van Horne, *History of Otsego Lodge No. 138, F. & A. M. and Mark Lodge, Chapter, and Council*, (Cooperstown, 1896), 55.

8. James and Henry Phinney were the sons of Elihu Phinney and took over his publishing and printing business. Dr. Sumner Ely is not listed as having been present at the first meeting of the Board of Superintendents of the Poor held on 13 December 1826. The first meeting at which he is listed as being present is 8 February 1827. However, the records of the board of superintendents do not list who the Otsego County Board of Supervisors appointed to this board, nor do they mention any addition or deletions from their board in this period. Therefore, it has been assumed that Dr. Sumner Ely was among those initially appointed to this board.

9. Joseph P. Vidosic, *The Meadows and its Predecessors*, (Cooperstown, 1998), 6-13. Records of Superintendent of the Poor, 1826-1911, 13 December 1826, 8 February 1827, 8 April 1827, New York State Historical Association, Cooperstown.

10. Records of the Poor, 14 March 1828, 8 December 1828, 25 November 1829, New York State Historical Association. The Elihu Phinney on this board was the son of Elihu the publisher and bookseller who founded the *Otsego Herald*. The senior Elihu had died in 1813.

11. Ibid., 14 June 1828, 16 February 1829, 26 January 1830. Evan Coats had been appointed Keeper of the Poor by the Board of Superintendents of the Poor on 17 February 1827.

12. Ibid., 16 February 1829, 14 June 1828.

13. *Otsego Herald*, 23 April 1814.

14. Deed between Rensselaer Westerlo and Silas Devol recorded 11 July 1818, liber Y, 172, and Deed between Silas Devol and James Frazier recorded 17 April 1819, liber Z, 155, Otsego County Clerk, Cooperstown; Trustee Minutes of the First Baptist Society in Middlefield, Book 1, 1825-1833, 24 January 1825.

15. Records of the Poor, 29 November 1831, 21 November 1832, New York State Historical Association.

16. Sumner Ely to Lydia Ely, 29 August 1838, Collection of Dominick J. Reisen; Martha Reamy, *Early Families of Otsego County, New York*, (Westminster, 2001), vol. 1, 80.

17. Census for 1855, United States Department of Commerce, Bureau of the Census. *Owego Gazette*, 1 June 1882.

18. Practice Book of Doctor E. W. Spafford of Cherry Valley from 1834 to 1836, Collection of Dominick J. Reisen; Vieve Metcalfe, "The Metcalfs of Middlefield, Otsego County, New York," unpublished paper, 1; Copy of Metcalf certificate to practice medicine, Collection of Rodney and Jeanne Johnson.

19. Records of the Poor, 1 December 1832.

20. James Arthur Frost, *Life on the Upper Susquehanna, 1783-1860*, (New York, 1951), 34; *Otsego Herald*, 23 April 1814.

21. Deed between Joshua L. and Mary Pinney and John Hayden and Benjamin D. North recorded 2 May 1835, liber 54, 23, Otsego County Clerk. This store building was moved to the grounds of the Farmers' Museum in Cooperstown in 1951.

22. *The Freeman's Journal* (Cooperstown), 7 September 1835.

23. Frost, *The Susquehanna*, 104. One such poster has been preserved in its original location in North's tavern and is now in the collection of Rodney and Jeanne Johnson, the current owners of this building.

24. Barnabus M. Gilbert, "A Part of Farm No 17 in the Outhout Patent, formerly owned by Gilbert Ely" (1861), George Hyde Clarke Family Papers, #2800, Division of Rare and Manuscript Collections, Cornell University Library, Ithaca; Frost, *The Susquehanna*, 20; Alf Evers, *The Catskills: From Wilderness to Woodstock*, (New York, 1972), 333-334.

25. Freemasons in Middlefield to Grand Lodge of New York, 23 December 1823, vol. 123 of the Grand Lodge of Free and Accepted Masons of the State of New York Archives, The Chancellor Robert R Livingston Masonic Library and Museum, New York; Trustee Minutes of the First Baptist Society in Middlefield, Book 1, 1825-1833.

26. Frost, *The Susquehanna*, 104.

27. *The Freeman's Journal*, 8 July 1839.

28. George Rogers Taylor, *The Transportation Revolution 1815-1860*, (New York, 1951), 16.

29. Letter from Rufus H. Hibbard to Joshua (?) L. Phelon, 22 November 1847, Collection of Dominick J. Reisen.

30. Taylor, *The Transportation Revolution*, 23-25; L. Ray Gunn, *The Decline of Authority: Public Economic Policy and Political Development in New York State, 1800-1860*, (Ithaca, 1988), 36-37; *Cherry Valley Gazette*, 12 January 1830; Joseph Austin Durrenberger, *Turnpikes: A Study of the Toll Road Movement in the Middle Atlantic States and Maryland*, (Valdosta, 1931), 156-158.

31. *The Freeman's Journal*, 20 July 1830.

32. William Cooper, *A Guide in the Wilderness*, (Cooperstown, 1936), 21-22.

33. Taylor, *The Transportation Revolution*, 33.

34. Beardsley, *Reminiscences*, 214.

35. Carol Sheriff, *The Artificial River: The Erie Canal and the Paradox of Progress, 1817-1862*, (New York, 1996), 23; *The Freeman's Journal*, 17 April 1826; Taylor, *The Transportation Revolution*, 33-34.

36. Sheriff, *The Artificial River*, 123.

37. David Maldwyn Ellis, *Landlords and Farmers in the Mohawk-Hudson Region 1790-1850*, (Ithaca, 1946), 123, 172; Frost, *The Susquehanna*, 75-76.

38. Ralph Birdsall, *The Story of Cooperstown*, (Cooperstown, 1954), 68-69.

39. Beardsley, *Reminiscences*, 275.

40. Ellis, *Landlords and Farmers*, 160-161, 173.

41. *Owego Gazette*, 25 October 1855, 3 March 1898; Dorothy Scott Fielder, *Otsego County Postal History*, (Walton, 1994), 92.

42. Deed between William A. Ely and Joshua L. Pinney recorded 27 July 1838, liber 36, 9, Tioga County Clerk, Owego.

43. Metcalfe, *The Metcalfs*, 2. Deed between Erek and Jane Howard and Azel E. Metcalf recorded 31 September 1834, liber 52, 131; Deed between Henry Guy and George Clarke recorded 11 December 1828, liber OO, 214-215; Deed between Jane Howard and Henry Guy recorded 3 September 1834, liber 52, 129-130, Otsego County Clerk.

44. School Bill, 17 March 1828, Diary of George Washington Johnson, Town of Middlefield Historical Association. See also Appendix 8. Deed between Erek Bradford and Azel Metclaf recorded 10 November 1833, Liber ZZ, 219-221, Otsego County Clerk.

45. Taylor, *The Transportation Revolution*, 29-31; George Geddes, "Plank Roads," *Scientific American* (April 27, 1850).

46. Daniel B. Klein and John Majewski, "Plank Road Fever in Antebellum America: New York State Origins," *New York State History: Quarterly Journal of the New York State Historical Association* LXXV/1 (1994): 45, 47.

47. Taylor, *The Transportation Revolution*, 29-31.

48. Ibid., 31; Ellis, *Landlords and Farmers*, 182.

49. Beardsley, *Reminiscences*, 219, 222; Taylor, *The Transportation Revolution*, 76; Terri L. Premo, *Winter Friends: Women Growing Old in the New Republic, 1785-1835*, (Chicago, 1990), 137.

50. Taylor, *The Transportation Revolution*, 79, 103; Sheriff, *The Artificial River*, 78. Gunn, *The Decline of Authority*, 104-105.

51. Jim Loudon, "Pioneer Railroads of Otsego County, 1827-1837," *Leatherstocking Journal* (Third Quarter, 1997), 3-6.

52. Ibid.

53. Ibid.

54. Thomas Summerhill, *Harvest of Dissent*, (Chicago, 2005), 121

55. *The Freeman's Journal*, 3 March 1854, 23 May 1856.

56. Hurd, *History of Otsego County*, 189.

57. Ibid.

58. Dominick J. Reisen, *Inscriptions from the Middlefield Baptist Cemetery: With Select Genealogical Information*, (Middlefield, 2002), 3. Christian Deyo's grave is the oldest extant grave in the Baptist cemetery in Middlefield. "A Bit of Middlefield History," *Otsego Farmer*, 1912; List of Students and School Bill, Johnson Diary. See Appendices 6 and 8.

59. Methodist Church Records, Book 2 (1863-1881), Middlefield Town Historian Files. These records were copied from the originals by Harriet Rogers, Middlefield Town Historian, in 1981. The originals were borrowed from Danny Moore and were unable to be located by Dominick J. Reisen. In 1981, Book 1 of these records was reported lost. Hallesville was later known as Pleasant Brook and became part of the town of Roseboom when that town was divided from Cherry Valley in 1847.

60. Reisen, *Inscriptions*, 4.

61. Deed between George Clarke and the Trustees of the Methodist Episcopal Society of the Town of Middlefield recorded 12 January 1829, liber OO, 303-304, Otsego County Clerk.

62. Johnson Diary, 21 June 1823.

63. The Methodist church has undergone significant alterations since its construction, most notably in 1910 when the belfry was moved and the interior was redesigned. This description of the original appearance of the church is based on a c. 1908 photograph taken before these renovations were made. Photographic postcard, Collection of Rodney and Jeanne Johnson; Hurd, *History of Otsego County*, 190.

64. Trustee Minutes, Book 1, 5 June 1833, and Book 2, 7 September 1835, First Baptist Society in Middlefield. For Daniel North's note see a loose sheet in Book 2 entitled "Balance Sheet" which records monies clearly collected and expended for the purchase of this house. Although, a search of deeds in the Otsego County Clerk's office did not reveal a deed for this house held by the Trustees of the First Baptist Society in Middlefield, it seems clear that the Baptists took possession of this house as a parsonage. The house is listed as their parsonage on Barnabus M Gilbert, "Map of Subdivisions No's 17 & 18 in Great Lot No 12, and a part of Subdivision No 21 in Great Lot No 13, Oothout Patent" (1851), George Hyde Clarke Family Papers, #2800, Division of Rare and Manuscript Collections, Cornell University Library, Ithaca.

65. Deed between Joshua Pitney and Sumner Ely and Erastus Sterling recorded 30 December 1833, liber ZZ, 368-369, Otsego County Clerk.

66. Deed between Benjamin and Elizabeth North and Erastus S. Sterling recorded 4 September 1834, liber 52, 132-133, Otsego County Clerk.

67. Deed between Richard M. Kemball and Silas Devol recorded 9 June 1835, liber 54, 301, Otsego County Clerk.

68. Reamy, *Early Families*, (Westminter, 2001), vol. I, 40, 80.

69. *The Freeman's Journal*, 18 January 1828.

70. Hurd, *History of Otsego County*, 190.

71. *The Freeman's Journal,* 9 November 1835.

72. Beardsley, *Reminiscences,* 446-447.

73. *The Freeman's Journal,* 10 July 1826.

74. Will of George Clarke dated 25 August 1835, Otsego County Surrogate's Court.

75. Hurd, *History of Otsego County,* 30.

76. Waldo Ellsworth, "Cooperstown's First Bank," *New York State History: Quarterly Journal of the New York State Historical Association* XXII (1941), 404-405.

77. Deed between Anthony and Hannah Lynes and Eben B. Morehouse recorded 3 March 1834, liber 51, 119, Otsego County Clerk.

78. Van Horne, *History of Otsego Lodge,* 54; Birdsall, *Cooperstown,* 225-229; Deed between Eben B. and Eliza C. Morehouse and Samuel W. Beall recorded 14 June 1936, liber 57, 54-55, and Deed between Samuel W. Beall and Eben B. and Eliza C. Morehouse recorded 1 July 1839, liber 64, 178-180, Otsego County Clerk.

79. Will of George Clarke, Otsego County Surrogate's Court.

80. Birdsall, *Cooperstown,* 239.

81. Deed between George Clarke and Ebenezer Pratt recorded 1 July 1829, liber RR, pages 184-185, and Deed between Ebenezer and Mary Pratt and Clark D. Parshall recorded 11 April 1836, liber 53, page 458, Otsego County Clerk.

Chapter Five: A STEADY PROSPERITY

1. Horatio Gates Spafford, *A Gazetteer of the State of New York: Embracing an Ample Survey and Description of its Counties, Towns, Cities, VIllages, Canals, Mountains, Lakes, Rivers, Creeks, and Natural Topography,* (Interlaken, 1981), 316; Duane Hamilton Hurd, *History of Otsego County, New York, with Illustrations and Biographical Sketches,* (Ovid, 1978), 188.

2. *Otsego Herald* (Cooperstown), 10 May 1819.

3. Henry Conklin, *Through "Poverty's Vale": A Hardscrabble Boyhood in Upstate New York, 1832-1862,* (Syracuse, 1974), 26.

4. Donald B. Marti, "In Praise of Farming: An Aspect of the Movement for Agricultural Improvement in the Northeast, 1815-1840," *New York State History: Quarterly Journal of the New York State Historical Association* LI/4 (1970): 352.

5. Hurd, *History of Otsego County,* 43; *Otsego Herald,* 4 September 1817.

6. *Otsego Herald,* 12 June 1820, 9 October 1820; *The Freeman's Journal* (Cooperstown), 10 March 1828.

7. *The Freeman's Journal,* 5 June 1826, 16 November 1835, 8 July 1839.

8. Spafford, *Gazetteer,* 316, 393; Census for 1835, United States Department of Commerce, Bureau of the Census; *The Freeman's Journal,* 1854.

9. Spafford, *Gazetteer,* 316; L. Ray Gunn, *The Decline of Authority: Public Economic Policy and Political Development in New York State, 1800-1860,* (Ithaca, 1988), 101; Barnabus M. Gilbert, "A Part of Farm No 17 in the Outhout Patent, formerly owned by Gilbert Ely" (1861), George Hyde Clarke Family Papers, #2800, Division of Rare and Manuscript Collections, Cornell University Library, Ithaca.

10. E. Pomeroy Staats, *Town of Middlefield, Otsego County, New York*, (Middlefield, 1991), 38, 42; *The Freeman's Journal*, 3 April 1826.

11. David Maldwyn Ellis, *Landlords and Farmers in the Hudson-Mohawk Region, 1790-1850*, (New York, 1967), 196-197; Census for 1855, United States Department of Commerce, Bureau of the Census.

12. Horatio Gates Spafford, *A Gazetteer of the State of New York: Carefully Written From Original and Authentic Materials, Arranged on a New Plan In Three Parts*, (Albany, 1813), 238; Spafford, *Gazetteer [original]*, 316; Conklin, *Through Poverty's Vale*, 111.

13. For a general discussion of the phenomenon of the rural division of labor in nineteenth century New York, see Nancy Grey Osterud, *Bonds of Community: The Lives of Farm Women in Nineteenth Century New York*, (Ithaca, 1991).

14. Ibid., 33; Henry Hilton Wood, *Experiences and Activities of a Lifetime*, (Longbeach, 1934), 52; Manning and Mortimer Gilbert Store Ledger (fragment), Collection of Rodney and Jeanne Johnson.

15. Hurd, *History of Otsego County*, 188, 52; *The Freeman's Journal*, 21 February 1846.

16. Eunice R. Stamm, *The History of Cheese Making in New York State*, (Endicott, 1991), 33; Eric Brunger, "A Chapter in the Growth of the New York State Dairy Industry, 1850-1900," *New York State History: Quarterly Journal of the New York State Historical Association* XXXVI/2 (1955): 137; Hurd, *History of Otsego County*, 188; Ellis, *Landlords and Farmers*, 203.

17. Stamm, *Cheese Making*, 36; Hamilton Child, *Gazetteer and Business Directory of Otsego County, N. Y. for 1872-3*, (Syracuse, 1872), 193; Deed between Lucinda Storms and James H. Pope recorded 1 April 1851, liber 92, 527-528, Otsego County Clerk, Cooperstown; *The Freeman's Journal*, 21 February 1846.

18. Jacob Morris, *Address of Gen. Jacob Morris, President of the Otsego County Agricultural Society*, (Cooperstown, 1817), 6.

19. Simon W. Rosendale, "Closing Phases of the Manorial System in Albany," *New York State History: Quarterly Journal of the New York State Historical Association* VIII (1909): 235; Dorothy Kubik, *A Free Soil - A Free People: The Anti-Rent War in Delaware County, New York*, (Fleischmanns, 1997), 11, 21, 66; Henry Christman, *Tin Horns and Calico: A Decisive Episode in the Emergence of Democracy*, (New York, 1945), 17-18.

20. Thomas Summerhill, *Harvest of Dissent: Agrarianism in Nineteenth-Century New York*, (Chicago, 2005), 75.

21. Christman, *Tin Horns and Calico*, 151, 206.

22. Will of William Cooper as stated in David M. Ellis, "The Coopers and New York State Landholding Systems," *New York State History: Quarterly Journal of the New York State Historical Association* XXXV (1954): 413; Ellis, *Landlords and Farmers*, 237; Christman, *Tin Horns and Calico*, 39, 41.

23. Christman, *Tin Horns and Calico*, 291.

24. Summerhill, *Harvest of Dissent*, 80; Martha Reamy, *Early Families of Otsego County, New York*, (Westminster, 2001), vol. I, 80.

25. Summerhill, *Harvest of Dissent*, 83; Kubik, *A Free Soil*, 123.

26. Christman, *Tin Horns and Calico*, 292-293. Child, *Gazetteer*, 192-193.

27. Thomas Summerhill, "Farming on Shares: Landlords, Tenants, and the Rise of the Hop and Dairy Economies in Central New York," *New York State History: Quarterly Journal of the New York State Historical Association* LXXVI/2 (1995): 130-132.

28. Conklin, *Through Poverty's Vale*, 27.

29. George Potts to William B. Campbell, 2 September 1836, Campbell Family Papers, Box 1, New York State Historical Association, Cooperstown.

30. Summerhill, *Harvest of Dissent*, 88, 91; *The Freeman's Journal*, 14 March 1878.

31. Chattel Mortgage, George Clarke to John Chamberlain, 25 June 1857, Clarke Family Papers, #2800.

32. Michael A. Tomlan, *Tinged With Gold: Hop Culture in the United States*, (Athens, 1992), 18-19; Hurd, *History of Otsego County*, 52.

33. Wood, *Experiences and Activities*, 50-52.

34. Tomlan, *Tinged With Gold*, 85.

35. Summerhill, *Harvest of Dissent*, 96.

36. *The Freeman's Journal*, 15 May 1826.

37. Ibid., 29 August 1862.

38. Hurd, *History of Otsego County*, 52-53.

39. F. W. Beers, "Town of Middlefield, Otsego Co. N.Y.",, *Atlas of Otsego Co. New York*, 1868.

40. Tomlan, *Tinged With Gold*, 107-109.

41. *The Freeman's Journal*, 27 December 1845.

42. Barry L. Wold, *The George Hyde Clarke Family Papers, A Guide to the Collection at Cornell University*, (Ithaca, 1977), 21.

43. Harriet R. Rogers and Grace North Parshall, "The North Family of Middlefield Genealogy," unpublished paper, Town of Middlefield Historian Files; List of Students and School Bill for November 12, 1827 to February 15, 1828, Diary of George Washington Johnson, Town of Middlefield Historical Association.

44. Deed between Harrison North and James Cornwall, recorded 23 March 1846, liber 77, 383, and Deed between Harrison North and George L. Briggs recorded 13 March 1847, liber 80, 266, Otsego County Clerk; Beers, *Atlas of Otsego County*.

45. Deed between Harrison North and Aaron Van Allen recorded 27 November 1846, liber 79, 487, Deed between Harrison North and Benjamin D. North recorded 13 March 1847, liber 80, 265-266, and Deed between Harrison North and Benjamin D. North recorded 18 June 1851, liber 92, 63-64, Otsego County Clerk.

46. Deed Between Harrison North and John F. Seymour recorded 21 June 1847, liber 81, 175-176, Otsego County Clerk.

47. Staats, *Town of Middlefield*, (Middlefield, 1991), 20. For much of the Brown family genealogy, the author is indebted to Karin Brown, for her painstaking research into this family.

48. Deed between Moses R. Brown and Azel and Anna Maria Metcalf recorded 6 October 1841, liber 69, 333, and Deed between Azel and Anna Maria Metcalf, and Benjamin D. and Elizabeth North recorded 26 March 1842, liber 70, 381, Otsego

County Clerk.

49. Deed between Harrison North and Moses Brown, and Orra Knapp recorded 15 March 1849, liber 85, 199-200, Deed between Harrison North and Moses Brown, and Eugene and Clarissa North recorded 19 June 1859, liber 89, 425, Deed between Harrison North and Moses Brown, and Luke Swan recorded 12 September 1851, liber 92, 196-197. Deed between Harrison North and Moses Brown, and George Clarke recorded 25 October 1851, liber 92, 381-382, and Deed between Harrison North and Moses Brown, and Nathan and Mary Watson recorded 30 March 1855, liber 102, 565, Otsego County Clerk.

50. Deed between Harrison North and Erastus Belknap, and Hiram Palmer recorded 10 May 1858, liber 112, 255, and Deed between Harrison North, Helen North, and Erastus Belknap, and heirs of Zimri Palmer recorded 22 December 1859, Otsego County Clerk.

51. Deed between Harrison North and Joseph Chiles recorded 17 April 1854, liber 101, 217-218, Deed between Harrison North and Daniel Aldrich, and Levi Cummings recorded 8 March 1864, liber 128, 168-170, and Deed between Harrison North and the estate of Peleg Coffin recorded 11 May 1872, liber 161, 494-495, Otsego County Clerk; Wayne Franklin, *A Rural Carpenter's World: The Craft in a Nineteenth Century New York Township*, (Iowa City, 1990), 216.

52. Otsego County Agricultural Society, *Transactions for the Year 1862*, (Cooperstown, 1863), 3, 8, 13, 19.

53. Deed between Harrison North and George Clarke recorded 14 December 1850 liber 90, 102-104, Otsego County Clerk; "A Map of a Lot of Land sold by George Clarke to Harrison North," George Hyde Clarke Family Papers, #2800, Division of Rare and Manuscript Collections, Cornell University Library, Ithaca; Beers, *Atlas of Otsego County*; G. W. Parshall, "Middlefield Fifty Years Ago," *Otsego Farmer* (Cooperstown), 1903.

54. Franklin, *A Rural Carpenter's World*, 31-35, 206. The date of the construction of Harrison North's house is taken from the cornerstone which also notes Ashley as the builder.

55. The information on Daniel Green is from Marian Holmes, who is his direct descendant. The house along the Cooperstown Road is no longer extant, having burned in the mid-twentieth century. An undated letter from Helen Pitts, a descendant of Harrison North, in the author's collection states that Daniel Green built the staircase in the North house. Deed between Alfred G. Cross and George L. Briggs recorded 23 July 1844, liber 75, 247, Otsego County Clerk.

56. Vieve Metcalfe, "The Metcalfs of Middlefield, Otsego County, New York," unpublished paper, 2; Deed between Azel E. Metcalf, and Benjamin D. and Elizabeth North, recorded 26 March 1842, liber 70, 381, Otsego County Clerk.

57. Metcalfe, "The Metcalfs of Middlefield," 4; Deed between Daniel A. and Esther Cummings, and Stephen F. Wickham recorded 1 October 1841, liber 71, 67, Otsego County Clerk.

58. *The Freeman's Journal*, 12 November 1858.

59. Rogers and Parshall, "The North Family."

60. Filing between Anson C. Parshall, assignee, and Sumner Ely and Alexander Murray recorded 16 July 1851, liber 93, 5-8, Otsego County Clerk.

61. Barnabus M. Gilbert, "A Map of Great Lots No's 11, 12, 13 & 14 in the Oothout Patent, Resurveyed and mapped" (1851), Clarke Family Papers, #2800; Deed between Anson C. Parshall, assignee of Sumner Ely and Alexander Murray, and Harrison North and Moses R. Brown recorded 14 October 1851, liber 92, 330-331, and Filing between Anson C. Parshall, assignee, and Sumner Ely and Alexander Murray recorded 16 July 1851, liber 93, 5-8, Otsego County Clerk.

62. Parshall, "Middlefield Fifty Years Ago."

63. *The Freeman's Journal*, 8 July 1858.

64. His name is alternately spelled LeRoy or Leroy, and his surname is alternately spelled as Bow or Bowe.

65. *Biographical Review*, (Boston, 1893), 84.

66. Ibid.; Deed between Benjamin D. and Elizabeth North, and Leroy E. Bow recorded 17, April 1848 liber 56, 83-84, Otsego County Clerk.

67. *Biographical Review*, (Boston, 1893), 83.

68. Deed between Samuel Shipman, and Robert and William Shipman recorded 15 May 1819, liber Z, 215-216, Deed between Jonah and Clarissa Griffin, and William Shipman recorded 16 December 1842, liber 71, 417-419, and Deed between Daniel M. and Marcia Green, and William Shipman recorded 17 January 1852, liber 93, 150-151, Otsego County Clerk.

69. Parshall, "Middlefield Fifty Years Ago;" List of Students and School Bill, Johnson Diary; *The Freeman's Journal*, 10 November 1883.

70. *Biographical Review*, (Boston, 1893), 417; Deed between Daniel Gilbert and Sumner Ely, and Carlton Briggs recorded 11 January 1836, liber 55, 215-216, Otsego County Clerk.

71. *Biographical Review*, (Boston, 1893), 417; Dominick J. Reisen, *Inscriptions from the Middlefield Baptist Cemetery: With Select Genealogical Information*, (Middlefield, 2002), 13; Barnabus M Gilbert, "A Map of Subdivisions No's 17 & 18 in Great Lot No 12, and a part of Subdivision No 21 in Great Lot No 13, Oothout Patent" (1851), George Hyde Clarke Family Papers, #2800, Division of Rare and Manuscript Collections, Cornell University Library, Ithaca; Deed between Sumner Murphy and Elihu C. Briggs recorded 28 February 1849, liber 85, 121-122, Otsego County Clerk; Parshall, "Middlefield Fifty Years Ago."

72. James M. Greiner, *Subdued by the Sword: A Line Officer in the 121st New York Volunteers*, (Albany, 2003), 3-4.

73. Gilbert, "A Map of Subdivisions No's 17 & 18 in Great Lot No 12," Clarke Family Papers, #2800; *Map of Otsego Co. New York from Actual Surveys by C. and R. C. Gates*, (Philadelphia, 1856); Trustee Minutes, First Baptist Society in Middlefield. All three of these men list their occupation as blacksmith in "Enrollment of Persons Liable to Military Duty in the Town of Middlefield," January 1864, Town of Middlefield Historian Files; Copy of letterhead for J. J. Allen & Son, blacksmith, Collection of

Dominick J. Reisen.

74. Gerald Carson, *The Old Country Store*, (New York, 1954), 21.

75. *The Freeman's Journal*, 21 February 1846.

76. Congregational Minutes of the First Baptist Society in Middlefield, 18 November 1854; Franklin, *A Rural Carpenter's World*, 41.

77. Manning and Mortimer Gilbert Store Ledger, Johnson Collection.

78. Carson, *The Old Country Store*, 23, 67.

79. Deed between Benjamin D. North and Harrison North recorded 18 June 1851, liber 92, 63-64, Otsego County Clerk; Gilbert, "A Map of Subdivisions No's 17 & 18 in Great Lot No 12," Clarke Family Papers, #2800; Dorothy Scott Fielder, *Otsego County Postal History*, (Walton, 1994), 92; *Map of Otsego Co. New York from Actual Surveys by C. and R. C. Gates*, (Philadelphia, 1856).

80. Deed between James Parshall Jr. and Clark D. Parshall recorded 11 September 1827, liber MM, 450, Otsego County Clerk. The information regarding the store being painted red comes from a reference in the deed between James Cook and Stephen Wickham recorded 1 August 1842, liber 71, 67-68, which uses Parshall's "red store" as the starting boundary point. Results of the Auction of Slips for the Baptist Church, Trustee Minutes, First Baptist Society in Middlefield; Child, *Gazetteer and Business Directory*, 193.

81. Deed between John F. and Frances Seymour, and Luke Swan recorded 8 June 1853, liber 97, 237, and Deed between Luke Swan and Chauncey Yager recorded 29 May 1856, liber 107, 105-106, Otsego County Clerk; Child, *Gazetteer and Business Directory*, 195.

82. Deed between Stephen F. and Irene Wickham, and Mortimer and Barnabus M. Gilbert recorded 2 August 1841, liber 75, 261-262, and Deed between Amanda M Gilbert and Barnabus M. Gilbert recorded 17 October 1868, liber 148, 526-527, Otsego County Clerk; Child, *Gazetteer and Business Directory*, 195.

83. These wings were later altered to become porticoes only, extending along the entire sides of the house. The mortise marks for the hinges of the connecting doors are still evident in the window casings of each one of the two front parlors in the central block.

84. Trustee Minutes, First Baptist Society in Middlefield.

85. Carson, *The Old Country Store*, 42-43; Parshall, "Middlefield Fifty Years Ago."

86. *Map of Otsego Co. New York from Actual Surveys by C. and R. C. Gates*, (Philadelphia, 1856).

87. Deed between Hannah Howard and Nathan Watson recorded 10 December 1853, liber 99, 181, Deed between Nathan and Mary A. Watson, and Harrison North and Moses Brown recorded 30 March 1855, liber 102, 565, and Deed between Harrison and Helen North, and Moses Brown recorded 30 March 1855, liber 102, 565, Otsego County Clerk.

88. *Map of Otsego Co. New York from Actual Surveys by C. and R. C. Gates*, (Philadelphia, 1856).

89. Gilbert, "A Map of Subdivisions No's 17 & 18 in Great Lot No 12," Clarke Family

Papers, #2800; Deed between James S. and Diana Jones, and John F. Newell recorded 5 April 1847, liber 80, 391-392, and Deed between George Clarke and James S. Jones recorded 25 May 1847, liber 81, 80-81.Otsego County Clerk.

90. Deed between James S. Jones and Charles Warner recorded 21 February 1849, liber 85, 88-89, Otsego County Clerk.

91. Trustees Minutes, 14 January 1845, First Baptist Society in Middlefield. The Brockham tavern is only mentioned in a deed between Daniel and Marcia Green, and William Shipman in the Otsego County Clerk's office liber 93, 150-151. There is reference to the lot Shipman is purchasing as a "house lot in Clarksville on the road near Gilbert Mills toward a tavern kept by Peter Brockham." Brockham did not own this tavern, though. The only reference in the County Clerk's office to Brockham owning property is a purchase of a lot on Pine Street in Cooperstown in 1857 liber 111, 506-507.

92. This schoolhouse is clearly noted on the following maps: Gilbert, "A Map of Subdivisions No's 17 & 18 in Great Lot No 12," Clarke Family Papers, #2800; *Map of Otsego Co. New York from Actual Surveys by C. and R. C. Gates*, (Philadelphia, 1856); Beers, *Atlas of Otsego County*.

93. Parshall, "Middlefield Fifty Years Ago."

94. Deed between Clark D. Parshall and Orra Knapp recorded 29 May 1835, liber 54, 110-111, Otsego County Clerk.

95. Lease between Erastus and Hannah Belknap, and Jesse Brown recorded 1 April 1865, liber 132, 342-346, Lease to Robert W. Taylor recorded 1 April 1865, liber 132, 346, and Lease to Henry Guy recorded 1 April 1865, liber 132, 347, Otsego County Clerk; Gilbert, "A Map of Subdivisions No's 17 & 18 in Great Lot No 12," Clarke Family Papers, #2800.

96. Trustee Minutes, First Baptist Society in Middlefield.

97. Deed between Harrison and Helen North and Moses and Ellen Brown, and Jordan Follett recorded 3 March 1865, liber 132, 86-88, Otsego County Clerk.

98. *The Freeman's Journal*, 8 July 1839, 21 February 1846, 21 November 1856.

99. Frederick Shelly, *Early American Tower Clocks*, (Columbia, 1999), 135-136.

100. Ibid.

Chapter Six: An Abstraction Called War

1. For a detailed review of this Supreme Court case see James F. Simon, *Lincoln and Chief Justice Taney: Slavery, Secession, and the President's War Powers*, (New York, 2006).

2. James M. McPherson, *Battle Cry of Freedom: The Civil War Era*, (New York, 1988), 81; *The Freeman's Journal* (Cooperstown), 9 June 1854.

3. Henry Conklin, *Through "Poverty's Vale": A Hardscrabble Boyhood in Upstate New York, 1832-1862*, (Syracuse, 1974), 210; James M. Greiner, *Subdued by the Sword: A Line Officer in the 121st New York Volunteers*, (New York, 2003), 9, 216 n27.

4. *The Freeman's Journal*, 3 May 1861.

5. *Oneonta Herald*, 30 July 1862.

6. Conklin, *Through Poverty's Vale*, 212.

7. Vieve Metcalfe, "The Metcalfs of Middlefield, Otsego County, New York," unpublished paper, 4-5.

8. Ibid., 5.

9. Henry Hilton Wood, *Experiences and Activities of a Lifetime*, (Longbeach, 1934), 7-8.

10. *The Freeman's Journal*, 8 August 1862, 22 August 1862.

11. Colonel J. Lafayette Rider to Mrs. Lyman Foote, excerpted from *The Freeman's Journal*, 21 June 1861; *The Freeman's Journal*, 17 January 1862.

12. Congregational Minutes of the First Baptist Society in Middlefield, Book 2, 15 November 1862.

13. William Goodell, *Slavery and Anti-Slavery: A History of the Great Struggle in Both Hemispheres, with a view to the Slavery Question in the United States*, (New York, 1853). For a general discussion of abolition and the Protestant sects in America, see Ronald G. Walters, *The Antislavery Appeal: American Abolitionism After 1830*, (Baltimore, 1976), chapter 3.

14. Jennifer L. Weber, *Copperheads: The Rise and Fall of Lincoln's Opponents in the North*, (Oxford, 2006), 51.

15. This incident is related in great detail in Ralph Birdsall, *The History of Cooperstown*, (Cooperstown, 1954), 308-318.

16. Weber, *Copperheads*, 52.

17. Ibid., 89.

18. Ibid., 153; Birdsall, *Cooperstown*, 316.

19. Conklin, *Through Poverty's Vale*, 222-223.

20. "Enrollment of Persons Liable to Military Duty in the Town of Middlefield," January 1864, Town of Middlefield Historian Files.

21. Ibid.

22. "Enrollment of Persons," Town of Middlefield Historian Files; Methodist Church Records, Book 2 (1863-1881), Middlefield Town Historian Files.

23. "Enrollment of Persons," Town of Middlefield Historian Files; Weber, *Copperheads*, 90.

24. McPherson, *Battle Cry of Freedom*, 413, 572; Wood, *Experiences and Activities*, 16.

25. Thomas Summerhill, *Harvest of Dissent: Agrarianism in Nineteenth-Century New York*, (Urbana, 2005), 147; Wood, *Experiences and Activities*, 44; E. Pomeroy Staats, *Town of Middlefield, Otsego County, New York*, (Middlefield, 1991), 11.

26. Metcalfe, "The Metcalfs," 4-5; Wayne Franklin, *A Rural Carpenter's World: The Craft in a Nineteenth Century New York Township*, (Iowa City, 1990) 225.

27. Methodist Church Records, Book 2; Congregational Minutes, 17 December 1864, First Baptist Society in Middlefield.

28. Congregational Minutes, 16 October 1864, First Baptist Society in Middlefield.

29. Dominick J. Reisen, *Inscriptions from the Middlefield Baptist Cemetery: With Select Genealogical Information*, (Middlefield, 2002), 12.

30. Deed between Elihu and Amanda Briggs, and Alanson Briggs recorded 7 October 1879, liber 183, 339-342, Otsego County Clerk, Cooperstown.

31. Olive Cook, *The English Country House: An Art and a Way of Life*, (New York, 1974), 109. The clear evidence for this closet was still apparent in a shadow on the floor of the painted parlor demarcating the door and walls of the closet when the current owners, Rodney and Jeanne Johnson, purchased the house in 1962.

32. Martha Reamy, *Early Families of Otsego County, New York*, (Westminster, 2001), vol. 1, 40.

33. "Enrollment of Persons," Town of Middlefield Historian Files; Reamy, *Early Families*, 40, 80.

34. Congregational Minutes, 19 May 1866, First Baptist Society in Middlefield. In 2007 this organ was the oldest pipe organ in Otsego County and among the oldest in the United States.

35. Methodist Church Records, Book 2; *Biographical Review*, (Boston, 1893), 83-85.

Key to Index: n = endnote; *illus.* = see illustrations; *map* = see maps.

abolition. *See* slavery

academies. *See* schools

alcohol. *See* distilleries; farming, hops; taverns; temperance

Allen, C. F., 167

Allen, James and Samuel, 152

American Hotel. *See* hotels

Anti-Rent Wars, 131-36. *See also* leasehold system; share farming; tenant farmers

architects, *see* Benjamin, Asher; Ashley, William O.; Hooker, Philip; Jones, Inigo; Plaw, John

architectural styles: Egyptian Revival, 120; Federal, 12, 16, 31-32, 35, 38-39, 42, 45-47, 61, 75, 77, 115, 120, 122, 145, 147, 149, 159, 177; Gothic Revival, 115, 120, 152, 160-62, 177; Greek Revival, 39, 45-47, 71, 75-77, 107, 115, 120, 122, 145-46, 149-50, 156, 159-60; Italianate, 145, 154, 159, 177; Palladian, 38, 41-42, 55, *illus.*; Regency, 32

Ashley, William O., 145, 145n54, *illus.*

attorneys. *See* lawyers

Averell, James Jr., 14-15, 29

Bailey family, 24

Bailey, Harrison, 150-51

Bailey, Nathan, 53, 61, 65

Baptist church, 24, 36, 49, 51, 54-55, 57, 60, 63, 67-68, 70-71, 73, 79, 94, 98, 112-116, 116n64, 118, 122, 148, 151-53, 155-56, 158, 160-62, 167-68, 172-73, 176-78, *illus., map. See also* cemeteries; Methodist church; Cooperstown, Presbyterian church

Banyar, Goldsbrow, 5, 7, 10-11, 10n24, 17, 17n48, 33

Barnum, Abijah, 27

Beardsley, Levi, 60, 91, 106, 109, 118

Belknap, Erastus, 69, 143, 160

Benjamin, Asher, 55, 58, 115, 156, 177, *illus.*

Bennett, Ebenezer, 27

Bennett, Jonathan, 27

Besancon, Peter, 42-43, 49-50, 133

blacksmith, x, 49, 51, 59, 150-52, 152n73, 176-77, 179

Boid, George, 27

Bow, Leroy, 149-50, 149n64, 149n66, 156, 159, 167, 174, *map*

Bowers, Henry, 10, 21, 28-29, 35, 120

Bowers, John, 35, 120

Bowers Patent, 21, 120

Bowerstown, 10, 21, 22, 28, 35, 167

Boyce, Susan, 172

Brant, Joseph (Thayendanegea), 3, 9

Briggs, Alanson, 172

Briggs, Carlton, 151

Briggs, George L., 141, 145, *map*

Briggs, Elihu C., 151-52, 172, *map*

Brookins, Thaddeus, 27

Brown, Jesse, 160-61

Brown, Moses R., 139, 142-46, 148, 154, 157-58, 161, *map*

Buel, Oliver, 27

burial grounds. *See* cemeteries

Burlington (Otsego Co., NY), 14, 16, 29, 39, 69, 168

Butternuts (Otsego Co., NY), 42, 52

Cameron, Andrew, 28

Campbell, Jonah, 170

Campbell, Robert, 22, 110-11, 120

Campbell, William B., 67, 110, 135

canals, 99, 103-04, 106-10, 176; Champlain, 104; Chenango, 105-6; Erie, *ix*, 56, 87, 99, 103-6, 109-10, 128, 132; Susquehanna, 105-6

cancer, 172

carding machines, 48-49, 63, 124, 127-28, 130, *illus.*

Carroll House, 76

Caryl, Leonard, 118, 173

cemeteries, *xi*, 36, 69, 113-14, 113n58, 117-18, 145, 147-48, 172. *See also* churches

Cherry Valley (Otsego Co., NY), *ix*, 3-5, 7-8, 10-11, 13, 16, 21-23, 26-28, 36, 45, 61, 96, 101, 105, 108-109, 114, 114n59, 159, 166

Cherry Valley Creek, 3, 23-24, 26, 28, 37, 40, 42, 50, 70, 98, 101, 105, 108, 111, 124, 127-28, 130, 150-51, 158-59, 175-76

Cherry Valley Massacre, 3, 7-8

Cherry Valley Patent. *See* land patents

churches. *See* Baptist church; Cooperstown, Presbyterian church; Methodist church. *See also* cemeteries

Clark, James F., 139-41

Clarke family, 72, 132

Clarke, George: portrait, *see frontispiece*; life in England, 10, 17; homes, 12, 16, 48, 75, 146, 172, 175, 177, *see also* Hyde Hall; as landlord and speculator, 10-11, 16-20, 23, 25-26, 30-35, 38, 42, 46, 50, 54, 75, 77-78, 89, 107, 111, 114-16, 119, 121-22, 125, 132, 136, 146, 175, *see also* leasehold sytem; land title and tenant disputes, 10-11, 17, 33, 42, 133-34; and DeWitt Clinton, 33; and Richard F. Cooper, 119, 121; and William Cooper, 16; and Eben Morehouse, 119; and Joshua Pinney, 30; death of, 118-19, 121

Clarke, George Hyde (son): as landlord and speculator, 88-89, 119, 121, 127, 131-40, 143-44, 154-55, 158, 160; land title and tenant disputes, 131-136, *see also* Anti-Rent Wars, share farming; as gentleman farmer, 127, 131, 135-41, 144; bankruptcy, 141

Clarke, George (Lieutenant Governor, great-grandfather), 4-7

Clarkesville: names and spelling variations, *ix*, *xi*, 5, 48; municipal definition and boundaries, 21-22, 123; origins and early settlement, 4-13, 16-20; population trends, 19, 28-30, 47-48, 63, 88, 106, 109, 146, 177. *See also* Middlefield, Town of; Newtown-Martin

Clinton, James (General), 9, 105

Clinton, DeWitt (Governor), 33, 104-05, 126; Clintonians, 13

Coats, Evan, 93-5, 93n11

Cockburn, William, 30

Coffin, Peleg, 141, 143

Colbert, William (Reverend), 112-13

Collier, Peter (Colliersville), 111, 139

Compton, William, 143-44

Cone, Eilhu, 53

Conklin, Brewster, 138

Conklin, Henry, 135, 165, 169

Cooper family, 34, 72

Cooper, James Fenimore, 32, 39, 69, 126, 133

Cooper, Richard, 32, 119, 136

Cooper, Richard F., 119, 121

Cooper, William, 4, 13-16, 18-20, 25, 32, 34, 39, 71, 89, 95, 101, 103, 119-20, 133

Cooperstown, 15-16, 21, 23, 25, 28, 34, 36, 43, 45, 48, 52, 61, 63, 67, 70-71, 73, 76, 94, 101-02, 105-06, 110-11, 120-21, 137, 161, 165, 167; Presbyterian church, 29, 37, 71, 126

Council of Appointment, New York State, 13, 43, 50, 90, 97

Crandall, William, 126

Crandall family, 24

Crandall, John J., 52, 54-55, 57, 59

Crandall, Robert R. 167-68

Crippen, Silas, 36

Crippen, Schuyler, 110-11

Cummings, Daniel A., 39, 46-47, 60, 77, 89, 122, 147, 149, *map*

Cummings, Hosea, 31-32, 48, 77, *map*

Cummings, James, 57

dairy production. *See* farming

Devol, Silas, 54, 56, 61, 65, 67, 93-95, 117

Dewey, Joshua, 14-15

Dietz, Jacob, 110

distilleries, *x*, *xi*, 48-51,49n9, 61, 63, 71, 73-75, 99, 106, 116, 142, 147-49, 153,

178, *map. See also* taverns; temperance

divorce, 32, 74, 77

doctors, x, 38-40, 51, 66, 88, 90-93, 96, 117, 119, 146, 148-50, 172-73, 177. *See also* Ely, Sumner; Metcalf, Azel; Metcalf, George Washington; North, Jeremiah; Otsego County Medical Society; Spafford, E.W., Warren, Erastus; White,Joseph

Dodge, Timothy, 170

Dongan Patent, 33

Duane, James, 10-11, 18, 33

Dunbar, James H., 138

Dunham, Abner, 126

Dunlop, Samuel (Reverend), 4-5, 7, 23

East Worcester (Otsego Co., NY), 117, 173

education (of children), *See* schools

Edson, Lewis, 15, 22

Ely, Adriel Gilbert, 117

Ely, Benjamin Cornwall, 117

Ely, Hannah Gilbert, 16n46, 39-40, 66-68, 95, 117, 173

Ely, Sumner (Doctor), 32, 38-42, 49-52, 49n9, 56-57, 64, 66-69, 74-75, 78, 87-93, 92n8, 95-96, 98-99, 106-7, 116-17, 122, 134, 141, 146, 147-51, 153, 160, 164, 173-74, 177-78, *map*

Ely, Sumner Stow, 173

Ely, Theodore, 173

Ely, William A., 107

Ely, William Horace

Exeter (Otsego Co., NY), 63, 67

farming: dairy, 124, 128-31, 136, 153, 171; hops, 135-45, 148, 171, *illus.*, *map*. *See also* leasehold system; share farming; tenant farmers

Federalists, 13-14

Follett, Jordan C., 152, 160-61, *map*

Freeman's Journal, The, 69, 99, 110, 112, 123, 136, 140, 153, 161, 164-65, 167

Freemasons, 15, 15n44, 38-39, 42-43, 45, 51-54, 54n19, 56, 71-75, 77-78, 92, 98, 112, 116, 120, 122, *illus.*

funerals. *See* cemeteries

Gallop, Nathanial, 27

Gibbs, Oliver, 27

Gilbert family, 90, 117

Gilbert, Barnabus M., 31, 144, 155, *map*

Gilbert, Benjamin, 12-16, 20, 22-23, 31-

32, 35-36, 39-40, 60, 87-88, 96, 117-18, 150-51, 160

Gilbert, Benjamin Jr., 52-53

Gilbert, Daniel, 49-51, 53-54, 56-57, 61, 64-66, 68, 73-74, 78, 87-88, 98, 116, 151, 177

Gilbert, Manning, 129, 154-56, 177, *illus.*

Gilbert, Mortimer, 129, 154-55, 177, *illus.*

Godfrey Miller Patent. *See* land patents

Goodell, William, 168

gravestones, graveyards. *See* cemeteries

Green, Daniel, 145-46, 146n55, 150, 177

Green, Isaac, 27, 113

Griffin, Samuel, 22-23, 26, 35, 40, 47, 87

Guy, Henry, 38, 107, 160-61, *map*

Harley, Nathaniel, 27

Hartwick Seminary, 14, 149

Hawkes, James (Sheriff), 40, 42

Hayden family, 24, *map*

Hayden, Alfred, 157

Hayden, John, 49, 52, 87, 97-98, 106, 116, 150, *map*

Hendrix, Cornelius, 27

Henry, Francis (Colonel), 14, 126

Herdman, George, 159

Hinds, Lucian, 135

Hinman, Carlton, 12, 173

Hodgson, Thomas, 37

Hooker, Philip, 34

hops. *See* farming

Hoskins, Daniel, 37, 73

hotels, 31-32, 38n47, 76-77, 107, 117, 157-59, *illus.*; American Hotel, 38n47, 158-59, *illus. See also* taverns

How, Jesse, 37, 73

Howard, Hannah, 31-2, 77-78, 107, 157, *illus.*

Howard, Jane, 68, 107

Howard, Nathan, 74, 77

Hubbell, Hannah, 22, 28

Hyde Hall, 32-5, 46, 54, 88, 118-9, 121, 136-41; in England, 10

inns. *See* hotels; taverns

Ingalls (Ingals), James, 26, 27

Ingalls (Ingals), Samuel, 69

Ismond Elias, 57, 113

Ismond, Louis, 170

Johnson, Benjamin, 28

Johnson, George Washington, 50nn11-12, 52n14, 64-68, 95, 107, 116, 141-42, 147,

150
Johnson, John (Sir), 8
Johnson, William (Sir), 6, 8-9
Jones, Amos, 37, 73
Jones, Inigo, 35
Jones, James, 32, 158, *map*
Jordan, Ambrose L., 42-43, 49-50, 119,
    121, 133
Judd, Oliver (Judd's Iron Works), 41-42
judges, local, 13, 16, 32, 35, 41, 50, 92-93,
    97, 147, 168. *See also* justices
justices: US Supreme Court, 3-4, 149, 164,
    168 (*see also* Nelson, Samuel; Taney, Ro-
    ger); NYS Supreme Court, 121, 134
Kaple, Bela, 52
Kent, Moss Jr., 14-15, 25
Killpatrick, Samuel, 26-27
Knapp, Orra, 24, 143, 159-61, *map*
Knox, Peter, 68
land patents: in New York, 3; Cherry Val-
    ley Patent, 4-6; Godfrey Miller Patent,
    4-5, 11, 16, 21-22; Long (Outhout) Pat-
    ent, 4-6, 11-12, 16, 19-20, 22-29, 34-35,
    41; Oriskany Patent, 4; Otsego Patent,
    5; Springfield Patent, 11
Lawson, Benjamin, 57
lawyers, x, 7, 10, 15, 17, 43, 65, 120-21,
    133, 136, 149-50, 173. *See also* judges;
    justices
leasehold system, 17, 18, 131-32. *See also*
    Anti-Rent Wars; farming; share farming;
    tenant farmers
Lindsay, John, 4
Livingston family, 16, 25, 33, 72, 89, 136
Livingston, Robert R., 30, 109
Long (Outhout) Patent. *See* land patents
Long Patent Road, 11, 16, 21-22, 38-41,
    46, 48, 60, 68, 77, 122, 143, 146-7, 152,
    160, 173, *illus. See also* roads
Macumber, Edwin, 159
mail service. *See* postal service
Manzer, John, 57
Marks, Benoni, 69, 172
Marks, Egbert, 155, 172
Marsh, Emma, 171
Mason, Daniel, 126
Masons. *See* Freemasons
McCollum family, 24
McCollum, Alexander, 7, 28
McCollum, Daniel, 7, 113

Meneely Bell Foundry, 162
merchants and stores, x, xi, 6, 11, 14, 25,
    28-29, 40, 43, 48, 50-51, 59, 64, 67, 75,
    78, 93, 97, 103-4, 106, 110, 112, 117,
    124, 129-31, 139, 142, 146, 152-58, 161,
    164, 170-71, 173, 175-79. *See also* ped-
    dlers
Metcalf, Anna Maria, 146
Metcalf, Azel (Doctor), 95-96, 107, 109,
    122, 142, 144, 146-50, 157, 172, *illus.*
Metcalf(e), George Washington (Doctor),
    146-48, 166, 171-74, *illus.*
Metcalf(e), Nancy Wickham, 166, 172
Methodist church, 112-15, 114n59,
    115n63, 122-23, 143, 152, 161, 170-72,
    174, *illus., map. See also* Baptist church;
    cemeteries; Cooperstown, Presbyterian
    church
Middlefield, Hamlet of. *See* Clarkesville
Middlefield, Town of, 21-22
Middlefield Centre. *See* Newtown-Martin
Milford (Otsego Co., NY), 52, 122, 134-
    135, 149-50, 158-59
Milford Center (Otsego Co., NY), 73, 153
mills, x-xi, 5-6, 19, 25-29, 41-43, 48-51,
    63-64, 74, 89, 92, 98, 101, 124, 127-28,
    130, 133, 150-51, 159-60, 175-77, 179,
    illus., map
Moake, John, 28
Morehouse, Eben, 69, 87, 119-21
Morell, George (General), 92, 111
Morris, Jacob (General), 14, 20, 69, 89,
    125-26, 131
mural painting. *See* Price, William
Murphy, James, 27, 57
Murphy, Smith, 53, *map*
Murray, Alexander, 147-49, 153, 178, 180,
    map
Nelson, Samuel (Justice), 41, 168
New Lisbon (NY) Congregational
    Church, 58
Newtown-Martin, 5, 7-8, 10, 14, 16, 21-
    22, 22n4, 28, 141; *See also* Clarkesville;
    land patents, Long Patent; Middlefield,
    Town of
North, Benjamin D., 28, 37, 50, 53-54, 59,
    61n34, 73, 96, 98n23, 127, 141-42, 146,
    157-58, 161, 177, *map*
North, Benjamin D. Jr., 40, 47-48, 50-51,
    54, 56-57, 75-79, 88, 96-99, 106, 116-17,

123, *illus.*

North, Daniel, 50, 56-57, 75, 113, 115, 116n64, 126-27, 141, 161

North, Elizabeth Gilbert, 16n46, 61n34, 75-76, 116, 149, 177

North, Harrison, 139-47, 145n54, 153-54, 157, 159, 177, *illus., map*

North, Harry, 147, 155, *map*

North, Jeremiah (Doctor), 147-49, 155

North, Waity, 147

North, William (Colonel), 18, 35

Oaksville (Otsego Co., NY), 53, 128

Olds, Ephraim, 59

Oneonta (Otsego Co., NY), 73, 105, 109-12, 153

Oneonta *Herald*, 165

Oriskany Patent. *See* land patents

Otsego County Agricultural Society, 125-26, 131, 144

Otsego County Bank, 120

Otsego County Medical Society, 35, 90-91, 95-96. *See also* doctors

Otsego County Poor House, 90-96, 111

Otsego *Herald*, 10, 97, 106, 110, 125

Otsego Lake, 9, 11, 21-22, 32, 34-35, 45, 52, 54, 63, 105-06, 109-11

Otsego Patent. *See* land patents

Outhout (Oothout) Patent. *See* land patents

Outhout, Volkert, 4. *See also* land patents

Owego (Tioga Co., NY), 106-07, 109, 146, 171-72

Palmer, Zimri, 127, 143

Parshall, Anson C., 22n4, 147, 172

Parshall, Clark D., 39, 46, 78, 89, 97, 122, 154-55, 160, *map*

Parshall, George Washington, 151, 159

Parshall, James, 24, 159, *map*

Parshall, James Jr., 54, 154

Parshall, John, 24

Parshall, Phebe Coddington, 24

Parshall store, 59n30, 154-155, 155n80, *illus.*

patents, land. *See* land patents

Pearce, Nathan, 27

Peck, Jedediah, 14, 29, 39

Peck, Tabitha Ely, 39

peddlers, 157. *See also* merchants and stores

Phinney, Elihu, 14-16, 71, 92n8, 93n10,

106, 140

Phinney, Elihu (son), 69, 93, 93n10

Phinney, Henry, 92, 92n8, 106, 110

Phoenix Mills (Phoenixville, Otsego Co., NY), 21, 128, 139-40

Phoenix Woolen Mill, 128. *See also* wool production

physicians. *See* doctors

Pierce, Benjamin, 144, 167

Pinney family, 153, 74

Pinney, Charlotte, 67

Pinney, Eliza, 49, 52n14

Pinney, Gilbert, 24, 37

Pinney, Hammon, 106

Pinney, Joshua L., 19, 30-32, 30n26, 36-41, 46-50, 49n9, 52-57, 54n19, 59-61, 59n30, 61n34, 64, 66-68, 71-75, 78, 89, 97-99, 106-07, 116, 126, 141-42, 144, 146, 149, 153-54, 157, 178, *illus., map*

Pinney, Polly, 37, 61n34, 67, 73, 153, 178

Pitts, Betsey, 36-37, 113

Pitts, Hiram, 157

plank roads. *See* roads

Plaw, John, 34

Pomeroy, George, 69, 95

Pope, James, 131

postal service, x, 47-48, 51, 71, 75, 123, 154, *illus.*

pot ash manufacturing, 24-25

Potts, George, 135, 143

Powers, Ingraham (Elder, Reverend), 146, 172

Prentiss, John H., 120, 126

Preston, Samuel, 135

Prevost, G. W., 36

Price, William, 76, 97

Prigg v. Pennsylvania, 164

railroads, 99, 108-112, 139, 176

Rice, Daniel, 114

Rice, Leopold, 157

Rich, Elijah, 41, 46, 60-61, 151

Rich, Moses, 19, 25-28, 41, 42n58, 87, 142, 144

Rich Moses Jr., 42, 42n58, 46, 49-53, 89

Rich, Reuben, 40-42, 178

Risendorf, John, 135

rivers: Hudson, *ix*, 4, 11, 16-17, 19, 25, 33-34, 45, 76-77, 89, 103-104, 132, 175; Mohawk, 6, 8, 25, 45, 89, 104, 109, 132, 191; Susquehanna, 8-9, 17, 21, 105-06,

109, 111, 120

roads: development of, *x*, 5-6, 19, 21, 23-29, 31, 43, 46, 49, 78, 99-103, 108-9, 148, 153, 175-76, *illlus.*; plank roads, 100, 108-09; turnpikes (toll roads), 27, 99-103, 108-9, 153; State Route 166, 3. *See also* Long Patent Road

Roseboom (Otsego Co., NY), 101, 108, 114n59, 159

Roseboom, Abraham, 29

Russell, John, 93, 95

Sawin, Albert, 64

Sawin, Benjamin (Elder, Reverend), 24, 32, 36-37, 51, 64, 66, 70, 118

Schenevus (Otsego Co., NY), 48

Schenevus Creek, 109, 111

Schenevus Valley News, 143

schools in: Middlefield, *x-xi*, 5, 15, 22-23, 27, 28, 36-38, 43, 45, 54, 60-68, 61n34, 71, 76, 93, 95, 100, 107, 112-13, 116-17, 122, 124, 141-42, 145, 147, 150-51, 159, 162, 175-76, 178, *map*; Cherry Valley, 13, 22-23, 60, 65; Cooperstown, 14, 45, 60-61, 63; Exeter, 63, 67-68; Gilbertsville, 65

Seymour, John, 142, 155

share farming, 18, 135-138, 140. *See also* Anti-Rent Wars; farming; leasehold system; tenant farmers

Shipman, O. N., 144

Shipman, William, 141, 147, 150-151, 220en5:91, *map*

slavery (and abolitionism), *xii*, 29, 45, 68-71, 79, 164, 167-68, 171, 173-74, 178

Smith, Jonathan, 27

Smith, Stephen, 25

Snyder, Chancellor, 170

South Valley (Otsego Co., NY), 147

Spafford. E. W. (Doctor), 96

Spaulding, Dunham, 16n46, 40, 52

Springfield (Otsego Co., NY), 7-8, 11, 15, 21, 25-26, 34, 46, 76, 131, 137-38, 173

Springfield Patent. *See* land patents

stage coaches, 101-03

Starkweather, George, 69, 120

Starkweather, Samuel, 110-11

Sterling, Erastus, 61n34, 74-75, 87, 99, 116-17, 120, 159

Stetson, Oliver, 27-28, 30

Stillman, George, 69, 95

stores and shops. *See* merchants and stores

Sullivan, John (General), 9, 105

Swan, Luke, 143, 155

Sweet, John, 27

Taney, Roger (Chief Justice), 164

tanneries, *xi*, 49, 97-98, 147, 150-51, 177, *map*

taverns (inns), *x-xi*, 11-12, 14, 19, 21, 26, 28-32, 30, 30n26, 36-39, 43, 47-51, 49n9, 53, 54n19, 61n34, 67, 71-79, 89, 94, 97-98, 100n28, 106, 116, 124, 141-42, 144, 146-47, 149, 153, 157-59, 159n91, 175-79, *illus. See also* distilleries; temperance

temperance, *xii*, 31, 37, 45, 67, 71-75, 77, 79, 93-95, 106, 153, 178. *See also* distilleries; taverns

Temple, Daniel, 27, 169

Temple, William, 69, 92

tenant farmers, 4, 9, 23, 33, 88-89, 121, 127, 131-32, 134, 136-37, 139-40. *See also* Anti-Rent Wars; leasehold system; share farming

Thayendanegea. *See* Brant, Joseph

Tucker, Ebenezar (Ebeneezer), 55, 57

turnpikes (toll roads). *See* roads

Van Rensselaer family and estate, 16, 18, 35, 72, 89, 131-32, 136. *See also* Anti-Rent Wars

Van Rensselaer, Jacob, 43, 133

Van Rensselaer, Stephen (Old Patroon), 13, 17, 35, 131-32

Van Rensselaer, Stephen IV, 132-34, 136. *See also* Anti-Rent Wars

Van Riper clocks, 161-62

Vincent, Dinah Ann, 70

wagon-making, 46, 89, 151-52, *map*

Walker, Timothy, 27

Warren, Erastus (Doctor), 172

Watters, Hayden, 68, 70

Westford (Otsego Co., NY), 49, 61, 69, 96, 107, 116, 122, 134, 143, 145, 148, 150, 153, 164-65, 169, *illus.*

Westville (Otsego Co., NY), 19, 21-22, 24-25, 28, 41-43, 42n58, 48, 142

Wetmore, Chester, 57

wheat production, 23-25, 28, 43, 105, 124-25, 128, 133, 141

White, Joseph (Doctor), 90, 90n3

Wickham, Stephen, 142, 146-47, 155, *map*
Wilson, Andrew, 25
Worcester (Otsego Co., NY), 21, 36-37, 173
Wood, Henry Hilton, 129, 137-38, 166, 171
wool production, 48, 93-94, 124, 126-128, 130, 139, 144. *See also* Phoenix Woolen Mill
Wright, Henry Clarke, 23, 60
Yager, Chauncey, 155
Yale University attendees, 14, 39, 42, 68, 95

Discover *upstate New York history*
through these other exciting offerings
available from Square Circle Press

A Romance Map of the Finger Lakes Region of Central New York
It's the return of a classic! This vintage illustrated history map has been
reissued and is available exclusively from Square Circle Press.

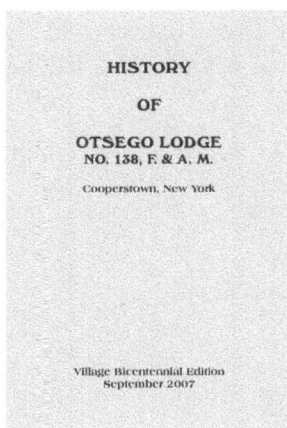

HISTORY

OF

OTSEGO LODGE
NO. 138, F. & A. M.

Cooperstown, New York

Village Bicentennial Edition
September 2007

Otsego Lodge No. 138, F.&A.M., Cooperstown, New York:
A Collection of Historical Miscellanea, 1795-2007
A vivid portrait of the Masonic fraternity's involvement in the daily life
of one of America's most scenic and legendary villages. Illustrated.

For more information about these items and more, visit
www.squarecirclepress.com

About the Author

Dominick J. Reisen is a 1989 graduate of Bard College with a degree in Social Sciences. He is a founding member and the first president of the Otsego County Historical Association, a position he held from 2003 to 2008. He has served as the treasurer of the Town of Middlefield Historical Association since 1999 and has been on its board of directors since 1994. From 2002 until 2004 he served as the Town Historian for the town of Middlefield. His previous books include: *Middlefield: Otsego Lake's Eastern Shore; Inscriptions From the Middlefield Baptist Cemetery;* and *The Middlefield Hamlet Historic District: A Guide for a Walking Tour.* He makes his home in the Daniel Cummings house in Middlefield, the hamlet once known as Clarksville.

www.ingramcontent.com/pod-product-compliance
Lightning Source LLC
Chambersburg PA
CBHW030940150426
42812CB00064B/3078/J